The Kaminski Brigade

The Kaminski Brigade

Rolf Michaelis

Schiffer Military History
Atglen, PA

Book translation by David Johnston.

Book Design by Ian Robertson.

Copyright © 2011 by Schiffer Publishing.
Library of Congress Control Number: 2011928157

All rights reserved. No part of this work may be reproduced or used in any forms or by any means – graphic, electronic or mechanical, including photocopying or information storage and retrieval systems – without written permission from the copyright holder.

Printed in China.
ISBN: 978-0-7643-3765-9

This book was originally published in German under the title
Die Brigade Kaminski by Michaelis-Verlag

We are interested in hearing from authors with book ideas on related topics.

Published by Schiffer Publishing Ltd. 4880 Lower Valley Road Atglen, PA 19310 Phone: (610) 593-1777 FAX: (610) 593-2002 E-mail: Info@schifferbooks.com. Visit our web site at: www.schifferbooks.com Please write for a free catalog. This book may be purchased from the publisher. Please include $5.00 postage. Try your bookstore first.	In Europe, Schiffer books are distributed by: Bushwood Books 6 Marksbury Avenue Kew Gardens Surrey TW9 4JF, England Phone: 44 (0) 20 8392-8585 FAX: 44 (0) 20 8392-9876 E-mail: Info@bushwoodbooks.co.uk. Visit our website at: www.bushwoodbooks.co.uk

Contents

Foreword 6

The Kaminski Brigade and The National-Socialist Party of Russia 9

The 29. Waffen-Grenadier-Division der SS "RONA"(russische Nr. 1) 43

Bronislav Kaminski 50

The Russian Mentality 52

Document Appendix 60

Sources and Literature 190

Foreword

Hundreds of thousands of members of the Soviet multiracial state served in the Wehrmacht, Waffen-SS, German police and civilian organizations between 1941 and 1945. In the process a distinction was made between non-Russian ethnic groups (e.g. Turks, Cossacks and Tatars), most of whom opposed Communism and regarded the mastery of the Russians as oppression, and the Russian peoples. In the military sphere the former were concentrated in so-called "East Legions" and received at least some concessions from the Germans.

The formations created using Russian personnel were designated *Osttruppen* (East Forces), and until 1944 had only limited rights compared to German units.

An exception was the Russian Kaminski Brigade, which was later given the title Russian Liberation People's Army (abbreviation RONA). Led by men oriented towards National-Socialism, for the German side it was more than just a part of the collaboration in the east.

It is intended that this book should describe the history of this unit in the military, economic and political spheres and make a contribution to the history of German – Russian relations.

Berlin, April 1999
Rolf Michaelis

The Kaminski Brigade
and the National-Socialist Party of Russia

"*1) When the Minsk front collapsed, the Wehrmacht handed the Kaminski Brigade over to Himmler, as it had no further use for it. The brigade was transferred to Himmler as soon as it set foot on East Prussian soil. From that moment on, Gottlob Berger also had to look after the Kaminski Brigade. After I had Kaminski shot, the brigade was leaderless and I gave it to Berger again.*

2) There were matters to be dealt with that were not of a military nature, for example where to send these masses of civilians that had belonged to Kaminski. Himmler placed Berger in charge of these measures, as it was he who was leading the negotiations to find accommodations for the Kaminski people."

Not only did these few sentences uttered by former *SS-Obergruppenführer und General der Waffen-SS und Polizei* Erich von dem Bach[1] at the Nuremberg Trials describe the end of a Russian volunteer formation that had fought on the German side, but also of a National-Socialist movement in Russia that was unique. Its beginnings went back to the

---

[1] Erich von dem Bach (-Zelewski) was born in Lauenburg on 1 March 1889. He fought in the First World War and was decorated with the Iron Crosses, First and Second Class. In 1919 he served in the Eastern Border Guard and Upper Silesia. He left the service in 1924 as a Leutnant. In 1930 he joined the NSDAP and one year later the SS (No. 9,831). On 15 December 1934 Bach attained the rank of an SS-Gruppenführer and became SS Senior Sector Commander "Northeast" (East Prussia). After conflicts with Gauleiter Koch he was relieved, and on 15 February 1936 took over Senior Sector "Southeast" (Silesia). On 28 June 1938 he was named Senior SS and Police Commander "Southeast". On 10 April 1941 he received the supplementary rank of Generalleutnant der Polizei. Three weeks later Bach was transferred to the personal staff of the Reichsführer-SS and on 22 June 1941 became Senior SS and Police Commander "Central Russia". Effective 9 November 1941 he was promoted to the rank of SS-Obergruppenführer und General der Polizei. Having been named Commissioner of the Reichsführer-SS for Anti-Bandit Operations on 23 October 1942, on 21 June 1943 he was placed in command of all anti-bandit units. From 1 July 1944 he was permitted to bear the title of General der Waffen-SS. After the retreat from White Russia, from August to mid-October 1944 he led Corps Group von dem Bach, which was responsible for suppressing the Warsaw uprising. On 30 September 1944 he was awarded the Knight's Cross of the Iron Cross for his actions. From 10 November 1944 until 25 January 1945 Bach commanded the corps headquarters of XIV SS Army Corps, which was deployed on the Upper Rhine. From 26 January to 10 February 1945 the command of X SS Army Corps assembled in Posen-West Prussia. One week later he took over the so-called "Oder Corps". Bach was held prisoner by the Allies until 1950 and at the Nuremberg Trials he testified against the principal war criminals as a witness for the prosecution. Not until 1961 was he sentenced to 4½ years in prison for manslaughter. One year later he was given life imprisonment for multiple murders. He died in prison on 8 March 1972.

Soviet Union of the 1920s, when various intellectuals got together to oppose the Stalinist system. As usual in a totalitarian state, the regime strove to destroy these groups, and the best fate their members could hope for was imprisonment in a labor camp.[2]

One such person was the former director of the Moscow Bureau of Standards, Voskoboynik[3], who was in Lokot when the war began and who was installed as mayor by the German military administration.[4]

As a result of the Wehrmacht's rapid advance towards the east, the occupation troops that followed became completely overburdened, leaving areas that could not be watched over, especially in the many forests. In such a vacuum, Voskoboynik and several others—including Kaminski—became politically active again in the autumn of 1941. They hoped to be able to pursue a new direction without foreign tutelage, in which the quality of life of the loyal citizens would be improved. They set up a police force[5] which even fought Red Army troops in the *rayon*[6] of Brasovo, unnoticed by the Germans. The Soviet troops, left behind from the battle of encirclement at Briansk, caused unrest amongst and plundered the peaceful population—in some cases on their own initiative and in others under direction.

Then, on 25 November 1941 Voskoboynik established the National-Socialist Party of Russia. The party began printing its own newspaper "Voice of the People". Moscow did not remain unaware of this development in the Lokot area, and in January 1942 paratroopers were sent into the *rayon* to kill Mayor Voskoboynik, who was on friendly terms with the Germans, and intimidate the population. Following the assassination Kaminski, who had been part of Voskoboynik's inner circle, became the new mayor of the Lokot District and leader of the party.

---

[2]"Operation Barbarossa" began on Sunday, 22 June 1941. From East Prussia to central Poland, at 03:15 hundreds of guns opened fire on the Soviet border fortifications. By the beginning of July Baranovichi, Minsk, Borisov and Polotsk were in German hands. Army Group Center's objective was Smolensk. From there an attack could be launched towards Moscow and depending on the situation a turn could be made to the north or south. On 18 July 1941 the Wehrmacht encircled 12 Soviet divisions in Smolensk. Four days later the battle was over: the Wehrmacht communiqué reported 348,000 Soviet prisoners and about 6,000 tanks and guns destroyed or captured.
The offensive towards Moscow began on 2 October 1941. Panzer Group Guderian, renamed the 2nd Panzer Army four days later, formed a pocket around Briansk. A second pocket was sealed at Vyazma. Despite the arrival of snow, constant counterattacks by the Red Army and growing supply problems, the German divisions succeeded in reducing the pockets. On 19 October the Wehrmacht High Command announced the conclusion of the double battle at Briansk and Vyazma: 657,948 prisoners had been taken and countless weapons captured.
[3]There he called himself Lomashkov.
[4]The areas of the Soviet Union occupied by the German military were under military administration near the front (to about 200 km behind the main line of resistance) and behind that the civilian administration. At the top of the military administration was the Quartermaster-General in the OKH (Dept. VII Military Administration). The army groups engaged Commanders of the Rear Army (Heer) Areas, the armies Commanders of the Rear Army (Armee) Areas (Korück). The Military Administration Headquarters and Town Headquarters represented the lowest levels of the military administration.
[5]By the end of 1941 the militia under Sub-Lieutenant Paulowitz already numbered 500 men.
[6]A rayon was roughly comparable to a German Landkreis (rural district).

At the same time, the German military became aware that the Lokot militia was fighting partisans on its own initiative. While repairing the Briansk to Lgov line, German railroad workers came upon Russian volunteers who had already achieved a number of victories [against the partisans]. In May 1942 the 216th Infantry Division[7] moved into the area. The local militia, which by then numbered about 1,400 men, was placed under its command. To ensure orderly coordination of the struggle against the partisans, the division commander established the von Gilsa[8] Group. It consisted of:

> the division headquarters with military police squad
> Signals Battalion 216
> one company from Pioneer Battalion 216
> Infantry Regiment 348
> IV (Heavy) Battalion/Artillery Regiment 216
> Anti-Tank Battalion 216[9]

In addition to the Lokot militia, the von Gilsa unit, which was ultimately expanded into a corps group (*Korpsgruppe*), included the 102nd and 108th Hungarian Security Divisions. The unit's headquarters were in Lokot. Members of the von Gilsa Group described their impressions at the time:

"In addition to its military experiences, during those summer months in Lokot the group formed impressions that were probably unique. We got to know the Russian people as friends; we found them to be extremely hospitable; we participated in the cheerful music and dance of which they were capable even under such pitiful conditions."

As a result of Kaminski's success against the partisans, on 19 July 1942 the Commander-in-Chief of the 2nd Panzer Army (*General* Schmidt[10]) placed him in charge

---

[7]The 216th Infantry Division was a third wave division created by the Landwehr Commander Hanover on 26 August 1939, consisting of the 348th, 396th and 398th Infantry Regiments. The 398th Infantry Regiment was disbanded on 1 June 1942, followed by the entire division on 17 November 1943 after the fighting at Orel,
[8]Werner Freiherr von und zu Gilsa was born in Berlin on 4 March 1889. In 1909 he was a Leutnant in the Guards Fusilier Regiment. After the First World War he served in the Reichswehr and on 1 October 1936 became commander of the 9th Infantry Regiment with the rank of Oberstleutnant. On 1 March 1937 von und zu Gilsa was promoted to Oberst. Promoted to Generalmajor (1 February 1941), he commanded the 216th Infantry Division until 4 April 1943. Further promotions followed, to Generalleutnant on 1 October 1942 and General der Infanterie on 1 July 1943. While holding the latter rank he commanded LXXXIX Army Corps. Following this, he was the military commander of Dresden and commanding general of the Gilsa Corps. Decorated with the Knight's Cross with Oak Leaves, he elected to commit suicide in 1945.
[9]At that time the Anti-Tank Battalion consisted of just one anti-tank company and the attached 216th Bicycle Reconnaissance Troop.
[10]Rudolf Schmidt was born in Berlin on 12 May 1886 and on 25 September 1906 he began his military service as an officer candidate. On 27 January 1908 he became a Leutnant in the 83rd Infantry Regiment. After serving in the First World War he became a member of the Reichswehr and on 1 October 1937 became commander of the 1st Panzer Division with the rank of Generalmajor (1 October 1936). Promoted to Generalleutnant on 1 June 1938, on 1 February 1940 he became commander of the XXXIX Panzer Corps and on 15 November 1941 of the 2nd Army. About one month later he was named commander-in-chief of the 2nd Panzer Army, on 1 January 1942 he was promoted to Generaloberst. Decorated with the Knight's Cross with Oak Leaves, Schmidt retired on 30 September 1943 and died in Krefeld in 1957.

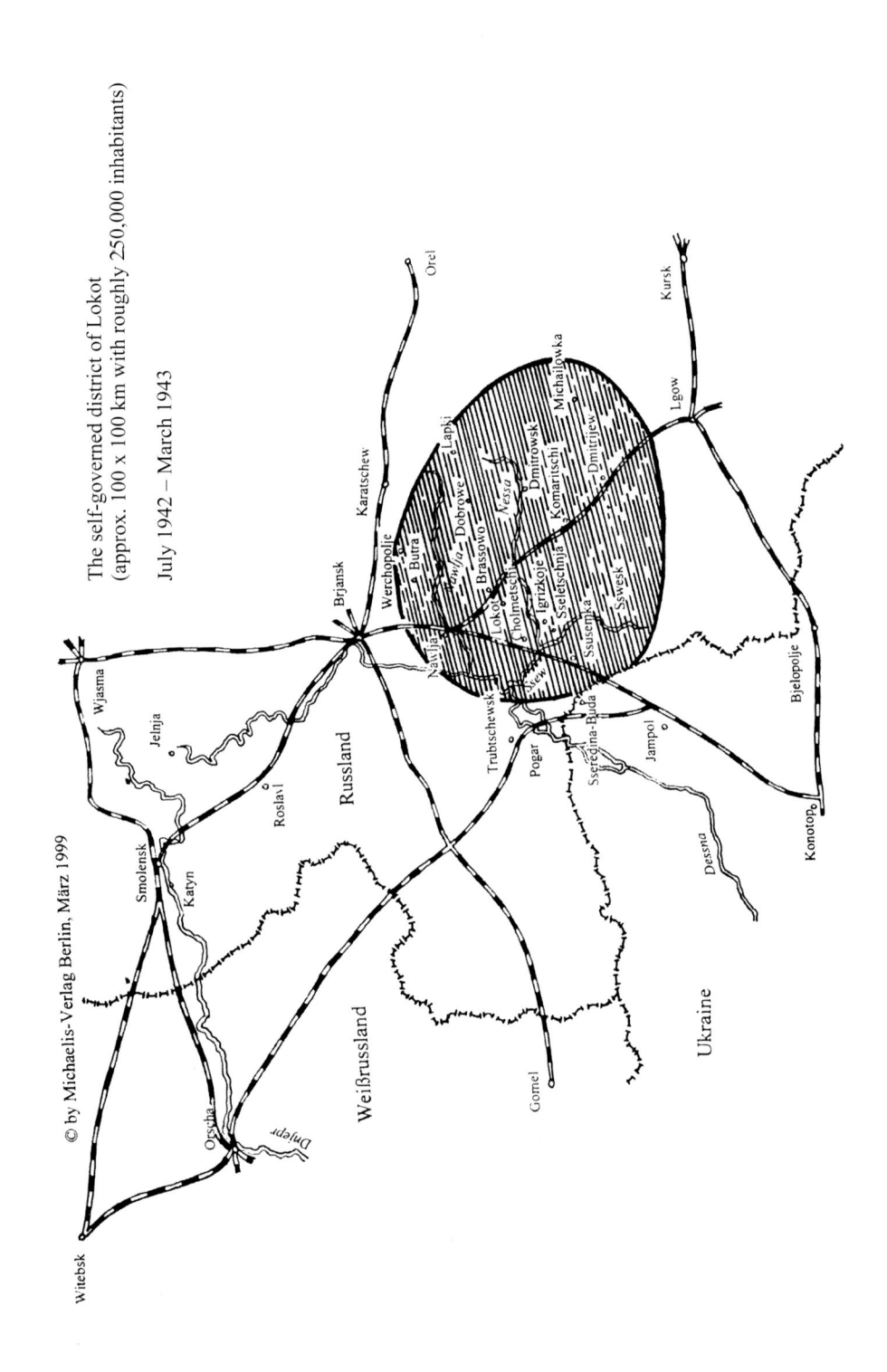

The self-governed district of Lokot
(approx. 100 x 100 km with roughly 250,000 inhabitants)

July 1942 – March 1943

of a self-governed district that also included the *rayons* of Navlya, Brasovo, Susemka, Dimitrovsk, Dimitriyev and Komarichi, and named him brigade commander.[11] This action was unprecedented and had no equal in the entire German *Ostpolitik*—a Russian was placed in almost total economic control of a region.

In September 1942 the commander of Rear Army Area 532 was sent to the Lokot area to monitor the military administration of the area. In December 1942 the 216th Infantry Division was sent to the Spass-Demensk area and the militia's subordination to Korpsgruppe von Gilsa came to an end. The new tactical command unit in the area was the Rübsam Group, which had been formed from the headquarters of the 17th Panzer-Grenadier Brigade.[12] In January 1943 Kaminski's militia took part in "Operations Polar Bear I to III" as part of the Rübsam Group. During the fighting in the Dimitriyev – Mikhailovka area the People's Defense was employed mainly to screen to the north along the Briansk – Roslavl railway line.

By spring 1943, Kaminski had formed five regiments (each of three battalions) with about 9,000 men in the Lokot Self-Governed District. Each battalion had three or four companies, which were stationed in the various villages. The People's Defense members helped work the land (farmer-soldiers) and were usually deployed near their base villages.[13] A former officer recalled:

"In the Lokot area the partisans laid mines on the roads, and many cows and pigs, as well as farmers, lost their lives. Units of the RONA set an ambush and watched as two partisans laid mines. In the ensuing firefight one partisan was killed and the other wounded... The mining came to an abrupt end in this area—word of what happened had spread quickly among the partisans. The partisans were so afraid that they stopped carrying out their orders. Instead, if they were supposed to blow up this or that bridge, they instead blew up a large tree near the bridge—and the bridge remained intact! I personally had contact with the local partisan leaders and we even exchanged newspapers!"

---

[11] In September 1942 the rayon of Mikhailovka was incorporated into the self-governed district.
[12] The 17th Panzer Grenadier Brigade was created from the 17th Rifle Brigade, which had been established on 1 November 1940, and was attached to the 17th Panzer Division.
[13] At that time the self-governed district had good propaganda value because of the living conditions there—better than under German or Soviet rule. As a result, many voluntarily joined the People's Defense. When the force began suffering casualties, in some cases 150 to 200 men per month (killed, wounded, missing), increasingly the ranks were filled with forced recruits. Finally, by 1944, only about 25% of its personnel were volunteers.

The Kaminski Brigade

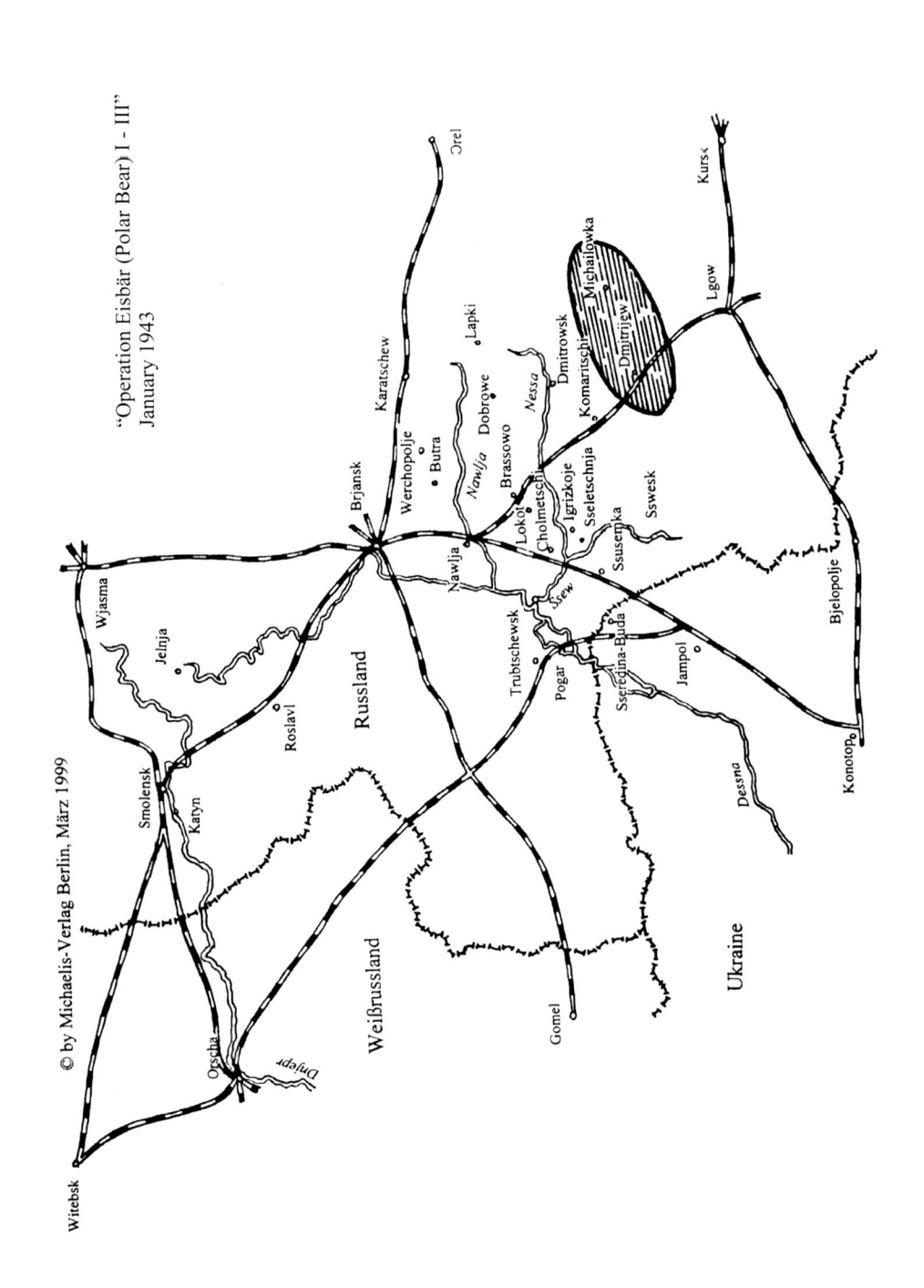

The Kaminski Brigade 15

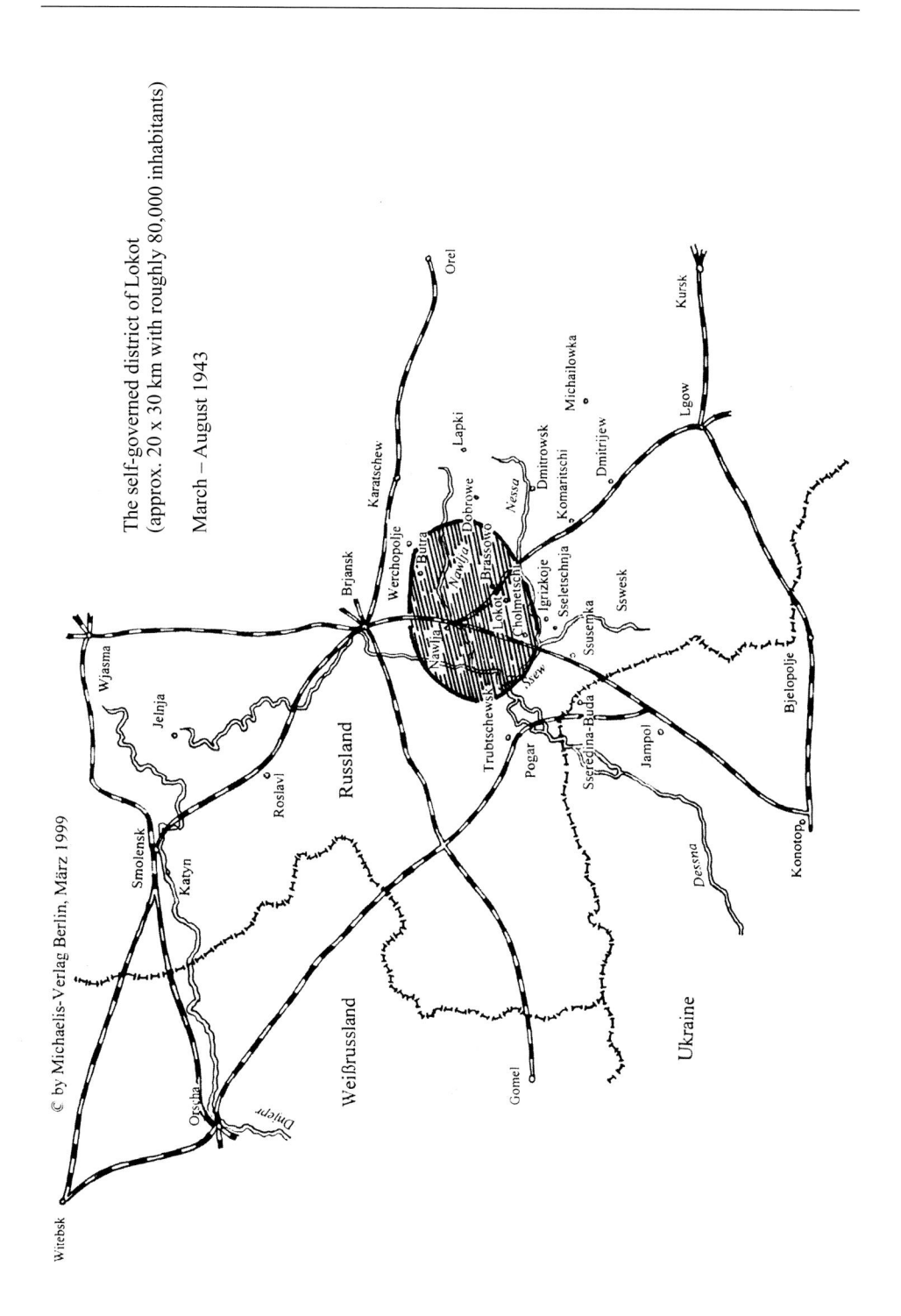

Following the collapse of Army Group B in the spring of 1943, Stalin ordered the "Briansk Front" to roll up the German Army Group Center from the south. On 12 February 1943 the Soviet attack struck the 2nd Army with full force, but ran into a determined defense and gained little ground. The Central Front then came to the aid of the Briansk Front by attacking the 2nd Panzer Army. To counter the enemy advance near Dimitrovsk, elements of the nearby VIII People's Defense Battalion were attached to SS Battle Group Zehender.[14,15] Other elements saw action under Headquarters, XX Army Corps. *Hauptmann* Korbel, the former commander of Headquarters, 72nd Infantry Division, part of XX Army Corps, recalled:

"I remember the Kaminski Brigade well. Some of our girls—Frontline Stage Entertainers 72nd Infantry Division—were friends and acquaintances. They certainly had a variety of motives; some to avoid deportation to Germany; in some cases they were also motivated by the bad feelings between the Russians and Ukrainians. The headquarters was in Lokot. Ina—one of the girls—reported that her friends had been roughed up so badly that she couldn't recognize them."

While the German formations were able to repulse the attacks by both Soviet army groups near Orel and the Red Army subsequently halted further attacks at the end of March, the *rayons* of Komarichi, Dimitrovsk, Mikhailovka and Susemka were again placed under direct *Wehrmacht* command: they had become frontline zones. As the Soviet Army had conquered the *rayons* of Sevsk and Dimitriyev in the recent fighting, Kaminski's administration had been reduced to the *rayons* of Navlya and Brasovo with about 80,000 inhabitants, of whom 6,575 were refugees from the other *rayons*.

In March 1943 Headquarters, Special Purpose Division 442[16] (*Generalleutnant* Karl Bornemann[17]), which had taken overall command of the anti-partisan effort, reported frequent confrontations between the Hungarian security troops and Kaminski's militia. In April 1943, after Bornemann recommended that the Hungarian troops be removed from the

---

[14] SS Cavalry Division
[15] Appendix to the XXXXVII Panzer Corps war diary.
[16] The 442nd Special Purpose Division (Division z.b.V. 442) was established in the west for Korück 580 on 18 October 1939 from regional defense battalions (Landesschützen-Bataillonen). At the end of October 1942 the unit went to central Russian, where it was placed under the command of the 4th Army, and at the end of January 1943 it was attached to 2nd Panzer Army. The unit was disbanded on 24 August 1944.
[17] Karl Bornemann was born in Austria on 15 September 1885 and on 1 October 1906 joined Infantry Regiment 99 of the Imperial Army as a volunteer. On 1 January 1908 he was promoted to Leutnant der Reserve and on 1 November 1910 he became an active officer. After taking part in the First World War Bornemann served in the Federal Austrian Army and following promotion to Generalmajor on 26 June 1937 he commanded the 2nd Austrian Division. At the outset of the Second World War he commanded Division No. 148 and from 10 January 1940 Special Purpose Division Command 442. While in this position he was promoted to Generalleutnant. From 5 January to 31 March 1944 he commanded Special Purpose Division Command 410. Decorated with the German Cross in Gold, Bornemann subsequently became Wehrmacht commander of Würzburg and on 15 March 1945 entered the officer reserve in Defense District XVII.

Operations by Elements of the People's Defense Brigade within XX Army Corps and XXXXVII Panzer Corps February – April 1943

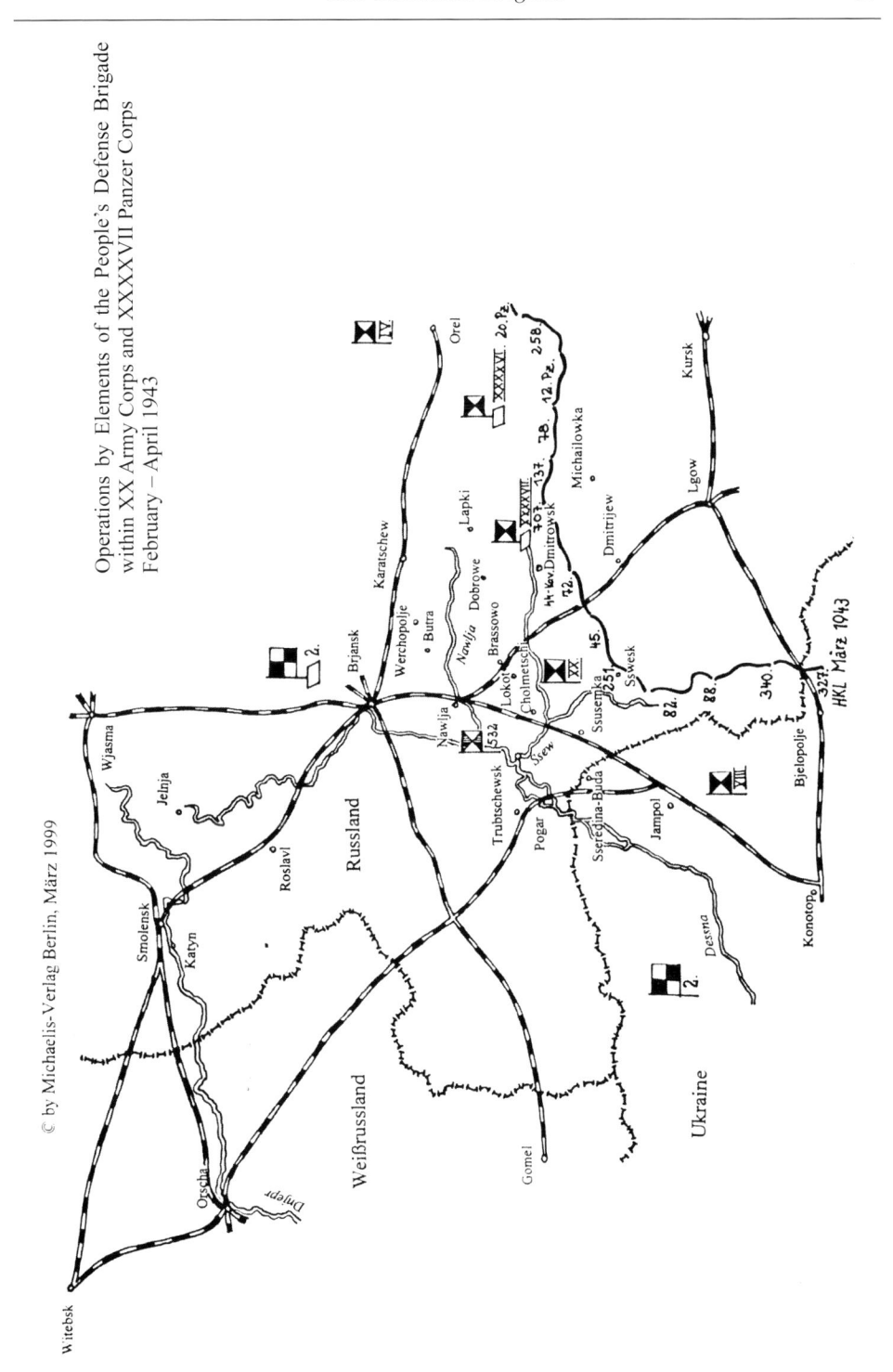

18   *The Kaminski Brigade*

Tank Badges and Insignia of the Russian Liberation People's Army
RONA

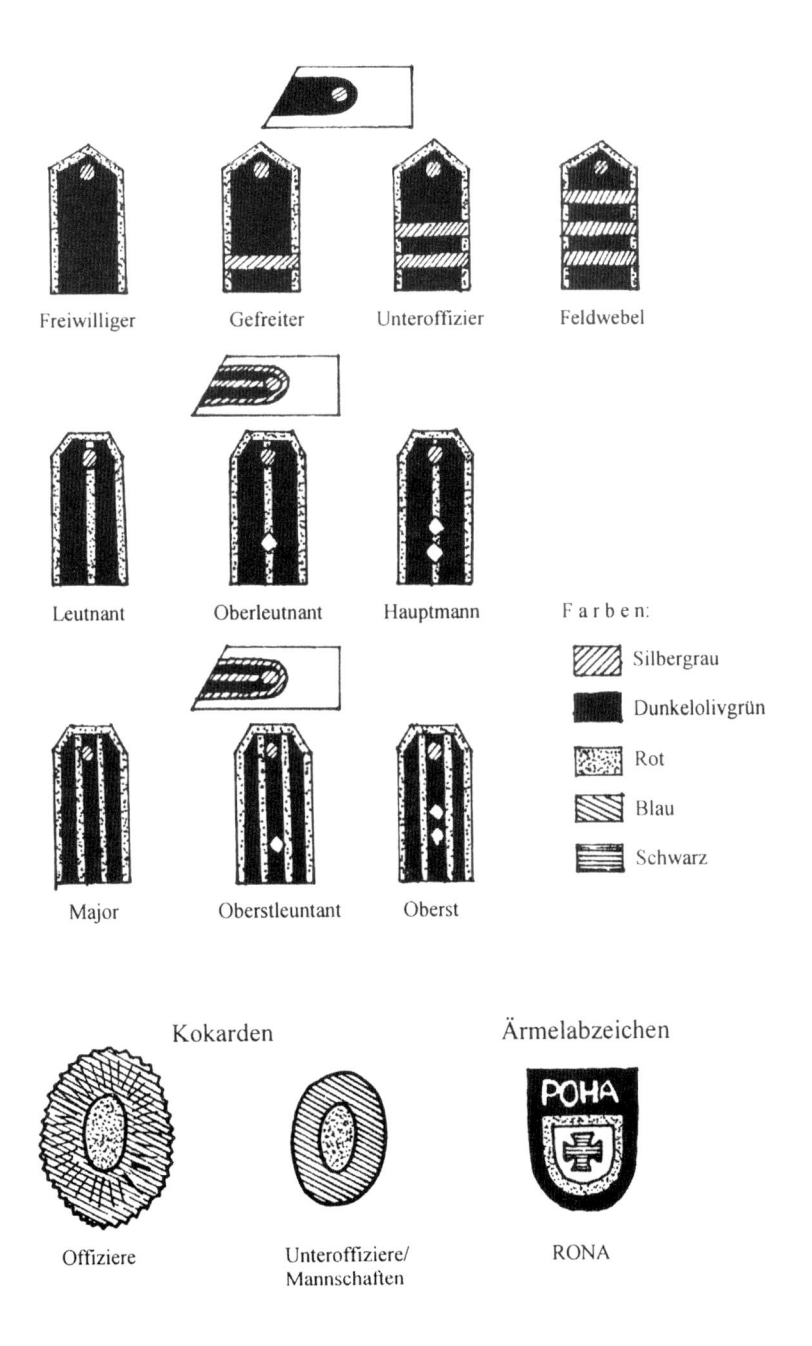

Freiwilliger   Gefreiter   Unteroffizier   Feldwebel

Leutnant   Oberleutnant   Hauptmann

Farben:
- Silbergrau
- Dunkelolivgrün
- Rot
- Blau
- Schwarz

Major   Oberstleutnant   Oberst

Kokarden   Ärmelabzeichen

Offiziere   Unteroffiziere/Mannschaften   RONA

The Kaminski Brigade

Armbands and collar patches of the 29. Waffen-Grenadier-Division der SS "RONA" (russ. Nr. 1)

area and replaced by German units, the 108th Hungarian Division was withdrawn. Initially only the 102nd Hungarian Division remained in the area of Korück 532 (Rear Army Area 532).

In May 1943 the OKH introduced Russian-style rank badges, and the officers' shoulder boards were based strongly on those worn by the Tsarist army.[18] At the same time, rank titles were introduced for native officers.[19] Russian equivalent officer ranks were:

Leutnant	Podporuczik
Oberleutnant	Poruczik
Hauptmann	Kapitan
Major	Major
Oberstleutnant	Podpolkovnik
Oberst	Polkovnik

The People's Defense, which so far had mainly worn Soviet uniforms with white bands on the left arm—on which there was an Iron Cross—now began receiving growing numbers of German uniforms as well as the designation RONA.[20] As well, sleeve badges bearing the Cyrillic letters POHA were produced by local tailors.[21]

From 16 May to 6 June 1943, Headquarters, XXXXVII Panzer Corps carried out "Operation Gypsy Baron" in the forested area south of Briansk with the following units:

7th Infantry Division
292nd Infantry Division
4th Panzer Division
18th Panzer Division
10th Panzer-Grenadier Division
Royal Hungarian 102nd Light Division
security forces of Korück 532
RONA People's Defense Brigade
Special Purpose East Battalion

From 20 to 30 May 1943, LV Army Corps (2nd Panzer Army) was supposed to pacify the area between the Bolva River and the Briansk – Zhukovka rail line. People's Defense Battalions I, II, III and XI took part in the operation, which was code-named "Freischütz".

On 14 June 1943 the XII People's Defense Battalion was committed in "Operation Tannhäuser". This was followed by "Operation Seydlitz" in the area south of Dorogobuzh from 25 June to 27 July 1943.

After the failed German summer offensive at Kursk ("Operation Citadel"), the Red Army succeeded in breaking through 2nd Panzer Army's front. On 26 July 1943 Hitler

---

[18] Order from OKH/Gen.StdH/GenQu/Iva (III, 3) Az 985 d, Nr. I/14124/43 of 29 May 1943.
[19] Order from OKH/GenStdH/Gen.d. Osttruppen III, Nr. 1200/43 of 9 May 1943.
[20] RONA = Ruskaya Ozvobododitielnaya Narodnaya Armiya (Russian Liberation People's Army).
[21] See the emblem illustrated on the cover.

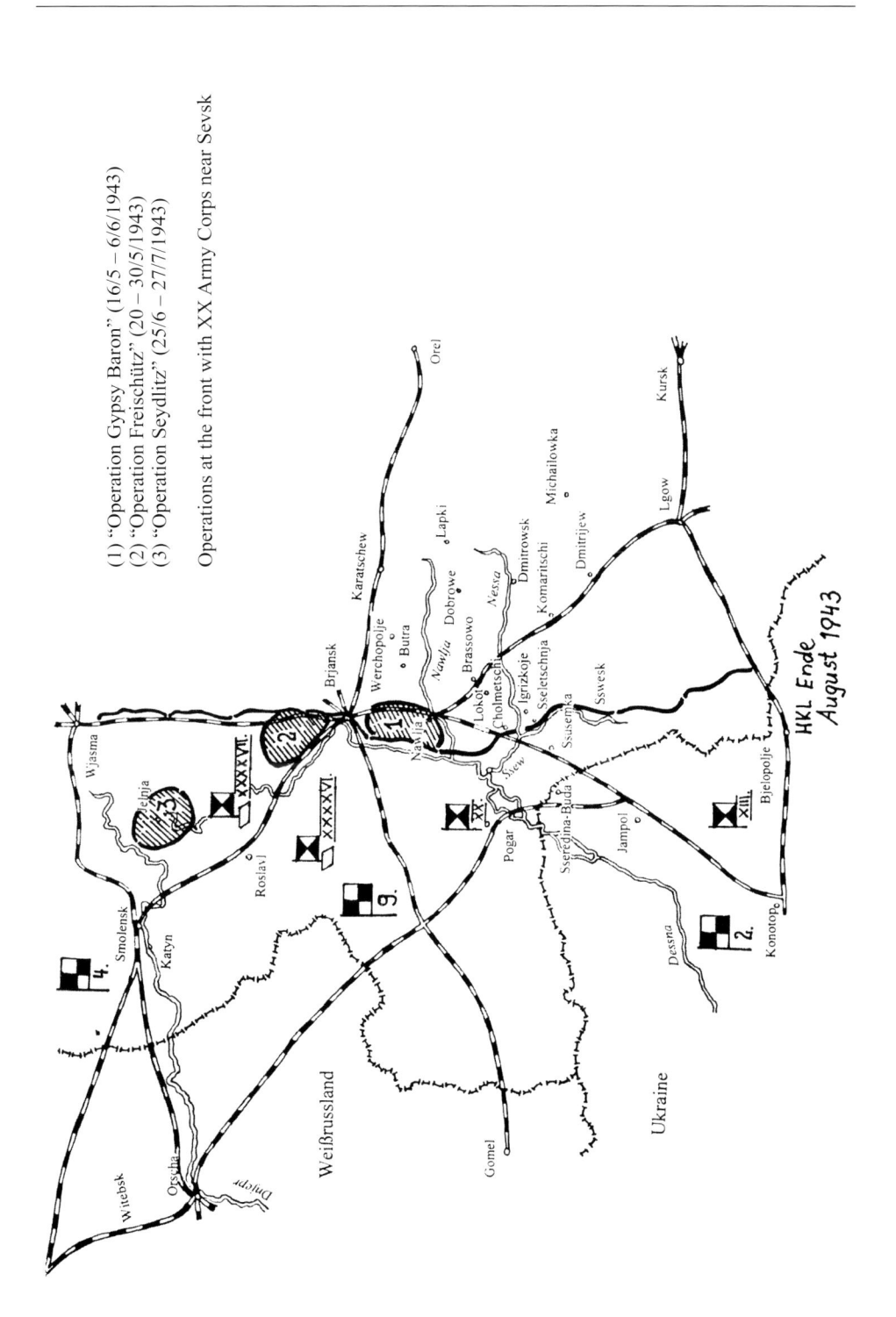

The Kaminski Brigade

(1) "Operation Gypsy Baron" (16/5 – 6/6/1943)
(2) "Operation Freischütz" (20 – 30/5/1943)
(3) "Operation Seydlitz" (25/6 – 27/7/1943)

Operations at the front with XX Army Corps near Sevsk

authorized the abandonment of Orel. On 4 August 1943 forward elements of the 3rd and 63rd Armies reached the city. At the end of the month the German forces withdrew towards the "Hagen Position", which extended north to south along the Bolva and Desna Rivers following the line Kirov – Briansk – Sevsk.

On 26 August 1943 the Central Front struck the seam between the German 2nd and 9th Armies in the Sevsk area. Among the units deployed there was the 4th People's Defense Regiment. Attached to XX Army Corps (45th, 137th, 86th and 251st Infantry Divisions), part of the 2nd Army, it was supposed to help cover the general retreat. The regiment was shattered in fierce fighting and the next day the Red Army occupied the city

The Kaminski People's Defense Brigade left the 2nd Army and, with the self-governed district having become a frontline zone, was sent to Lepel (area of Military Administration Headquarters 181). The population was initially moved from the Lokot area via Seredina Buda west of the Desna into the Gremyach – Pogar area. On 29 August the People's Defense and the civilians crossed the Desna at Peretorgi, over a bridge guarded by East Artillery Battalion 621 (*Major* Keiling). He recalled:

"The bridge at Peretorgi, which was guarded against partisans and air attack by a battery of East Artillery Battalion 621 made up of Russian volunteers, was so hermetically sealed by an easily-surveyable all-round defensive position that even German generals had to show their pass to the bridge commander before being allowed through the lines to cross the bridge. Units passing through, both large and small, were closely inspected. The security measures were handled strictly according to regulations so as to render pointless any attempt at sabotage.

RONA was no exception in this regard and had to be reported by the responsible officer. Some senior officers wearing the POHA sleeve emblem, cap braid and shoulder boards asked me to come see their commanding officer, but I stayed at my command post as per regulations and referred these officers and my own ranks to the official procedure, to which even German generals had to submit. Then a Russian, plain looking, but obviously held in high respect by his entourage, stepped forward. He said, 'I am brigade commander Kaminski' and produced a typewritten pass from Headquarters, 2nd Panzer Army, which confirmed that he had been named brigade commander. He then vigorously expressed his indignation over the treatment he had received, and his German liaison officer had to explain to him that he had in no way been slighted.

The remaining armed members of the RONA stood in stark contrast to the group of officers. They wore pieces of Soviet Army uniforms, sometimes supplemented by civilian things or articles of German service dress. Their equipment and weapons, also of Soviet origin, completed the picture. Tractors towing heavy guns and horse-drawn anti-tank guns were interspersed among the groups [of soldiers] *carrying small arms. Some groups appeared to be unarmed, so that they could have been taken for prisoners of war. The long rows of wagons and carts of the civilian column seemed endless."*

---

[22]In mid-August the 2nd Panzer Army was withdrawn from the central sector of the Eastern Front and sent to the Balkans. Part of its sector of front was taken over by the 2nd Army.

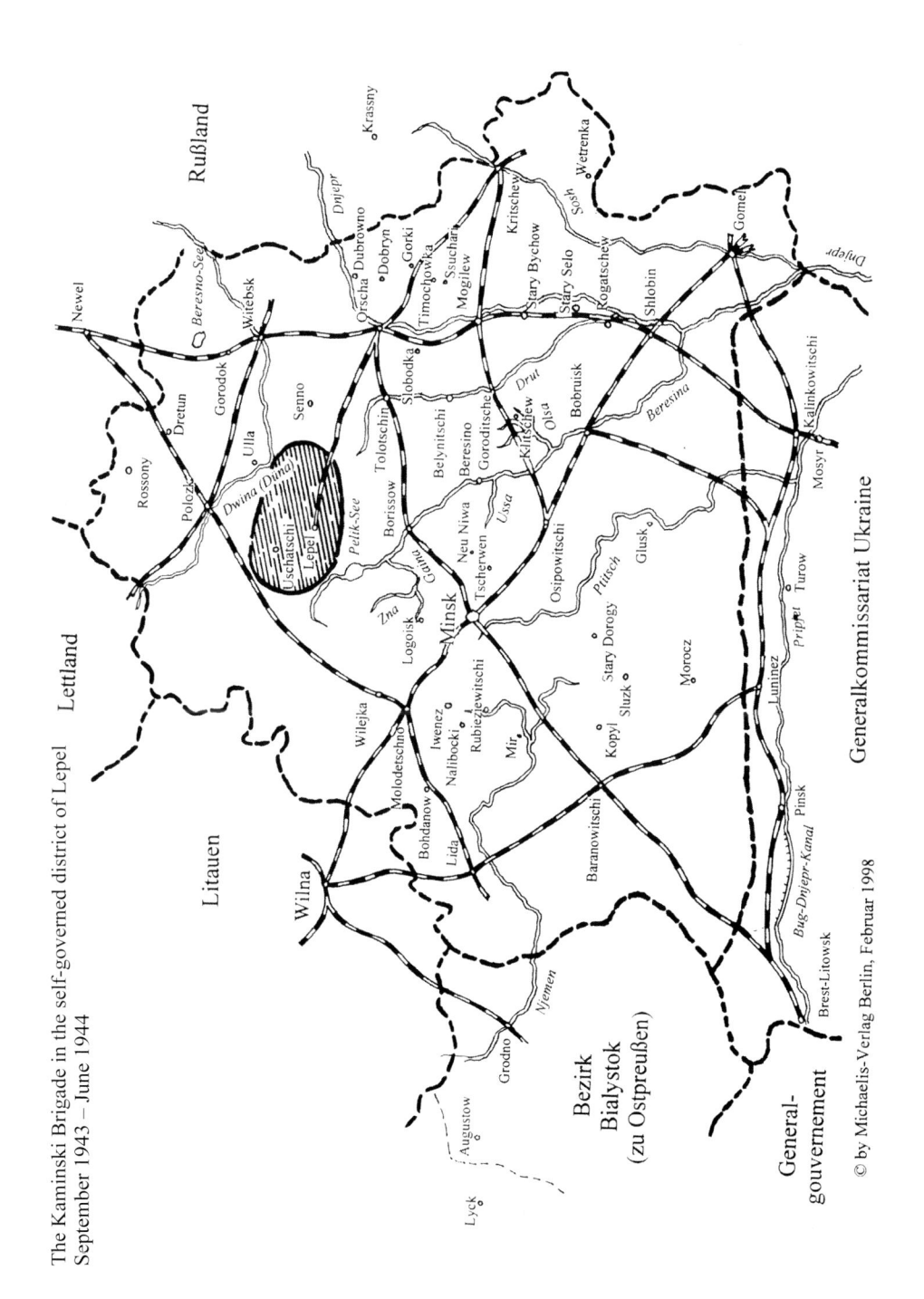

The Kaminski Brigade in the self-governed district of Lepel
September 1943 – June 1944

The column passed through Vitebsk to Lepel. The area and its inhabitants had been given over to Kaminski as a new self-governed district. With the withdrawal of the 3rd Army's border to the south, the entire area of the Lepel self-governed district was the responsibility of the 3rd Panzer Army.[23] Kaminski's authority was limited to the *rayons* of Lepel, Chashniki and Ushachi, and the latter was under the total control of the partisans. The area had previously been secured by troops of the Commanding General of Security Troops and Commander in Rear Area Army Group Center, *General* von Schenkendorff.[24,25] *Hauptmann* Köneke became the new liaison officer between Headquarters, 3rd Panzer Army and RONA. The German military administration headquarters were withdrawn from the area. The 286th Security Division,[26] which was still in the area, proposed that the People's Defense Brigade be assigned to certain villages. Kaminski rejected the idea, as he was conscious of the fact that his unit, which still numbered about 6,000 men in the late summer of 1943, was not as reliable as it had been in Lokot in 1942.

In autumn 1943 RONA's organization was as follows:

1st Rifle Regiment (*Oberstleutnant* Galkin[27])
2nd Rifle Regiment (*Oberleutnant* Golyakov, previously *Major* Tarasov)
3rd Rifle Regiment (*Major* Turlakov)
4th Rifle Regiment (*Major* Proshin)
Fast Special Purpose Guards Battalion
Armored Company[28] (*Hauptmann* Samsonov)

---

[23]The new border ran along the southern border of the rayons of Lepel – Chashniki – Senno – Bogushevskoye.
[24]Max von Schenkendorff was born in Prenzlau in 1875. In 1894 he joined the infantry and by 1908 rose to the rank of Hauptmann. He took part in the First World War as a battalion commander and in July 1918 was a special duties Major attached to the Chief of the Army General Staff. From 1922 to 1925 he worked in the Reichswehr Ministry and in 1924 was promoted to Oberst. In 1929 he became a Generalleutnant and in February 1930 he left the service. After the start of "Operation Barbarossa" he was named commanding general of security forces and commander in Rear Army Area Center. He died in the summer of 1943.
[25]At that time he commanded the 201st, 203rd, 221st and 286th Security Divisions and on 8 October 1943 his title was revised to Commanding General of Security Troops and Commander of Army Area White Ruthenia. On 19 April 1944 the position was renamed Wehrmacht Commander White Ruthenia.
[26]The 286th Security Division was created from elements of the 213th Infantry Division on 15 March 1941 and consisted of the reinforced 354th Infantry Regiment, the II Battalion of Artillery Regiment 213, the 704th Guard Battalion and division units. Since August 1941 the unit had been in Rear Army Area Center in the greater Orsha area. In February 1943 the division command also commanded the 931st Grenadier Regiment and the Commander of Eastern Troops 700. One year later the French 638th Infantry Regiment, Security Regiments 44 and 78, Special Purpose Regiments 631 and 632, and Grenadier Regiment 931 were attached to the division.

The 3rd Panzer Army regarded the brigade's move into the Vitebsk – Polotsk – Lepel – Senno area with mixed feelings, for if the militia defected to the partisans it would threaten the army's rear. "Operation Hubertus"[29] began on 16 October 1943 with the objective of restoring communications between Senno and Chashniki.

While fierce fighting[30] was raging at the front, Kaminski tried to wrest control of the new self-governed area from the partisans and restore order. The White Russian population wanted nothing to do with the Russian refugees, however, as the massive influx resulted in a serious deterioration in the supply situation. Consequently there were numerous confrontations between them and RONA members.[31]

Since the brigade's arrival in White Russia, Curt von Gottberg,[32] Senior SS and Police Commander Central Russia and White Ruthenia, had been in direct contact with the Waffen-SS. Himmler was interested in Russians with National-Socialist ideas, however, he was not

---

[27]In February 1945 Oberstleutnant (Lieutenant Colonel) Galkin commanded the Russian-staffed Panzerjagd-Brigade R (Russian Anti-Tank Units 10, 11, 13, 14). Armed with assault rifles and Panzerfaust anti-tank weapons and equipped with trucks, in April 1945 the brigade was placed in the Wotan Position (Altlandsberg – Werneuchen area). Shortly before the big Soviet offensive it received orders to join the 600th Infantry Division in the Friedland area.
[28]However only one T-34 and one KV I were serviceable.
[29]Battle Order No. 3 of the People's Defense Brigade RONA of 2 October 1943.
[30]At the beginning of January 1944, 56 Soviet rifle and 3 cavalry divisions plus 5 rifle and 22 tank brigades launched an offensive against the 18 divisions of the 3rd Panzer Army. The offensive achieved relatively little success, and after 10 days of fighting the troops of the 1st Baltic Front halted their attacks. After this First Winter of Vitebsk died down, forces were taken from the already weakened 3rd Panzer Army for other sectors of the front.
Stalin wanted a breakthrough at Vitebsk before the end of January and therefore ordered the 11th Guards Army, the 4th Shock Army and the 5th, 33rd, 39th and 43rd Armies to undertake a new offensive against 3rd Panzer Army. Although the defenders suffered heavy casualties, in mid-February 1944 the Red Army was forced to call off the offensive—mainly on account of heavy snow. The 3rd Panzer Army used the respite to withdraw its troops north of Vitebsk to a new line, for otherwise it could not have withstood another assault. Proposals by Army Group Center to withdraw either to the Dniepr or the Beresina were rejected by Hitler. Instead he ordered the cities of Bobruisk, Mogilev, Orsha, Vitebsk and Minsk to be turned into so-called "fortified places".
[31]The moral effect of leaving Russia and resettlement in White Russia should not be disregarded. The fleeing population was extremely depressed, as well it was obvious that Kaminski's political goal—to take power in Russia—had failed. The individual RONA member now saw that he was fighting a losing battle.
[32]Kurt von Gottberg was born in Preußisch Wilten on 11 February 1896. After graduation he joined the army and took part in the First World War from 1914, winning the Iron Crosses, First and Second Class. Discharged as an Oberleutnant, from 1919 to 1924 he was a member of the Erhard Brigade. He joined the NSDAP and the SS (No. 45,913) in 1932 and from 1937 to 1939 worked in the Race and Settlement Head Office. As an SS-Oberführer he led the land office in Prague. From 1 October 1940 until 21 July 1942 Gottberg was head of the requisitioning office in the SS Head Office. With promotion to SS-Brigadeführer and Generalmajor der Polizei he took over the post of SS and Police Commander "White Ruthenia" and on 24 March 1943 he became deputy to the Senior SS and Police Commander "Central Russia". On 15 July 1943 he was promoted to SS-Gruppenführer and Generalleutnant der Polizei. On 21 June 1944 he assumed the position of Senior SS and Police Commander "Central Russia", and nine days later was promoted to SS-Obergruppenführer and General der Waffen-SS und Polizei. On 20 July 1944 von Gottberg was awarded the Knight's Cross. Captured by the Allies, on 31 May 1945 he committed suicide in Flensburg.

The Kaminski Brigade

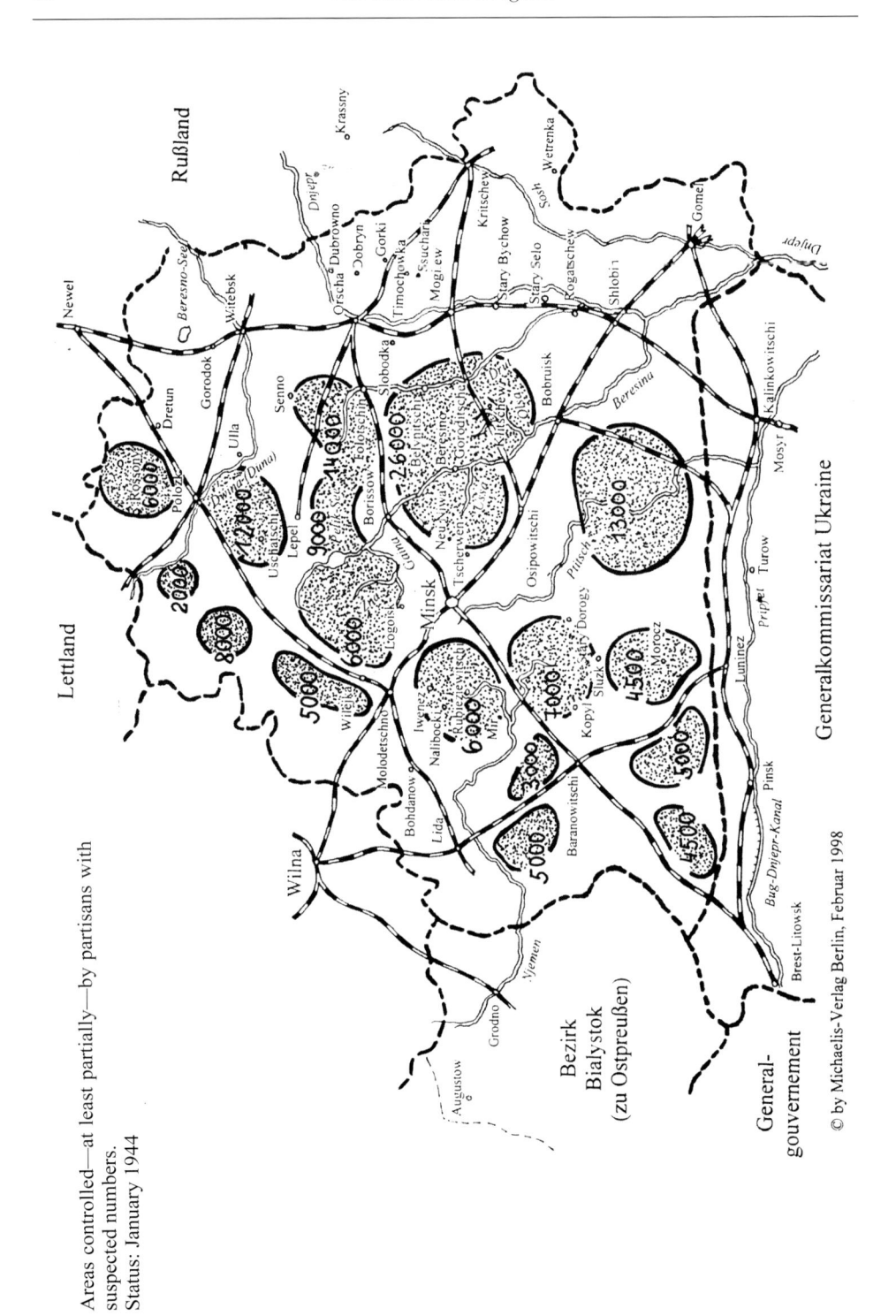

Areas controlled—at least partially—by partisans with suspected numbers.
Status: January 1944

© by Michaelis-Verlag Berlin, Februar 1998

The Kaminski Brigade

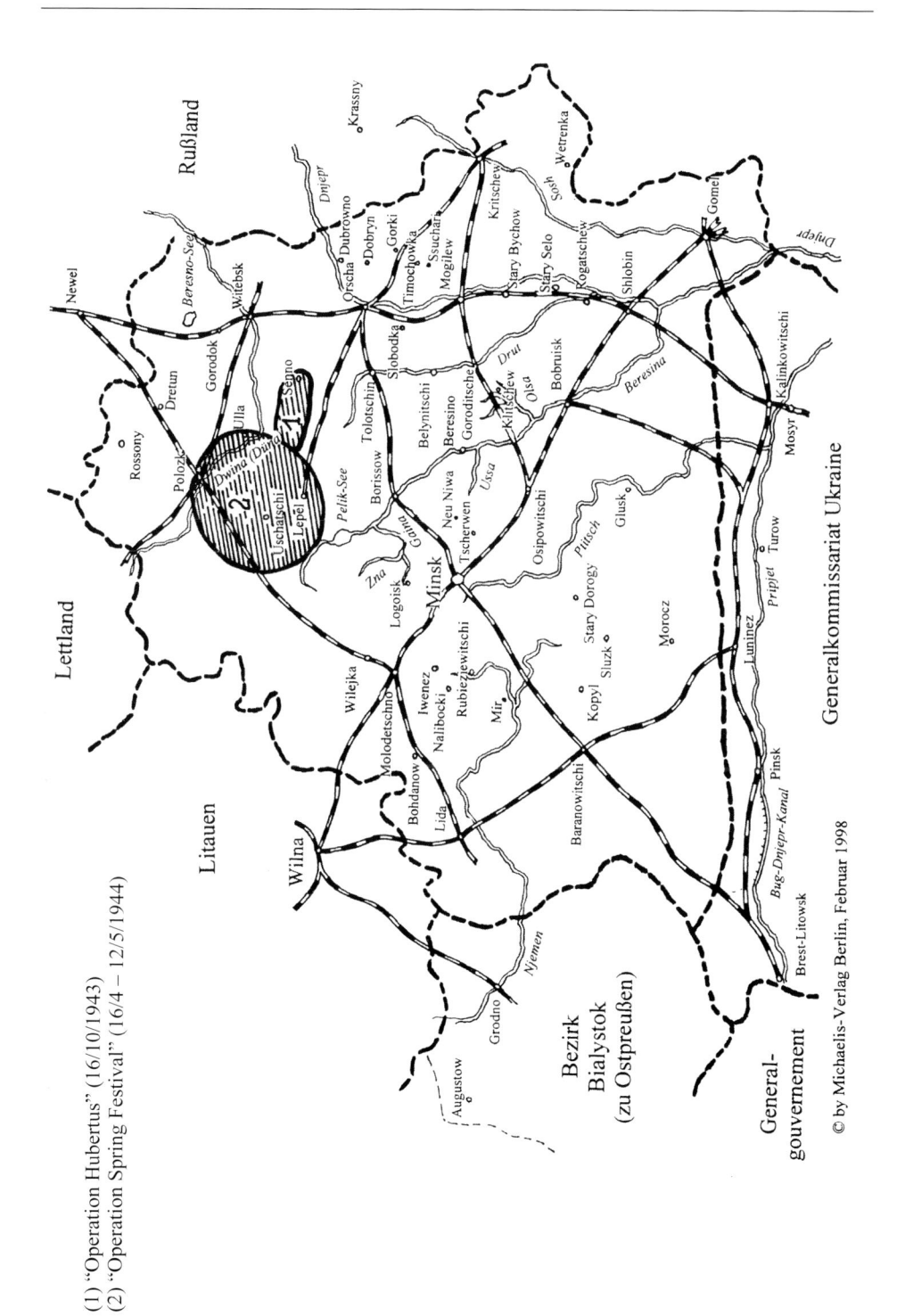

(1) "Operation Hubertus" (16/10/1943)
(2) "Operation Spring Festival" (16/4 – 12/5/1944)

Members of the German liaison staff assigned to the People's Defense Brigade "RONA" in the summer of 1943.

The People's Defense Brigade "RONA" in action in February 1944.

Members of "RONA" with Caucasian volunteers.

Generalmajor Heidkämper, chief-of-staff of the 3rd Panzer Army, Generalmajor Wolf, commander of a Flak Brigade, and Brigadeführer Kaminski in Lepel to celebrate the Russian Easter holiday on 16 April 1944.

The wife of Brigadeführer Kaminski.

The Kaminski Brigade

In the center General Staff Oberst Ludendorff with the brigade commander.

In the center Kaminski. Next to him Generalmajor Heidkämper. On the far right is General Staff Oberst Ludendorff.

yet prepared to bring about a fundamental resolution of the question of incorporating the unit into the Waffen-SS. Himmler instead wanted to wait for development of the NSPR.[33]

Generalmajor Otto Heidkämper met Kaminski on 16 April 1944 during the Russian Easter celebrations:

"Today I and several officers of the high command were invited to join the commander of the RONA in Lepel for the Easter celebration, which is also to be a farewell party for the RONA.

The RONA was originally conceived as an organization of armed farmers. Then last autumn it had to be moved out of the Orel salient with women and children to its new home in the Lepel area, where its first task was to clear it of partisans. There are approximately 7,000 men under arms, who are soon to take part in our 'Spring Festival' anti-partisan operation. Lunch, which began with the famous 'sakuska', lasted more than four hours, and the principal drink was vodka. I gave to the commander of the RONA, Herr Kaminski, whose wife I escorted to the table, a certificate for an 8-cylinder Horch automobile, a gift from the commander-in-chief (of Army Group Center; author's note) in gratitude for clearing the area we are now taking over...."

The former 1st General Staff Officer of the 3rd Panzer Army General Staff, *Oberst* Ludendorff, also recalled:

"As the Lepel area lay in 3rd Panzer Army's rear area, Kaminski was frequently in contact with our supply administration section to discuss matters of supply. I met him officially when he and the Senior SS and Police Commander of 'White Russia', a General

---

[33] The NSPR was ultimately renamed the National-Socialist Russian Worker's Party (NSRAP).
[34] Otto Heidkämper was born in Lauenhagen on 13 March 1901. On 9 July 1918 he joined Pioneer Battalion 10 as an officer candidate (Fahnenjunker) and subsequently served in the Reichswehr. On 1 April 1922 he was promoted to Leutnant in Pioneer Battalion 6. After serving as operations officer of the 7th Panzer Division, Oberstleutnant Heidkämper (1 November 1940) took over the position of operations officer in the 4th Panzer Division until 6 April 1942, leading the unit from 2 March to 4 April 1942. Promoted to Oberst on 1 June 1942, until 6 March 1943 he was Chief-of-Staff of XXIV Panzer Corps. As a Generalmajor (9 November 1944) he held the same position with the 3rd Panzer Army and from 1 September 1944 to 25 January 1945 with Army Group Center. With the rank of Generalleutnant (9 November 1944), in April 1945 he commanded the Geysing sector plus the 464th Infantry Division. He was awarded the German Cross in Gold and the Knight's Cross.

der Waffen-SS von Gottberg,[26] *attended a big conference concerning an offensive against partisan units in our rear area. Somewhat later I also saw Kaminski while off duty. The first time was at a social evening at the headquarters of a flak brigade attached to us, the second time at his headquarters in Lepel.*

Several officers of the operations and supply sections were invited to Lepel to celebrate the Russian-Orthodox Easter holiday, which falls on the Sunday after our Easter. General Heidkämper and I flew in the Stork to Lepel, about 60 km away, where a lavish lunch with much alcohol was served in the home of Kaminski, who had been decorated with the Iron Cross, First Class by the way. Our conversations were translated by interpreters. As the host spoke little German, I didn't speak with him before or after the meal—I wasn't sitting at his table. I did, however, occasionally say 'Prost', and when we left late in the afternoon I thanked him for his hospitality. It was very curious that the wives of Kaminski's inner circle, who spoke only Russian, led by Madame Kaminski, took part in the meal and were seated as our partners at table. As conversation with them was impossible, such as there was was conducted among us Germans over them. For their part the women saw to it that we all had enough to eat and drink."

From 16 April to 12 May 1944 the People's Defense Brigade took part in "Operation Spring Festival" as part of Battle Group von Gottberg, and subsequently moved from the Lepel area into the Lida region. Since the start of the war against the Soviet Union the region had been part of East Prussia, and was under the *Gauleiter* and *Oberpräsident* of East Prussia, Erich Koch.[35] Koch approached the State Ministry for the Occupied Eastern Areas several times to voice his vigorous opposition to the entry into his area of Russian refugee columns (Kaminski movement, Cossacks, etc.).[36] RONA reached Lida at the end

---

[35]Erich Koch was born in Elberfeld on 19 June 1896. After taking part in the First World War he was a member of a Freikorps in Upper Silesia. He joined the Nazi Party in 1922 and by 1928 was a member of the Ruhr District Command. On 1 October 1928 he was named District Leader of East Prussia. In 1930 he became a deputy in the Reichstag and Prussian councilor of state and in 1933 he was named Senior President of East Prussia. In November 1941 Koch became Reich Commissar for the Ukraine. After the war he disappeared under a false name, but he was uncovered in Hamburg in 1949. Koch was handed over to Poland in 1950 and sentenced to death nine years later. The sentence was ultimately commuted to life in prison, and in 1986 he died in his nineties.
[36]In addition to alluding to the fact that the eastern territories of the Reich would soon be completely overfilled with refugees, he made reference to the veterinary laws with respect to the unverifiable number of cattle the Russian refugees were bringing with them.

Brigade commander Kaminski with Oberst der Schutzpolizei Weissig at an operations briefing during "Operation Spring Festival".

Bronislav Kaminski, who was awarded the Iron Cross, Second Class and First Class as well as the Wound Badge in Black and the Medal of Bravery for Members of the Eastern Peoples 1st Class in Gold. Next to him is Oberleutnant Alexei Bagaturia, platoon commander in a transport company of "RONA".

Operations briefing during "Operation Spring Festival".

Second from left is Oberst der Schutzpolizei Weissig, then Brigadeführer Kaminski and, on the far right, Oberstleutnant (Lieutenant Colonel) Shavykin.

Warsaw: the bridge over the Vistula to Praga.

Waffen-Brigadeführer Kaminski at a briefing with *SS-Gruppenführer* und Generalleutnant der Polizei Reinefarth in Warsaw.

After the fighting, Warsaw had been reduced to ruins.

of May 1944 and economically was subordinate to the Senior SS and Police Commander Bialystok. After Koch's unwelcoming attitude, in June 1944 he took over the relocation of the brigade and about 21,000 civilians[37] to Czenstochau in the *Generalgouvernement*.

On 17 June 1944 the Waffen-SS took over the Kaminski Brigade. The brigade was given the military postal number 45 155 and from that point onward was designated:

Waffen-Sturmbrigade der SS RONA (russ.)

A new-style *SS-Sturmbrigade* (assault brigade) was supposed to consist of:

1 grenadier battalion (4 companies)
1 heavy battalion (infantry gun, anti-tank, flak and pioneer companies)

Authorized unit strength was between 1,700 and 2,000 men. At that time the RONA had a total strength of about 5,000 men, however, many of these were not fit for duty. Those who were fit for duty were used to form the *Sturmbrigade*, and there were sufficient personnel to form a second grenadier battalion of four companies. *SS-Sturmbannführer* Gerhard Reußner was named Waffen-SS liaison officer. Issuing of German uniforms was hampered by the rapid pace of events, and most of the brigade's personnel retained their captured Soviet equipment.

On 22 June 1944, the third anniversary of the German attack on the Soviet Union, the Red Army launched its summer offensive.[38] Vilnius (Wilna), in the 3rd Army's sector on its boundary with 4th Army, had been declared a fortified place and was supposed to be a lynchpin in the German defense. The XXXIX Panzer Corps (131st and 170th Infantry Divisions) formed the 4th Army's left wing. To its south were Blocking Unit Weidling (5th Panzer Division, Battle Group von Gottberg, Battle Group Flörke and the 50th Infantry Division).

Battle-ready elements of the *Waffen-Sturmbrigade der SS RONA* located in the Lida region were sent to Operations Group Jacob, which formed part of Blocking Unit Weidling. Initially deployed at the western end of the Naliboki Forest, beginning 4 July 1944 the

---

[37] These were finally sent to Pomerania and some were employed as workers. At the beginning of 1945 they were taken into custody by the Russians.
[38] Within a few days Army Group Center's front collapsed under the Soviet onslaught. The 3rd Panzer Army found itself fighting for its existence. Army Group Center had nothing left with which to counter the Red Army and was virtually destroyed. On 27 June 1944 Soviet troops stormed Vitebsk. The bill for Hitler's order to turn Vitebsk into a fortified place was 10,000 German troops captured and countless dead in the ruins of the city. The next day the remnants of the 3rd Panzer Army withdrew into the Lepel area. The resulting gap between Army Group Center and Army Group North could not be closed. After leaving behind their heavy weapons and losing the equipment they had taken with them in the swamps, the various German battle groups tried to make their way to the west through the vast area of forests and swamps. On 29 June 1944 the Soviets reached the Beresina. On 2 July 1944 the Red Army severed the Minsk – Molodechno road. Coming from Bobruisk, enemy troops arrived south of Minsk. When Soviet tanks advanced from the north through Lagoisk toward the White Russian capital, they trapped elements of the fleeing 4th Army east of Minsk. In the pocket east of Minsk were 28 German divisions with about 350,000 troops. Except for a few that managed to fight their way back to the west, the units were captured or destroyed.

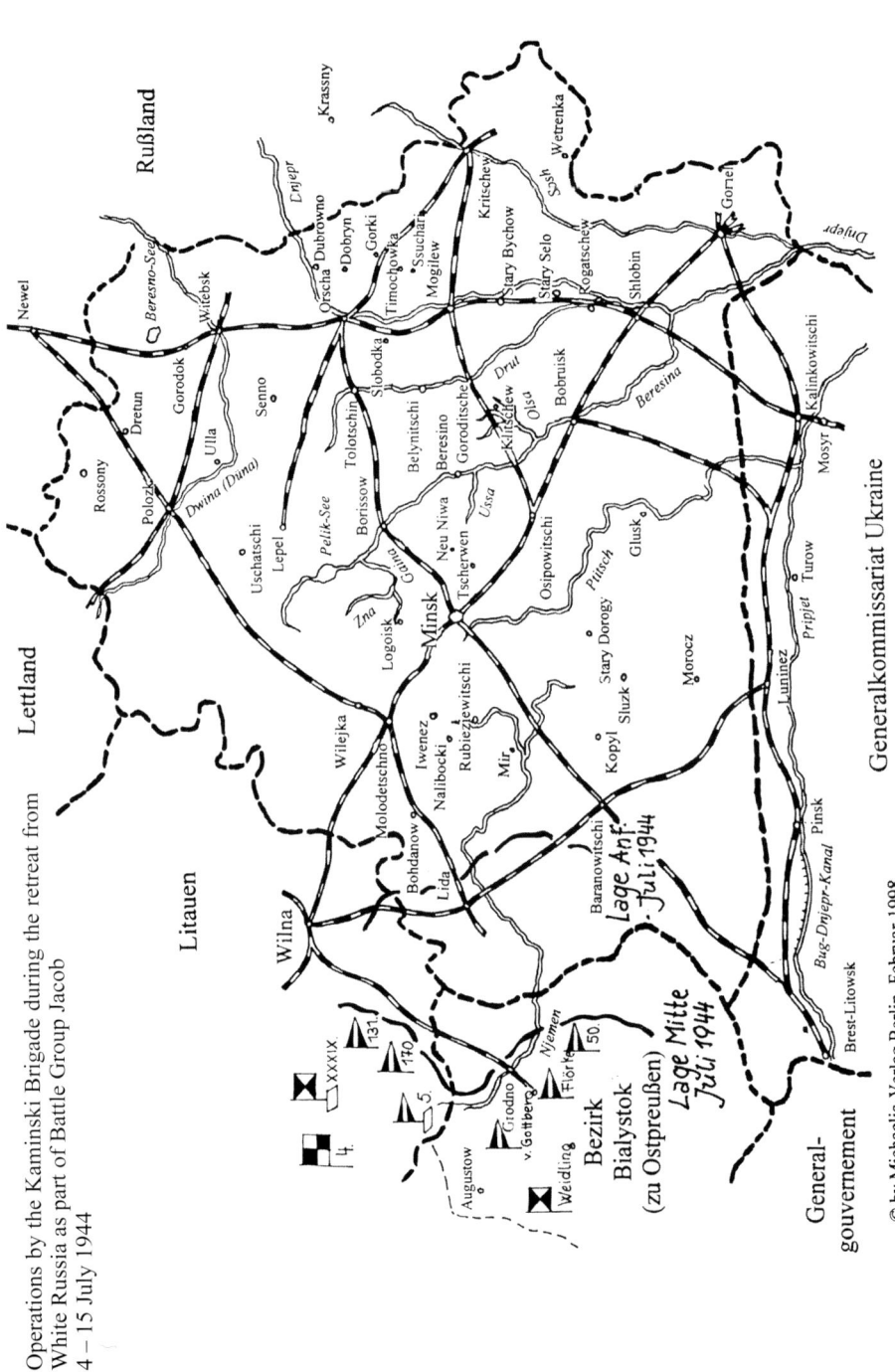

Operations by the Kaminski Brigade during the retreat from White Russia as part of Battle Group Jacob
4 – 15 July 1944

nominally Russian Waffen-SS members fought partisans near Nieniewicze. Committed against regular Soviet troops in the 50th Infantry Division's sector, by 8 July 1944 it had been forced back to the line Wsielub – Novogrodek. With the Red Army storming forward,[39] after a few days the committed RONA elements received orders to withdraw from the front and follow the units that had already pulled out and the civilians.

No sooner had it arrived in the Czenstochau area when the Russian *Waffen-Sturmbrigade der Waffen-SS* was ordered to Warsaw to help put down the uprising.[40] Those personnel fit for duty were used to form a regiment of about 1,700 men. Its organization was almost identical to that of the *Waffen-Sturmbrigade der SS (russ.)*:

2 grenadier battalions
1 artillery battalion with two Soviet 122-mm guns
1 armored unit with four T-34s and a Russian assault gun[41]
1 anti-tank unit with eight Russian anti-tank guns

On 4 August 1944 the regiment arrived in Warsaw via Petrikau, under the command of the RONA's operations officer, Major Frolov.[42] Because the troops had no standard uniform, the 9th Army sent a radio message to the Wehrmacht commander in Warsaw:

"RONA Regiment committed to clean up Warsaw, some personnel without uniforms, probably yellow arm bands, confusion with bandits possible. Troops deployed in Warsaw must be given detailed briefings to avoid run-ins!"

The next day the regiment, which had been designated Attack Group South of Battle Group Rheinefahrt, was reinforced through the addition of 2nd Company, Anti-Tank Battalion 743 with 12 anti-tank guns and 1st Company, Armored Pioneer Assault Battalion 500. At 08:00 the RONA launched an attack in the direction of Warsaw's main train station. Advancing from the southwest down Radomska Street, on this day the regiment reached

---

[39] The Soviets occupied Brest-Litovsk on 28 July 1944 and thus reached the western border of the USSR. In the previous four weeks alone, Army Group Center had lost more than 200,000 soldiers killed or captured.

[40] At 17:00 on 1 August 1944 the Poles launched an uprising in Warsaw. Their objective was to link the part of the city west of the Vistula with the suburb of Praga east of the Vistula, where there were already Soviet troops. They wanted to liberate Warsaw from the Germans with their own forces. The Polish attempt failed, however, as they were unable to take possession of any of the bridges over the Vistula. Instead, what followed was two months of fierce fighting in the streets and houses. The bulk of the German units committed there were training and replacement units, security and alert units, approximately 50% of which were Azerbaidzhaini, Cossacks, Lithuanians, Russians and Volga Tatars. Among them were elements of the Waffen-Sturmbrigade der SS RONA. The units deployed against the Polish Home Army were:
-- SS Special Regiment Dirlewanger
(see Michaelis, Rolf: Die Grenadier-Divisionen der Waffen-SS (Vol. III), Erlangen 1995)
-- Security Regiment 608 (Oberst Schmidt) from Defense District XXI Posen (620 men)
-- Group Posen, 16 military police companies of the SS and Police Commander Posen (about 2,750 men)
-- the Azerbaidzhaini Special Unit Bergmann (5 officers and 677 men)

[41] The armored vehicles were lost in the first days of street fighting.

[42] Frolov was designated a Major. As Himmler made Kaminski a Waffen-Brigadeführer effective 1 August 1944, it is reasonable to assume that the staff officers, at least, were also given rank designations for foreign members of the Waffen-SS. Frolov was therefore probably given the rank of Waffen-Sturmbannführer. In autumn 1944, during the formation of the 600th Infantry Division (Russian), he was a Major and head of the operations section.

the railway crossing, the church in Narutowicza Square, the University Quarter in Academy Square (all in the Ochota Quarter), and was halted before the mahorka [cigarette] factory. The 9th Army's war diary recorded:

"Kaminski Regiment, from the south on the Reich Road, has drunk its way up to the mahorka factory."

An important point in this first day of operations is the radio message sent by the Kaminski group to the "Rheinefahrt Group" at 1726 hours:

"5,000 captured civilians at Point 27. Request immediate transport out."

There is no dispute that more than 10,000 Poles were shot on 4-5 August 1944. To date the blame has been placed on the Dirlewanger and Kaminski units. According to this radio message, however, the captured Poles should have been handed over to other units on 5 August.[43]

The next day the Kaminski group was still fighting in the suburb of Ochota, where the enemy was putting up fierce resistance. The RONA was also still in Ochota on 7 August. It appears, however, that its lack of progress was only partly due to enemy resistance. The following entry appears in the 9th Army's war diary on 10 August:

"The Kaminski group is still fighting in Ochota; at present, however, it appears to regard looting as more important than continuing the attack."

On 11 August the 9th Army's diarist recorded:

"Kaminski huge bust, today they raped German KdF girls.[36] *Our pillaging directive is making itself felt uncomfortably."*

There is no doubt that Himmler gave Kaminski permission for his troops to loot. It is therefore not surprising that the Russians placed more value on booty than in risking their lives by attacking. The Commander-in-Chief of the 9th Army now also found himself with cause to ask von dem Bach for overall command of the effort to suppress the revolt so that, in the face of the flagrant behavior by RONA, he could at least prevent future excesses against Reich Germans and ensure that the attacks to restore contact with the German forces at the central station were vigorously pursued.

On 18 August 1944 the Frolov Regiment still had a strength of 75 officers and 1,510 NCOs and men.[44] The next day Kaminski left Warsaw by order of von dem Bach—the regiment was pulled out of Warsaw on 27 August 1944 and deployed to screen towards Puszca Kampinoska.

---

[43]The many cases of looting and rape committed by the Russians have been documented. Because of the path the regiment followed in Warsaw during the period from 5 to 27 August and statements by witnesses before the Polish committee for the investigation of German crimes in Poland, it appears that the regiment was responsible for killing about 300 civilians.

The *29.Waffen-Grenadier-Division der SS "RONA" (russische Nr. 1)*

The SS-FHA issued orders for the formation of the *29. Waffen-Grenadier-Division der SS RONA (russ. Nr. 1)* at Camp Neuhammer in Silesia, with an effective date of 1 August 1944. The approximately 5,000 remaining members of the *Waffen-Sturmbrigade der SS RONA* were to form the core of the new division. Roughly one-third of these were deployed in Warsaw beginning 4 August 1944. During a visit with Himmler in Rastenburg on 31 July, Kaminski was promoted to *Waffen-Brigadeführer und Generalmajor* and named commanding officer of the *29. Waffen-Grenadier-Division der SS*. One of the brigade's officers who was present recalled:

"When we arrived in Rastenburg Himmler behaved very courteously. Referring to the recent attempt on Hitler's life, he remarked to us that he would feel safest if he had a bodyguard of members of our RONA, because at the moment it appeared that there were no Germans left who could be trusted. This revealed Himmler's opinion of us."

Himmler subsequently drove to Posen to give his famous speech to the Gauleiters. During the speech he touched briefly on the RONA:

"Three of my units escaped the collapse at Minsk or beyond Minsk. One was the Russian Kaminski Brigade with 6,000 or 7,000 men, led by a Russian. I had to listen to my German operations staff relate to me how many cigar boxes of Iron Crosses the Russians had picked up as souvenirs along the wayside because they had been thrown away!"

On 2 August 1944 von dem Bach wrote in his diary:

"I saw the RF-SS again the day before yesterday and I also met Guderian. Also present was Kaminski, leader of the Russian volunteer corps, with whom I had to conduct lengthy negotiations."

With the operation in Warsaw imminent, plans existed to place the *29. Waffen-Grenadier-Division der SS (russische Nr. 1)* and the *30. Waffen-Grenadier-Division der SS (russische Nr. 2)* at the disposal of the Commander-in-Chief West. The following entry appears in the latter's war diary under 4 August 1944:

"Order for transfer of the 29. and 30. Waffen-Grenadier-Division der SS (russische Nr. 1 and 2) into the area of the Commander-in-Chief West for anti-terrorist operations

---

[44] At 4% of its personnel, the regiment had an unusually high number of officers.

(divisions are currently involved in putting down the uprising in Warsaw: strength 6,000-7,000 and 9,000 men). Further orders from the Chief Intelligence Officer."

After the shooting of Kaminski on von dem Bach's order at the end of August 1944, the unit was commanded by *Waffen-Standartenführer* Belayev. The division's planned organization was:

Waffen-Grenadier-Regiment der SS 72 (russische Nr. 1) – 2 battalions
Waffen-Grenadier-Regiment der SS 73 (russische Nr. 2) – 2 battalions
Waffen-Grenadier-Regiment der SS 74 (russische Nr. 3) – 2 battalions
Waffen-Artillerie-Regiment der SS 29 (russische Nr. 1) – 4 battalions
SS-Füsilier-Bataillon 29 (fusilier battalion)
SS-Pionier-Bataillon 29 (pioneer battalion)
SS-Panzerjäger-Abteilung 29 (anti-tank battalion)
SS-Nachrichten-Abteilung 29 (signals battalion)
SS-Versorgungs-Regiment 29 (supply regiment)
SS-Veterinär-Kompanie (veterinary company)
SS-Sanitäts-Kompanie 29 (medical company)
SS-Feldersatz-Bataillon 29 (replacement battalion)

Developments in the situation resulted in cancellation of the division's transfer to France, and consideration was given to deploying the RONA and *SS-Sonderregiment Dirlewanger* to Slovakia to help put down the national uprising taking place there. *SS-Brigadeführer und Generalmajor der Polizei* Diehm[45] was named interim commander of the division. On 27 September 1944 *SS-Obergruppenführer* Berger replaced him with *SS-Gruppenführer* Jürs.[46] Jürs was supposed to reorganize the brigade in the German defense

---

[45] Christoph Diehm was born on 1 March 1892 and participated in the First World War as an officer in the 60th Prussian Infantry Division. After serving in a Freikorps after the war, he joined the SA and on 1929 became adjutant to the SA commander in Wurttemberg. On 22 March 1932 Diehm was taken into the SS with the rank of Oberführer. After just two years he was an SS-Brigadeführer and commanded SS Sector XIX and until 1939 SS Sector I. Diehm was attached to the staff of the SS Senior Sector West. He was then attached to the Reich Central Security Office until 1943. From June 1943 until 25 July 1944 he held the post of SS and Police Commander Lvov. As of 20 August 1944 Diehm was initially considered for command of the 29. Waffen-Grenadier-Division der SS "RONA" (russische Nr. 1); instead, however, he went to the SS Head Office and on 9 November 1944 was given the supplementary rank of Generalmajor der Waffen-SS.

[46] Heinrich Jürs was born on 17 January 1897 and was an early member of the SS (membership number 11, 362). On 30 January 1933 he received the rank of SS-Untersturmführer and on 3 September was promoted to SS-Obersturmführer. Soon afterwards, on 24 December, Jürs was promoted to SS-Hauptsturmführer. Further promotions followed unusually quickly: SS-Sturmbannführer on 12 April 1934; SS-Obersturmbannführer on 17 June 1934; SS-Standartenführer on 20 March 1935 and SS-Oberführer on 30 January 1936. From 1937 he was commander off SS Sector XXXII and on 30 January 1939 was promoted SS-Brigadeführer. On 1 October 1940 Jürs received the rank of a SS-Standartenführer der Reserve der Waffen-SS and until 1943 served as head of Department II in the SS Head Office. On 21 June 1943 he was promoted to SS-Gruppenführer and Generalleutnant der Polizei. Without receiving any additional promotions in the Waffen-SS, on 18 January 1945 the SS-Standartenführer der Reserve der Waffen-SS was promised promotion to the rank of Generalleutnant der Waffen-SS.

zone in Slovakia and from there lead it in action in the central part of the country. Of this Karl Albrecht wrote:[47]

"When the tragic uprising in Warsaw broke out, Kaminski's gang, with women and children, was about 100 kilometers north of the Polish capital. At that time the Kaminski people were still wearing field-gray uniforms with their own fantasy emblems. But during the action in Warsaw and later, when I carried out the inspection in Kattowitz, they wore Waffen-SS uniforms with the prescribed rank badges and could not be distinguished from the regular Waffen-SS.

Himmler had chanced across this gang during one of his trips to the east and had immediately bagged it for himself. That's how these bandits ended up in the Waffen-SS. He placed the brigade under the SS-Obergruppenführer [von dem Bach] responsible for anti-partisan operations. That was certainly the right place for it! Then, when the frightful acts of cruelty committed in Warsaw caused dismay and great anger, even in the German military command positions, and could no longer be hushed up, this SS general had Kaminski shot out of hand, in order to shake off responsibility for these horrible acts committed under his overall command. [...]

But Hitler and Himmler had ensured that they had absolutely no military reserves left and could only offer this Kaminski Brigade [to put down the Slovakian uprising]. And then I arrived with this bad news [about the condition of the brigade]. Was he [Berger] supposed to part with these, as he had been told, 10,000 [in fact about 2,500] well-disciplined soldiers? It was a tough battle that he had to fight. I saw this and made a suggestion: I would check out the Kaminski Brigade on his behalf and determine its tactical military worth as well as its moral disciplinary qualities.

General Berger agreed. That same night he called SS headquarters in Berlin and spoke to Himmler, who agreed to dispatch SS-Gruppenführer und General der Waffen-SS Lührs [correctly Jürs], whom I was to meet in Breslau or Kattowitz. Two days later I met Lührs in Breslau. As soon as we spoke I realized that Himmler had instructed Lührs to give a favorable report on the Kaminski Brigade no matter what.

I was unable to agree with Lührs. [...] We met again at the office of the SS commander in Kattowitz. The latter already had experience with the brigade, which was quartered in his area of responsibility. I did not know then that Kaminski was already dead, shot. While inspecting the camp, I heard that just prior to our visit his people had found his car in an isolated spot, empty with a large pool of blood in the back seat. They believed that

---

[47] See the book: Sie aber warden die Welt zerstören. Albrecht's account is tendentious and thus loses credibility. Nevertheless, his descriptions surely describe certain incidents accurately.

partisans had ambushed their general and carried him away! They were still looking for him when Gruppenführer Lührs and I carried out our inspection. The brigade had also played havoc in the Kattowitz area, plundering, raping and mistreating the population, exactly as had happened for years at Briansk and Smolensk.

I said frankly to Lührs that the brigade was a wild band of robbers, the worst kind of bandits, its officers a consortium of cunning rogues and murderers. Lührs laughed. You have to prove that, he said. Furthermore here's an order from Heinrich Himmler that you and Berger have to obey. What's more, I would be careful about expressing such opinions if I was soon to be the guest of this brigade.

I later heard that Himmler had considered Lührs to succeed the shot Kaminski as an SS-Obergruppenführer und General der Waffen-SS in the event that he successfully prepared the brigade for operations in Slovakia.

I didn't see Lührs again until the banquet given him and his aides in a gaily-decorated hall in brigade headquarters by Belayev, the acting commander of the brigade, who wore the uniform of an SS-Standartenführer. Lührs accepted, laughing. I refused. I had already inspected the 'brigade' camp and had formed a clear picture of everything I needed to be able to render an objective judgment. [...] Lührs, having arrived, had been collected by Belayev and his staff with much ceremony. To the strains of the German national anthem and the Horst Wessel Song, Lührs reviewed the parade, graciously shaking the hand of each battalion commander. I, however, had gone another way. I had taken along an escort consisting of my adjutant (SS-Untersturmführer) Anatoly Kaminin and two SS-Oberscharführer from Berger's staff. Together we had quietly inspected the brigade's open field camp and located everything that interested me. Each of us had a submachine-gun slung over our shoulder, ready to fire. One never knew with these bandits... Lührs needed only betray a single word of my opinion of this gang of murderers and my life wouldn't have been worth a brass farthing. [...]

I spoke with wounded who were hobbling around. They had no boots, no coats, they didn't even have on an intact shirt or pair of pants. All that mattered here was brute force, the bullet, club law. Those who failed to defend themselves forfeited their lives. It was like a horde of career criminals. [...] Many of the people had been recruited forcefully into the brigade. They cursed the day they had joined this band of murderers and wished only for an opportunity to escape. [...]

We watched the parade, Lührs' people, from the Wangenburg, and when it was all over we slowly walked toward the officers standing in front of the large officer's mess.

'Ah, there you are Albrecht. This is a wonderful unit, this discipline, these clear commands, this march pace, this soldierly bearing. You should have seen it.' I just looked at Lührs. [...]

'I also made an inspection, Gruppenführer. We walked through the camp and spoke with the wounded, with the women and children, of which there were several thousand.' At that moment Belayev joined the conversation, asking where I had been in his camp and who had given me permission to be there.

I replied that I was there by order of the German commander in Slovakia, SS-Obergruppenführer und General der Waffen-SS Gottlob Berger.

'I alone make the decisions and give the orders in my camp, tell that to your Obergruppenführer, he can …,' and there followed a vulgar curse commonly used by untrained and uneducated men in the east. Everyone laughed. Belayev, who couldn't speak a word of German, had spoken Russian. But next to him was a man, a German, who translated the conversation; he was a German liaison officer, Obersturmbannführer Rössner [Reußner]. This German officer knew about all of these frightful actions, and as constant advisor to Kaminski and now to this Belayev he had given his approval and taken part in them. Lührs now realized that it was time for him to step in before there was a terrible fight or even a wild shoot-out.

'Gentlemen,' he said, 'we all want to get along. We are fighting for a common cause and in the same formation. Come, let us drink a few glasses of good vodka together, that will cool our tempers. Albrecht, you're not going to be a wet blanket.' In the mess we were supposed to surrender our submachine-guns, in fact all of our weapons. We didn't do it, instead laying the submachine-guns at our feet and watching to see what developed. It was monstrous. While the women and children and the wounded I had just visited were starving, while the numerous children in that Wangenburg were without milk and often without bread, orderlies in white linen uniforms now carried in huge mountains of food–roast chicken, capons, suckling pig, sausage, baked fish. There was also rice, salad, fruit. Everywhere there were large bowls of bread, with an abundance of wine and liquor.

I was filled with disgust. My hand reached for my submachine-gun. I looked my adjutant in the eyes. I could see that he, too, wanted to open fire into the ugly faces of this devil's brew, this band of murderers. But Lührs kept on drinking lustily. To him this was all part of the 'merry soldier's life', the kind desired by such mercenary creatures. I assume that he understood only a fraction of what was said, that only a fraction was translated for him. Obersturmbannführer Rössner sat beside him. They were probably discussing this merry Kaminski Brigade's action in Slovakia. I couldn't listen to it all any longer. It was high time for me to disappear. Submachine-guns at the ready, we walked to our cars and drove back to Pressburg [Bratislava] as fast as we could go.

Then I described these frightful things to Obergruppenführer Berger. My adjutant confirmed everything I had said. Berger was appalled. He had never heard anything like it. That same evening a courier delivered my written report to Himmler with the request that he not employ such criminals in an operational role. At the same time Berger demanded that this brigade of bandits be transported to the troop training grounds at Münsingen, where they should be disarmed and called to accounts. […]

Although Lührs had sent Himmler a report about this 'wonderful, indeed magnificent unit', the Reichsführer chose to believe our report. He intervened in an exemplary fashion. More than 150 of these 'officers' were shot, the entire brigade disbanded, and many of its members were sent to punishment units or put in concentration camps. Many went to Matzkau. That was the end of the Kaminski Brigade, that brigade that some dare to claim was a famous unit."

48 The Kaminski Brigade

Whereas Kaminski had been able to exercise a certain measure of control over the RONA, all discipline disappeared with his death. The attempt to insert a German commander failed because a suitably qualified officer could not be found. As the unit was no longer operational in its present condition, Himmler authorized its disbandment.[48] Its remaining members were supposed to be used in the formation of the *600. Infanterie-Division (russ.)*[49] at Münsingen.

In November 1944 about 3,000 former RONA members arrived at the training camp at Münsingen, Württemberg. In keeping with the Russian mentality, many officers behaved in a very autocratic manner—including some who wore several watches—while many of the common soldiers had no boots, with only foot wrappings to protect their feet. Such was the impression that this made on the German commander of the training camp that a remustering was carried out. After the suitable men had been chosen, issued new uniforms, and given three months of training, the former RONA formed Grenadier Regiment 1602. Its commanding officer was *Oberstleutnant* Artemyev.[50]

On 6 March 1945 the 600th Infantry Division left Münsingen and marched via Weissenburg and Herzogenaurach, near Erlangen (20 March 1945), to Lieberose, arriving there on the 26th. On 13 April 1945 the I Battalion of Grenadier Regiment 1602 (battalion commander Major Solontavin) tried unsuccessfully to reduce the Soviet bridgehead across the Oder at Erlenhof.

Saying that he did not want to be drawn into Germany's inevitable defeat, *Generalmajor* Bunyatshenko, the willful division commander, gave orders that the attack on Erlenhof not be repeated. Instead, he ordered his division to march south into the Protectorate of Bohemia and Moravia. The *Wehrmacht* lacked the means to intervene.

What the opponents and skeptics had always feared was coming true: the fully-equipped Russian division was becoming a source of danger of the first order behind the German lines. On 18 April 1945 the division marched through Kamenz, and on the 29th

---

[48]The first two regiment numbers were assigned in 1945 to the two Waffen-Grenadier regiments (No. 72 and 73) of the 36. Waffen-Grenadier-Division der SS. No SS regiment with the number 74 was ever formed. The division number was assigned to the Italian Waffen-Grenadier-Brigade der SS, which became the 29. Waffen-Grenadier-Division der SS (italienische Nr. 1).

[49]The division was established at the end of November 1944 by the General of Volunteer Units in the OKH at Training Camp Münsingen as the first division of the Russian Liberation Army (Ruskaya Osvobodennaya Armiya). Formation of the division was supposed to be completed on 28 February 1945 with the following organization:

    Grenadier Regiment 1601 (2 battalions)
    Grenadier Regiment 1602 (2 battalions)
    Grenadier Regiment 1603 (2 battalions)
    Division Units 1600

was in Teplitz-Schönau (Sudetenland). On 5 May the unit reached Prague and joined the side of the Czech rebels, falling on the rear of German forces. Coming from the southwest, Grenadier Regiment 1602 reached the city center and drove back a counterattack by troops of the *Waffen-SS*. As a result, on 7 May 1945 Prague was, for the most part, in Czech-Russian hands. When the first Soviet troops under Marshall Konev reached the city from the east, the new Czech National Council dropped a bombshell, declaring that it wanted nothing to do with "*traitors and mercenaries of the Germans*". Faced with this turn of events and the opposing Red Army, Bunyatshenko changed his mind again and tried to get his division to the American lines.

General Vlasov,[51] who was with the division, came upon U.S. troops in Pilsen and unsuccessfully tried to negotiate an agreement for the ROA units not to be turned over. On 11 May 1945 the 600th Infantry Division (Russian) laid down its arms in Schlüsselburg. The next day Vlasov and Bunyatshenko tried to meet with the Americans again, but on the way there they were captured by Red Army troops. Both men were hanged in Moscow on 1 August 1946.

The Americans handed the former RONA members and other Soviet volunteers serving with the Germans over to the Soviets. There they were sentenced to death or forced labor.

The story of the Kaminski Brigade and the National-Socialist Party of Russia shows what could have been achieved if the German occupation policy had granted the Russians autonomy. After decades of oppression the population yearned for a better life. Quickly enthused by their new freedom and the—albeit modest—economic upswing, with the flight to White Russia before the Red Army a growing lethargy set in. With no positive outlook for the future, the political movement and Kaminski's combat unit fell apart. By then the force was of little use, and had instead become a burden to the responsible German commanders. The latter also had no further interest in helping Kaminski in any way. The movement, which had had such hopeful beginnings, finally reached its dramatic conclusion; Kaminski was shot and his troops and civilians were scattered to the four winds.

---

[50] On 11 May 1945 Artemyev stumbled into the Soviet lines, posed as a negotiator and established contact between the Red Army and the 600th Infantry Division (Russian). How Artemyev finally escaped Soviet custody is not known, however he survived and later wrote a book about the 1st Division.

[51] Andrei Andreyevich Vlasov was born in Lomashkino (Novgorod District) on 1 September 1901. After the October Revolution, in 1919 he joined the Red Guard and became an officer. In 1930 he became a member of the Communist Party and from autumn 1938 served as head of a division headquarters. During the Sino-Japanese War he served as an advisor and after returning in 1939 assumed command of a division. He was promoted to major-general on 4 June 1940. From January 1941 he commanded the IV Mechanized Corps, which was stationed in the Lvov area in June of that year. In December 1941 as a lieutenant-general he formed the 20th Army and successfully defended Moscow. In 1942 Vlasov was ordered to relieve Leningrad on the Volkhov. During the failed offensive, in July 1942 the commander of the 2nd Shock Army was captured by the Germans near Tukhovechi. As a POW Vlasov was used primarily as a propagandist against Stalin and at the end of 1944 was named commander-in-chief of the Russian Liberation Army (ROA).

Bronislav Kaminski

Bronislav Kaminski was born in Vitebsk on 16 June 1899, the son of a Pole and a German. He studied engineering in Leningrad and subsequently worked in the paint industry. Already an opponent of Stalin in the 1920s, in 1929 he signed the so called Bukharin Declaration opposing Soviet agricultural policy. In August 1935 he was arrested for alleged contact with Polish and German agents and was banned to the Urals for ten years. From the Butirka Prison in Moscow he was taken to the Soviet concentration camp in Nishi-Tagirski/Chelyabinsk, in the Urals. His mother's banishment ended in 1941. Kaminski was forced to settle in Lokot and worked as an engineer in the local distillery. There he met Constantine Voskoboynik, who opposed the Soviet regime and wanted to establish a national-socialist Russian state. After Voskoboynik's death on 8 January 1942, Kaminski took over the job of mayor and leadership of the Russian National-Socialist Party. During 1942 Kaminski became the leader of a self-governed district, and on 19 July 1942 was promoted to brigade commander of the local people's defense by the commander-in-chief of the 2nd Panzer Army, *Generaloberst* Schmidt. From November 1942 he was awarded several decorations for bravery for members of the eastern peoples, and on 27 January 1944 he was awarded the Iron Crosses, First and Second Class by *General* Burgdorf[52] of the OKH.

Meletij Sykov, who came from the office OKW/Wehrmacht Propaganda and who was a member of General Vlasov's closest staff (Russian Liberation Army), knew Kaminski. To him, he was a worse Nazi than any German. In a letter to Vlasov he declared:

"We are just Russians, not German mercenaries. What the Germans think of us is irrelevant. We believe we are serving our people with pure hearts and clean hands. Stalin, and Hitler too, be damned! As General Malyshkin said, our crime is striving for freedom.

But if we lay down the reins now, then opportunists will take our place. That would spell the end of the Russian people's struggle for freedom. We mustn't fool ourselves, Andrei Andreyevich. There are countrymen among us who are bigger Nazis than the German National-Socialists. They are just waiting for the Germans to place them in the saddle in your place, Andrei Andreyevich. They fall over themselves to talk like the Germans. Already one hears them chiming in in the old battle cry: bey shidov – spassai rossiya (Out with the Jews – save Russia!). If these spirits of reaction ever take the helm, then woe to the Russian people! Perhaps Kaminski, the little Russian Führer, who admittedly did contribute to the liberation of the Lokot District, is waiting for just that. And that is just one example. There are others who are pursuing their own unspecified goals but who do not believe in the freedom of our people, because they have sold themselves to the Germans…"

With events moving rapidly Himmler decided to incorporate Russian units into the Waffen-SS, and on 1 August 1944 he named Kaminski *Waffen-Brigadeführer und Generalmajor der Waffen-SS* and placed him in command of the *29. Waffen-Grenadier-Division der SS "RONA" (russische Nr. 1)*, which was then being formed.

During the operations to put down the Warsaw uprising it became apparent that Kaminski was not in control of his unit, whose discipline deteriorated steadily. In response to complaints by the Wehrmacht, police and Waffen-SS, Himmler ordered that "*the Kaminski problem be solved*".

Von dem Bach subsequently invited *Waffen-Brigadeführer* Kaminski to a meeting in Litzmannstadt. Kaminski left the Warsaw area on 19 August 1944 and was probably shot the same day after von dem Bach telephoned the *Schutzpolizei* in Litzmannstadt, in the Warthe District.

To cover up this action, the rumor was spread that Polish partisans had ambushed and killed Kaminski on his way to the meeting. Kaminski's death also resulted in the end of the NSPR (NSRAP)—which died just as quickly as it had been born in 1941.

---

[52] Wilhelm Burgdorf was born in Fürstenwalde on 15 February 1895. He entered the military on 1 August 1914 and on 18 April 1915 he was named Leutnant in Grenadier Regiment 12. After the First World War and the Reichswehr, on 1 October 1937 he became adjutant in IX Army Corps. In that position he was promoted to Oberstleutnant on 1 August 1938. At the end of April 1940, Oberst Burgdorf (1 September 1940) took over the 529th Infantry Regiment and commanded the unit until 4 April 1942. On 1 May 1942 he became a department head in the Army Personnel Office (W.P.A.) and on 1 October of the same year he was named deputy head of the W.P.A. and promoted to Generalmajor. Burgdorf was promoted to Generalleutnant on 1 October 1943 and General der Infanterie on 1 November 1944 and on 1 October 1944 he became head of the W.P.A. He had previously been awarded the Knight's Cross. Burgdorf took his own life in May 1945.

[53] For further reading on this interesting decoration see: Michaelis, Rolf: Die Tapferkeits- und Verdienstauszeichnung für Angehörige der Ostvölker, Erlangen 1997.

The Russian Mentality

The phenomena of Kaminski, the National-Socialist Party of Russia and the Russian Liberation Army had their breeding ground in the conditions of those times. These were summed up in a study compiled in autumn 1941 by *Oberstleutnant* Gehlen[54] and first presented to officers of the German general staff in Vinnitsa in June 1942. The style of speech reflects the spirit of the times, and many of the points can be attributed to a totalitarian state. Of particular interest are the statements that reveal why Kaminski had success and ultimately failed.

"[…] In the mental image of the Russian one first encounters a striking width of the emotional field, meaning a great wealth of feelings and effects, of motivations, which play a decisive role in the behavior of the Russian. The characteristic features are powerful feelings and motivations rising to extreme intensity, a frequent and sudden shift between emotional states with a great variation in their quality and content.

With the Russians, therefore, we experience brutality as well as the most tender sympathy, deep faith together with the crassest materialism, vivid enthusiasm next to apathy, bravery and cowardice, universal will and sudden failure. Today we are all witnesses to these conflicting natures in the breast of the Russian people! These opposite natures are both a strength and a weakness, and the Russian is conscious of both. Yet he does not perceive the strength within himself to balance out these contradictions; perhaps he doesn't even want to.

---

[54] Reinhard Gehlen was born in Erfurt on 3 April 1902 and entered military service on 20 April 1920. He was commissioned as a Leutnant with the 3rd Artillery Regiment on 1 December 1923. From 10 November 1938 he was commander of 8th Company, Artillery Regiment 18 and from 1 September 1939 1st General Staff Officer of the 213th Infantry Division. At the end of October 1939 Gehlen was transferred to the Army General Staff and in autumn 1940 became a group leader in the Army General Staff's operations section. Following promotion to Oberstleutnant on 1 July 1941, from spring 1942 Gehlen worked as head of the Foreign Armies East Department. There, on 1 July 1942, he was promoted to Oberst. After receiving the German Cross in Silver, on 1 December 1944 he was promoted to Generalmajor.

Power [...]

Whereas the German tribes chose the most noble of freemen from their own race to be leaders, we know that the Slavic tribes were subjugated and ruled by Viking nobles. The reign of the Tartars, also foreigners, left more deep scars. Power has thus always been a foreign and distant force.

"The Tsar is far away," the Russians used to say, and in fact the Tsar was far away. He sat in Moscow or in even more distant St. Petersburg, yet the reach of his henchmen extended to the most remote village. He drafted men for service in the army and let them die far from home. He punished and killed. In the Reich the Kaiser had to reckon with his nobles—secular and religious. Early on in England the counter-government—allied with popular sentiment—led to the Magna Charta and to parliamentarianism and thus found its refuge. [...]

The German princes, the kings and Kaiser, "the first servant of his state", all personified a close and gentle power. The Russian, on the other hand, knew only the foreign, distant and dark power that had always excluded him, which instead of inner ties demanded only unconditional obedience of him. I showed a captured Russian general the Reich Chancellery. "So this is where your Führer lives", he said, astonished, "right in the midst of the people... No Kremlin, no walls, no distance,... simply inconceivable..."

And the rulers of Russia have always realized that they could only control "the inner resistance of the Russian soul" through ruthless suppression and oppression. [...]

Bolshevism has control, not just of the legal system and the police power, but also of the body of the Soviet citizen, because it is absolute master of the economy and has chained the citizens to it. [...]

No Western European could have withstood such pressure for a quarter of a century without being completely crushed by it. It is a known fact that after 25 years of Bolshevik rule, the Western Europeans who remained in Red Petersburg are broken men. They are no longer Westerners.

The Russians on the other hand have endured their suffering differently. Only Russians could have survived this period, and even today they possess unimagined strengths which will enable them to become new men.

This special attitude of the Russian people toward power must not be overlooked if a new power is to be established, whether foreign and distant or gentle and near.

Possessions:
The different nature of the Russian becomes even more understandable to the Western man if he takes the trouble to examine the Russian's fundamentally different attitude towards possessions.

To the Russian possessions are not an end in themselves, rather always a means to an end, which is not to say that the Russian does not strive to have possessions as such. He, too, strives for possessions, and the gulf between him and the western man would probably not have become so great if the broad masses of the Russian people had become aware of the value of property at an earlier stage. Perhaps, too, it would not have come to chaos and Bolshevism if the Russian Prime-Minister Stolypin had realized his great agrarian reforms. In any event, today we find the Russians—"not hanging onto possessions, but instead standing over, or even more accurately—under possessions."

In Tsarist times a small Russian upper class lived in luxury, and some had no idea of the extent of the properties awarded them by the Tsar or inherited from their fathers. The great mass of the people, however, were poor and yearned for their own property—the farmers for their own land. This mass stood under possessions.

But when was the "muzhik" ever permitted to sample the blessings of property earned by his own labor and effort? He was betrayed over and over again.

The last giant swindle was the so-called de-kulakization in 1929, twelve years after the Bolsheviks had come to power with the slogan: "Land for those who cultivate it!"

At this point it should be noted that the expression of work as "output" is unknown in the Russian language. The words "output" and "produce" have no adequate expression in Russian. […]

Suffering:
As long as there have been people, suffering has been part of the lives of individuals and peoples—as a touchstone of growth and maturity.

Whereas the western man, by "making an effort", tries to overcome suffering through action, the Russian has learned to endure it.

The distant, dark powers of violence, the hopeless struggle against epidemics and the forces of nature, perhaps even his religion have taught him that suffering is an unavoidable part of his life. […]

The new Russian leader class:
Men and women of the people were given tasks that had to be accomplished one way or another, and they grew into these tasks. In so doing, however, they were also elevated from the mass of the people. At present, however, the face and conduct of this new intelligentsia is so foreign to us that we can scarcely distinguish the officers from the soldiers, the engineers from the workers. And why is this?

Because this new Russian leader class developed without a model. It will be our task to turn this face toward better models and to be an example if we in the new Europe wish to avoid continually looking into this alien face. The talents and intelligence of the Russians cannot be denied, for without them there is no explanation for their various high achievements, which we have acknowledged. Intelligence tests on Russian prisoners of war have revealed a very interesting picture.

As with most peoples, this picture of the Russians reveals common characteristics.

50 percent average or middle, 25 percent above, and 25 percent below average. Whereas intelligence testing of the average and below average produced results below the German average, the good 25 percent displayed outstanding intelligence and ability, surpassing the majority of Western Europeans.

It must be stated, however, that conversations with Russian engineers, chemists, etc. revealed that the knowledge possessed by these people was heavily one-sided and strongly focused on a specific specialty.

In September 1941 I wrote:

"In contrast to the earlier Russian upper class, that of today has neither firmly outlined national nor Slavophil objectives. At present its attitude is neither anti-German nor pro-Entente. Only the smallest minority have given any thought to the political reorganization of the eastern territories. At present, however, it seems that the national ideal is more and more moving the minds of the leading circle."

Since then, Stalin has kindled the nationalist flames that sprang up everywhere after the start of the war into a huge "patriotic fire". He has given the "Soviet citizen"—raised as an imperialist in the sense of the World Revolution and inherently proud of his vast, rich nation—a racial foundation. He has harnessed Russian history, the national spirit, indeed even the Orthodox Church, as naked terror had proved insufficient to whip the masses of millions into the greatest blood sacrifice of all times.

The Russian today is perhaps less doctrinaire than before. He wants to live according to some concept, however, and it is up to us to reveal this concept to him.

For he is certain of one thing: this vast land with its tremendous challenges can only be mastered with him and not against him. But because he is Russian and has learned patience, he can wait. […]

The Russian peasant:

The Russian peasant and the Russian village are both familiar phenomena. We know that the peasant has become much poorer since Russia became a so-called agrarian republic. We know that the peasant owns practically nothing apart from a garden plot, a cow and a few hens. And it is known that the peasant hates the collective system, because it has turned farmers into rural proletarians. The general flight from the land is characteristic of the "internal Soviet success in the field of agrarian politics". The Russian peasant is politically disinterested. He has just one desire—a piece of land of his own. It matters little to him who governs. He will welcome any authority which gives him land and is more just than its predecessor. The rural proletarian will again become the peasant and lead his own life, and therefore all theories about a "Russian mass soul" are wrong and irrelevant.

The Russian farmer has the same desires and the same hopes as the farmer in the Reich or elsewhere. Only fate has repeatedly barred his way to becoming an individual and establishing a hereditary farm.

It would be incorrect however, based on the statements above, to assume that the Russian peasant has no national consciousness. It will be said that his distress under the Soviet regime was so great that everything else had to move to the background temporarily. One must never forget that a national "intelligentsia" arose from the peasantry in spite of all the mistreatment. Not love of country in the Western sense—but a distinct sense of national community has been confirmed by many examples in even the simplest men—and this should not be overlooked.

The Russian peasant is calculating and mistrustful. Too often he has been lied to by his government. Only facts can convince him. The number of illiterate has decreased, because the Soviets prefer to disseminate their propaganda via the written word.

Everywhere in the Russian land where we encounter Soviet peasants, we again encounter the Russian--not the good-natured and gullible muzhik—for he never existed, rather the muzhik—good-natured to chaotic, gullible to mistrustful—in a word, the Russian peasant in whose soul every register and thousands of possibilities are alive.

We can all better understand this if we recall the psychological profile offered earlier. The worker:

If one compares today's worker with that of the First World War, one must plainly admit that today he seems much more enlightened and has learned much as a specialized worker. Nevertheless, in terms of performance he cannot compare to the German worker in the long run. Neither the joy he takes in his work nor his income measure up to European standards. […]

The working masses are the most heavily--and successfully—exposed to Soviet propaganda. In approaching the Russian worker one should remember not to bring up "freedom of religion" (of which he knows nothing) or the achievements of the "German Labor Front", of which he has no concept. "But", he says, "I know that our workers are being deported to Germany, where they are paid nothing and are forced to wear the symbol of an inferior person—the East Badge!" […]

Space and Numbers:

As scales are the topic of discussion, it seems fitting to quickly touch on the question of space and numbers, which have strongly influenced the character of the Russian man.

The Russian man is the product of the endless spaces into which he is born. Coming from a small space, the European must adapt himself, both intellectually and emotionally, if he is to master his task in the east. The Russian man has the correct feeling for the vastness and insurmountability of his land, and even the most modern means of transportation have not weakened this feeling in him. He knows that in this land the individual must disappear or die. He knows that the many are superior to the individual and that even the outstanding individual personality must serve the many if he is to master the land.

The vastness of the Russian spaces, with their impenetrable forests and unconnected rivers, must have the effect of hampering any real progress and every equally strong will. It is therefore not easy to alter the rhythm of life in this land, especially when faced with an indifferent mass. Vastness of space and isolation have formed the character of the Russian man—thus the attitude of "nichevo" [don't worry, let things take their course: translator's note] *and the chaos, the boundlessness in his character, but at the same time the mute, long-suffering bending under the unalterable forces of nature, the poverty and epidemics, under the force of the power exercised through the many. The master in Russia is he who commands space and masses. Perhaps we can now understand why, to the Russians, the fate of the individual is always of secondary importance.*

It is very characteristic, and should be said here in passing, that the western man—as the result of his different nature—has conquered space and isolation. America is an example of this.

So today we meet the Russian man everywhere—outwardly mired in distress and poverty, having few needs, will-less, frightened, apathetic and resigned. The Bolshevik economic order proved incapable of improving the individual citizen's standard of living.

But the heart of the problem shifted away from the originally-stated plan of reforming an ailing capitalist economic order to the arena of the cultural struggle, for the realization of the Marxist-materialist efforts resulted in a de-spiritualization and with it a rejection of our culture to the last sense of the conflict, and next to this state-ordered de-spiritualization stood the unused: "I know, that I know nothing!"—the searching, questioning and receptive man.

It is perhaps appropriate at this point to thoroughly investigate the reasons for the bitter and determined resistance offered us by the Red commissars and soldiers. I have already answered these questions, in part in the German officer's gazette and also within the scope of this study.

The Russian has always been a poor mercenary but a good soldier; obedient to every authority, resigned to his fate and so undemanding—so frightfully undemanding! This characteristic is benefiting the leaders in the Kremlin today. Patriotic and religious themes have also been used, and recently the peasants were again promised some land. Every possible means is being used to reach out to the "seekers", in order to pacify the range of motivations I have spoken about. Earlier I said that the Russian was a poor mercenary. Perhaps he is the worst mercenary in the world? Just by reading this necessarily limited study, it should not be difficult to explain why this is.

When we speak of the sum of the resistance and only consider tanks, guns, armaments capacity and fuel—we are justified in doing so, but many make the same mistake that the Allies make when they fail to include the German man—the real agent of passive or active resistance—in their calculations.

Therefore the Russian man is and will remain the object of the coming conflict in the Russian-settled area (like the Ukrainians in the Ukraine), especially and to a greater degree once the German military has swept away the Red regime.

Conclusion:

The Russian man, who knows nothing of our world and looks up to us, approaches us with a question that is also ours:

What happens now?

Before I was a railway worker, official, officer. What will become of me now? Before I was a Soviet man, all Soviet men were citizens of a state which, though it enslaved us, promised to lead us to a better future.

What will become of us now?

The question has a double meaning, one political and one psychological.

The political question is beyond the scope of this study. How the map of Eastern Europe will look is also of no importance to the questions touched on here. Within certain boundaries, however, we will have to meet 100 million Russians and deal with them! And there are only two possibilities for this process.

1. The Russians will not be won over, or

2. the Russians will be won over.

Failure to win them over can mean: rule by force.

In this case the mental and spiritual nature of the Russian is of little interest to us, and there will be no need to take them into consideration, just as there will be absolutely no need to consider his political and economic self-interests.

This is not entirely correct, however.

We saw previously that the Russian's relationship to power, to possessions and to suffering is something different, and now we arrive with our Western-European power. Compared to what he is used to, our power will seem imperfect to the Russian. If, however, this is not be the case, then we will have to change, which means that we, too, will have to set up an NKVD apparatus of 1.6 million men. If we fail to address the property question or do so with half measures, if we fail to turn misery into happiness—then sooner or later we will have to establish a total and probably brutal dominion over body and soul, the same as despised Bolshevism!

This would be a return to the old Russian methods—practiced by western men—presuming that they are in fact capable of it.

If we don't do all that, then we must take a second path, the path of winning over the Russian man.

This is the actual psychological possibility, but it depends on a thorough knowledge of the Russian man. […]"

Document Appendix

Document 1
Voskoboynik's Memo to Hitler Concerning Germany's Mistakes in Its Conduct of the War against the Soviet Union

I am writing this letter out of a sense of responsibility towards my homeland. The war in Russia has been going on for more than half a year now and it is still impossible to say when it will end. It was hoped that the war would be over in three months. But even though the Soviet Union is a tottering giant, the war still goes on.

One can cite the incredible vastness of Russia or the Russian winter, but these things were not new. It is interesting, therefore, to examine the particular reasons for the war dragging on.

In my opinion there are two such reasons:

1.) I did not expect that the Red Army's soldiers would be so held together by discipline. Two decades of Soviet terror have certainly had an effect here.

2.) And in my opinion this is the biggest reason — propaganda, the most powerful weapon in the war against the Soviets, has not been exploited.

I live in a forested area, Lokoty settlement, Orel district. We receive news even though the fighting has passed through our area. The Russian 13th Army was destroyed in our forests. We would have liked to see many anti-Soviet leaflets, which could have been dropped from aircraft. But we found just five air-dropped leaflets and these were not effective enough.

The Soviet system was a cruel prison for the entire Russian people that poisoned everything. To date there has been a lack of propaganda, which could save many millions of people. This propaganda must also disseminate new ideas to fill the masses of the Russian people and lead them against Stalin's ruinous regime.

The propagation of the new ideas must be synchronized with the new political and economic order. The completion of these tasks just now will have a great influence on the subsequent course of the war.

I understand well the world problems that the present war poses us, and it is therefore very important to bring this war to a speedy conclusion and to mobilize all German and Russian forces to solve the common world problems.

Completing these tasks is dependent on bolstering propaganda and solving the internal political problems. A war always brings tremendous difficulties for the population, and it is therefore important to give the people everything that can be given and is needed.

The peasant most of all wants his own field. The fields must therefore be allocated now, before the arrival of spring. Special committees can be created to deal with this. The allocation of land will create a new strong peasantry which will support the political order. Those who have fought against the Stalinist system with a weapon in their hand should receive the best land. We must also ensure that the peasant who lost his home under the Soviets is not denied it now. He waited many years for his own home and now watches with bitterness as his enemy continues to live in his house. It is also not right if the cattle needed to feed the German army are taken from the peasants but not from the communists. This will not make the communists better. You yourself realize that you must of course now step back. Every change of government and especially the present one benefits one and disadvantages the others. That is a fact and cannot be overlooked.

The second important peasant question is the distribution of horses. In many villages the peasants have received horses. They were very happy to have their own horses, but their joy was short lived. The local German commanders issued a decree to the effect that the collective farms were to continue in their old form (until the end of field work). Such an order was understandable in the autumn, but now in the spring it should be changed, for the political and economic conditions have changed. If the horses are kept together they cannot be fed as well as if they were with the individual peasants. This might result in the loss of all the horses.

The horses should be given to the peasants as their property, especially to those who are now joining the defense battalions to fight against the partisans. They form the core of the army which in the future will, shoulder to shoulder with the Wehrmacht, bring the war to a successful conclusion.

The third is the economic-industrial question. At present it is difficult to organize private companies in Russia. A certain amount of time is needed to complete the change from state to private economic order. For this purpose, all enterprises should be activated and then transferred to private hands in stages. This will allow the economy to develop and give work to the broad masses. We should not allow a business to remain closed and the workers and employees to be out of work. This would be wrong for political and economic reasons, but so far the representatives of the new order have shown little or no interest.

All of these problems are of major importance and must not be ignored. If they are addressed positively, one can say that the main task presented by the defeat of the hated Stalinist regime has also been positively solved. If Stalin then continues to speak of the collective economy, then the peasants will tear him apart with their forks.

The population in the areas still occupied by the Bolsheviks must be made aware of the satisfactory solution of the identified problems. Then everything will develop positively.

Document 2
Announcement by the Mayor of the Lokot Rayon Kaminski

On 20 January 1942 Zhukov Vasily Petrovich, the civilian guard in the village of Glodnevo, was shot for drunkenness, robbery and self-disgrace.

Document 3
Order No. 23 by the Mayor of the Lokot Rayon

Police officer Sergey Andreyevich is to be shot for drunkenness, mutiny and resistance while imprisoned. The sentence is to be carried out immediately.

Document 4
Announcement by the Mayor of the Lokot Rayon

On the night of 9 January seven partisans were shot for the murders of Voskoboynik, mayor of the Rayon, police officers Babarikin and Kovlar, and aides Katanova and Anopriev.

Document 5
Kaminski's Proclamation of War in the Rayon of Brasovo

A state of war has been declared in the Rayon of Brasovo for the purpose of eliminating the partisan movement. All road traffic will cease with the fall of darkness. Citizens found on the roads after darkness will be punished according to the rules of war.
To defend the lives and property of the peaceful population, a police station will be organized in each village under the responsibility of the village elder.
The village elder is authorized to employ all means, and he may call up all men between the ages of 17 and 50 for various indispensible jobs.
All those unwilling to comply with this order are to be arrested and transported to Lokot.

Document 6
Order No. 33 by the Administration of the Rayon of Lokot of 20 January 1942

1§

In order to maintain calm and order in Lokot, I order that all residents living on the Lipoveya Alleya and Vesenni Perenlok roads be resettled to the other roads within three days.

2§

Vacant houses are to be used by the families of the police.

3§

The following villages are to detach sleighs to the administration headquarters each day:

1. Rasoshka	*3 sleighs*
2. Snytkino	*5 sleighs*
3. Serp and Molot	*5 sleighs*
4. Goroelishche	*3 sleighs*
5. Mayski	*2 sleighs*
6. Aloshonka	*5 sleighs*
7. Pogreby	*5 sleighs*
8. Voron'or Lok	*1 sleigh*

Horses and wagons are to be sent with one day's fodder and rations.

4§

Battalion commander Mironeko is responsible for ensuring that the order is carried out.

Document 7
Proclamation by the Mayor of the Rayon of Lokot

The partisans have killed 4 men and 2 women in the village of Chutar Kholmetzki and 1 man in Kholmichi. As a reprisal, 8 male hostages from the families of the partisans were shot at eight in the evening on 20-21 January 1942.

Document 8

Report by Leutnant Glatz
(platoon leader attached to the commander of railroad pioneers/H.Q. 2nd Panzer Army)
Observations Made in the Area West of Lokot
26 January 1942

Voskoboynik, the mayor of Lokot who was killed in combat with partisans on 8 January 1942, organized a 20-man police station. It was enlarged to 50 men and later to its present strength of 200.

This police station is today a police school, where men with no previous training are trained under the direction of Mishtshanov. In the station itself, strict discipline is maintained. Failure to obey an order results in immediate punishment. A typical barracks routine is followed with scheduled shooting practice, drill, barracks housekeeping and periods of alert. The individual squads are housed in rooms, and each squad of ten to twenty men is commanded by a senior police officer. Several rooms in the police building have been set up as cells, in which partisans, suspected partisans and members of their families, including a number of women, are held as hostages. The new mayor is fully on our side and together with the commander of the entire battalion, Sub-Lieutenant Mironenko Daniel Paulowitz, has committed his entire force to combat the partisans.

From Lokot four more larger police stations have been established, and in addition 10-25 police, some of them armed, have been stationed in each village. The Lokot area encompasses 137 collective farms and 21 municipalities. Regular armed patrols maintain constant contact with these and also conduct reconnaissance.

Locations of the police stations, strengths and weapons:

1.) Lokot   200 men, 3 heavy MGs, 6 light MGs, 3 mortars,
*   300 rifles and 1 75-mm cannon*
2.) Krupets   90 men, 4 light MGs, 2 mortars, 100 rifles
3.) Brasovo   40 men, 4 light MGs, 40 rifles
4.) Vladimirovsky 60 men, 4 light MGs, 60 rifles
5.) Dubrovka   80 men, 3 light MGs, 40 rifles (being established)

Villages in which partisans have been discovered, strengths and weapons:
Susemka, Navlya, Komanichi

1.) Kokorevka: 15 men (spies). These organized the ambush of Leutnant Arnold's patrol.

2.) Terebuzhka: (see note) Headquarters, Kapralov Battalion, 80 to 100 men, 11 heavy MGs, 21 light MGs, 1 mortar (half of the men are mobilized civilians).

3.) Cherny: 100 men (Ukrainians) well armed.

4.) Borshchevo: 1 bunker, 85 men, also well armed.

5.) Demisovka: 100 – 200 men, well armed

Ikritskoye   )
Selechnaya   ) are occupied by the partisans
Gavrilla Gulla   )
Trubchevsk   )

Ostraya Kuka   ) partisan headquarters
Terepushka   )
Tvorankino Gorka)
Borshchevo   ) bunker
Kapralov   )
General:
Combined total: approx. 1,500 partisans
Weaponry: very good, adequate supply of ammunition
The typical captured partisan was carrying 2 pistols, 2 to 3 hand grenades and 1 submachine-gun.
Partisan Attacks:
1.) Navlya on 27 December 1941 (ambush of Ofw. Schubert's signals battalion).

2.) Attack on Lokot on 8 January 1942. Killed were the mayor and 1 police officer. Five police officers were wounded. 22 Russian police fought a well-armed partisan battalion—160 men—under the command of the Communist Kapralov. They were armed with 11 heavy machine-guns and 50 automatic rifles plus 21 light machine-guns.

3.) On 17 January 1942, after its position was betrayed by partisans in Kokorevka, Leutnant Arnold's reconnaissance patrol was ambushed in Neruski between the Kholmech railway station and Susemka. Lt. Arnold's patrol consisted of one officer, one NCO and 14 enlisted men. The ambush was planned, consequently our men had no opportunity to bring their own weapons into position. Eight men reached the troubleshooting team in Brasovo on 18 January 1942. Lt. Arnold, Fw. Hink and six men have not returned.

4.) The villages of Kholetsky Chutto and Kholmech' were attacked on 19 January 1942. Four policemen and three civilians were killed. Fifteen partisan hostages were shot.

5.) Altkhova was attacked on 24 January 1942. For the purpose of mobilizing the villages for the attack on Lokot, anti-German posters were handed out (telling of the German retreat from Orel and Kursk).

6.) A partisan patrol (four men) set out from Borshchevo to Klinskoye, where it was put to flight by the Russian police. Some of the partisans withdrew from Terebuzhka to Maltsova.

Operations by the Russian police:
On 24 January 1942 a Russian police battalion was sent to Govrillova Guta, where four armed partisans were captured.

Ongoing capture of partisans.
A reprisal raid on Terebuzhka (Lt. Arnold) was planned from Lokot. The nearby police stations were deployed for an encirclement. One paratrooper was captured near the village of Dubrovka on 27 January 1942 and brought back by the patrol to the Rear Army Headquarters in Briansk. (Report on the initial interrogation by the rear army headquarters is attached.)

Combating the Partisan Movement:
Operation in the area west of Lokot.

Required: one battalion equipped with small arms and light infantry guns. The first objective of this operation must be to establish contact with the reliable and German-friendly police school in Lokot. Only there is the objective of the attack to be determined with Russian police officers attached to the battalion for their knowledge of the roads and villages. The village elder in Lokot will provide 500 sleighs for use as transports during the operation.

Lengthy preparations in the local area are not required. Ruthless measures against non-residents in the individual villages, also seizure of family members of partisans.

Document 9
Observation Report by Leutnant Glatz for the Navlya Area

Towns where partisans have been discovered.
Area: Briansk – Vygonichi, Briansk – Bovanovo.
Peritonye, Trubchevsk, Altukhova, Pogrebi, Shcheklovka, Sokolova, Putre, Siderovka southwest of Sineserki, Soltanovka, southwest of Navlya, Pechki, Gretovo, Borshchevo.

Organization of the partisan movement is carried out by party functionaries from Navlya and officers of the Red Army. There are indications that the partisan units, previously independent and working alone, are being concentrated and are working according to common guidelines.

In the past 14 days there has been a partial mobilization of men from 16 to 60 years of age in the above described area.

The partisans are very well armed. Anti-tank guns, very many machine-guns and many automatic weapons. Ammunition is adequate for the scope of their plans.

The weapons were acquired from the encirclements of the Red Army around Briansk.

The concentrations in the villages of Sidorovka, Atrelok, Sytenki, Vsdrushov and south of the Shchegloneka railway were given orders to attack German units and destroy Russian police.

In general the efforts of the partisans are directed solely against the Russian police and the German-friendly mayors and their representatives (see Lokot).

Fear of open combat against German troops is great. Ambushes of German soldiers are only conducted when the partisans enjoy numerical superiority and after lengthy preparation.

In the villages where there is no German control, 60% of the population is sympathetic toward the partisans, as their relatives must also be with the partisans. Children as young as eight and old women are used to providing the partisans with accurate information about the strength and condition of the Russian police as well as the German military. Propaganda leaflets are distributed. The content of these leaflets, some of which are handwritten and some machine-printed, is as follows: The Germans are on the retreat and are taking away all the cattle, bread, grain, horses and warm clothing. They are also carrying off young men and women. If the Germans come the people are to hide everything and go into the forest. Death to the German officers.

Long live the great Stalin! The Red Army is coming, we are in contact with it. The signature is that of the commissar of partisans. On orders and air-dropped leaflets the officers are anonymous. Junior officers, lieutenants and sub-lieutenants are identified by first names only. In addition to these false reports there are also occasional reports on conditions at the front, which are surprisingly accurate and not exaggerated. This suggests a well-organized network of spies or radio communications.

The bunkers in the area south of Navlya, which are marked on the maps already delivered, are believed to house headquarters. The bunkers are well camouflaged and guarded by heavy weapons. The bunkers are manned by 100 to 200 men, who are housed in barracks and follow a camp routine. Training is good, as there are many former Russian soldiers and officers in the partisan battalions. We hear artillery and machine-gun fire in the forests.

The partisans possess numerous sleighs and skis.

Operations against bunkers south of Navlya.

Requirements: preliminary aerial reconnaissance and scouting of roads, production of maps indicating the positions of bunkers.

Employment of a reinforced battalion supported by infantry guns, anti-tank guns, flamethrowers and light mortars.

As the police station in Navlya is not reliable, the police cannot be called upon to play an important part.

Remarks: Own Operation

In mid-January 1942 the German side initiated an operation by the air signals battalion with a strength of 2 officers and about 80 men. Its objective was to attack and eliminate a bunker near Navlya (see bunker sketch). Operation failed. Several dead and wounded on our side.

Document 10
Appeal by the Leader of the National-Socialist Party of Russia Kaminski under his Pseudonym Engineer Zemlya

The crimes of the Stalin order are staggering.

Starvation and prisons, concentration camps and backbreaking labor, lies and provocation, misery and total destruction are the achievements of our land in the past ten years.

Almost all of the best, most honest and cleverest people of the country have been destroyed, almost all who failed to agree with the "brilliant" idiots from the Kremlin in minor matters.

Stalin doesn't even spare his intimates. The best and most honorable party members, the best commanders of the Red Army, the people who spoke the truth, are dead or rotting in prison.

Destroyed were: Pykov, Bukharin, Piatakor, Rakovski, also heroes of the army: Blücher, Yegorov, Kovtynch, Tukhachevski, Yakir and others.

The entire Leninist politburo had been destroyed. They disgraced them and branded them spies bent on sabotage.

Freedom was dragged through the mud.

Previously we fought for freedom of speech, under Stalin even silence was forbidden. Everyone had to praise the disgraceful order created by the ass from the Caucasus. Anyone who remained silent was politically suspicious.

People were forced to speak and to spread lies among the masses of the people. One could only be free if one stood and saluted Stalin, clapped and bowed before the Kremlin.

Thousands of the unworthy bowed before this "genius of humanity, before this friend and father of the people". The land became ever poorer, the people wore rags and even bark shoes became a rarity in many villages, while from the Kremlin the unworthy Stalin and his henchmen declared that we were living in prosperity and pleasure.

"We have made tremendous achievements" they said. "We have achieved socialism and now we are embarking on communism."

Yes, they were beginning to live better, they lived well twenty-four hours a day, but the people lived in terrible misery.

Not only did the people die of hunger and misery, they died of cold as well. The people froze in our country where there are so many forests. Many thousands committed suicide, they threw themselves in front of trains and hanged themselves, poisoned themselves, in a word they did everything to put an end to this unbearable "happy life".

13 million people died of starvation in the Ukraine.

Vast Siberia is decorated with crosses. They dared not print a word of this in the newspapers. The truth was silenced. For those brave ones who spoke a single word against it, it was death by shooting or exile.

Stalin was skillful in his handling of the unarmed people, but he knew of the German military and he used lies to maintain his power. He spread false reports using the radio, newspapers and posters, claiming that the German military raped women, killed peaceful citizens and poured petroleum on everything and burned it down.

Now everyone knows that it was lies.

The German military released us from the Stalinist yoke. It brought our people a free, happy life.

The war has been going on for six months already; millions of innocent children have become orphans and all of this has happened to maintain the existence of the bloody Stalinist order.

Now in winter Stalinist bandits are burning villages and towns, tossing the population into the street, where they starve and freeze to death.

The time has come to put an end to this mistake.

Down with the bloody Kremlin dog!

An awful death threatens our longsuffering people.

Soldiers and commanders!

You are destroying our own women and children! Be reasonable, it is still not too late!

The Stalinist order must disappear, but we must save millions of innocent lives.

Document 11
Manifesto of the NSPR

On 25 November 1941 the National-Socialist Party of Russia began its work.

The N.P. was born in secrecy in a Siberian concentration camp. For a short time the national-socialist party was called "Viking".

The N.P. makes itself responsible for the fate of Russia.

It commits itself to create a government which will bring about peace, order and all the necessary conditions for the blooming of peaceful work in Russia, for honor and dignity.

The N.P. will proceed according to the following program:

1.) Total destruction of the communist and collective agricultural order.

2.) The free transfer of all lands to the farmers for perpetual hereditary use, with the right to lease and trade, but not to sell. A farm in central Russian will encompass about 10 hectares.

3.) Free, perpetual, hereditary transfer of garden plots to the Russian citizens with the right to trade, but not to sell. The garden plots in central Russia are on average one hectare.

4.) Free development of private industry, on the basis of which every citizen has the right to pursue the career of his choice. Everyone has the right to establish a factory or business.

5.) Private capital will be limited to 5 (five) million rubles in gold. Every worker is entitled to a two-month vacation to establish and work his garden.

Note: for those in occupations detrimental to the health, the vacation will be extended to four months.

6.) Every citizen can receive wood from state lands free of charge for the construction of a home.

7.) The following are state property: forests, railways, mineral deposits and main factories.

8.) Amnesty for all members of the youth party.

9.) Amnesty for the secret members of the communist party who did not torment the people.

10.) Amnesty for all communists who took up arms against the Stalinist order.

11.) Amnesty (remainder untranslatable).

12.) Total destruction of the Jews who served as commissars. Free work, private property within the borders prescribed by the law. State capital increased and improved through private initiative. The spirit of the citizens will form the basis for the introduction of a new state order in Russia.

This program will be implemented after the end of the war and after the N.P. has come to power.

Essentially, privileges will be granted to those who have participated in the establishment and strengthening of the new order.

All good-for-nothings and thieves will be rooted out.

Our party is a people's party. It will protect and honor the history of the Russian people.

It knows that in the distant past Vikings, with the help of the people, created the Russian empire.

Our country has been destroyed by the Bolshevik government. The senseless and destructive war, brought about by the Bolsheviks, has left thousands of cities and factories in ruins.

But the "Viking" Party believes in the bravery and the civic courage of the Russian people and swears to rebuild the Russian empire from Bolshevik rubble.

The Russian army of old fought and triumphed with the picture of the victorious George, so it will also be in the future and therefore our national help is the white cloth with the picture of victorious George and the George Cross in the upper, left corner of the flag.

Every citizen who is in agreement with our party's program, should sign up those citizens who want to join our party. Viking Party committees shall be organized in every government and district center. The National-Socialist Party salutes the courageous German race, which has destroyed the Stalinist right of slavery in Russia.

Document 12
Order No. 35 of the Elders (Starosten) for the Rayon of Lokot
(formerly Brasovo) dated 21 January 1942

§1
Traffic from village to village is suspended. In urgent cases traffic may take place with the confirmation of the village elder.

§2
All gatherings in private homes and in the streets are forbidden.

§3
Walking about on the roads after nightfall is forbidden, and whoever fails to obey this order will be shot.

§4
The village elders shall collect personal documents and record in them the bearer's height, eye color and hair color. These documents shall be forwarded to the Rayon administration for the issuing of visas.

§5
All non-residents must report to the village elder.

§6
Each village is to form a sleigh guard, in order to report partisan ambushes to the administration.

§7
Each day the municipality of Krupets must keep 15 sleighs at readiness, the municipality of Krasny-Kolodets 15 sleighs. The village elders are responsible for the sleighs.

§8
The market in Lokot and the church in Brasovo are temporarily closed.

§9
Those who do not obey this order will be punished in accordance with martial law.

§10
Responsibility for the implementation of this order is entrusted to Senior Police Officer Ivanin Roman Tikhonovich.

§11
This order shall be posted in every village.

Document 13

Letter from the Mayor of the Lokot District Kaminski to Headquarters,
2nd Panzer Army in Orel
30 March 1942

We are sending to you those orders issued in response to the decision made by the army headquarters in Orel.
1.) *Order No. 53 of 1 March 1942*
2.) *Order No. 54 of 1 March 1942*
3.) *Order No. 55 of 2 March 1942*
4.) *Order to the police battalion in the Lokoty District of 11 March 1942*
5.) *Appeal to the population of the Lokoty District*
6.) *Open letter to the captured partisans*
7.) *Reply to the cadre bandits, former partisans*
8.) *Appeal to the soldiers and commanders mobilized by the partisans*
9.) *Text of the oath*
10.) *Report of 10 March 1942*
11.) *First issue of the newspaper "People's Voice"*

At the same time, I am advising you that a club for propaganda has been established in Lokoty. The newspaper "People's Voice" will be issued twice a month. We are asking that you send "Retsch" and other materials, such as books, brochures, posters. I am also requesting a 220-Volt radio receiver, foolscap and linoleum.

Document 14

Order No. 53
to the Population of the Lokot District
1 March 1942

At the conference held in the German general staff headquarters, General Brand expressed his thanks to me and the entire administration of the Rayon for our good work.

As an expression of his gratitude, the German military commander ordered that pastures and horses be given to all employees of the Rayon, the police and commanders.

As well, the Rayons of Susemka and Navlya have been transferred to us. This order is being brought to the attention of the population of the entire Rayon, and I am convinced that in the future we will be able to work with the friendly German people for the growth and benefit of the great Russian people and our beloved homeland.

Document 15

Order No. 54
to the Population of the Lokot District
1 March 1942

For the purpose of carrying out General Brand's order concerning the distribution of pastures to commanders, police officers and employees of the administration of the Rayon of Lokoty, I order:

§1
As soon as possible, Mr. Mossin shall provide the agricultural department with qualified workers, so that preparations for the distribution of pastures can be completed by 20 March 1942.

§2
Within three days battalion commander Mironenko shall produce lists of police and employees for the distribution of pastures and deliver them to the agricultural department.

§3
All senior police officers and village elders shall prepare lists of police and employees in the agricultural department with the name of the village.

§4
For the purpose of distributing the horses, Mrs. Kolokzeva and the village elders shall produce lists of the horses so that they can be properly distributed.

§5

Senior police officer Mr. Ivanin shall make a list of all the functionaries of the administration who have no horses and provide them with horses within one month.

§6

In distributing the pastures, the parcels will be selected in such a way that the police and employees receive the best pastures.

Document 16

Order No. 55 from Mayor Kaminski

I am issuing the following orders to the administration of the Lokot District in response to a decision by the staff of the German Army:

§1

The district administration is to establish a Department of Agitation and Propaganda.

§2

My aide Mr. Mossin Stefan Vasilyevich is to be made head of the propaganda department.

§3

Mr. Mossin is to select functionaries within three days and submit their names to me for approval.

Document 17

Order from the Deputy of the Head of the National-Socialist Party of Russia Kaminski

To the police battalions of the Lokoty District, 11 March 1942

Since the 3rd to the 10th of March this year, the communists and commissars who have become leaders of the partisan movement have attempted to interfere with our peaceful work. These attempts were unsuccessful, however, even though their attack preparations were lengthy and thorough. These traitors to the Russian people have deceived themselves. They have achieved nothing. They have only shed blood, as it was during the war against the German military.

These proper traitors have hidden in the forests instead of fighting at the front. Now, with the front far away, they have occupied villages and plundered and terrorized the population. They plunder and rob, they spill the blood of the Russian people here in the hinterland. They lie and betray the population. They speak of great successes by the bloody Stalin, they mobilize the population, which does not wish to follow them. Adding up all their successes, the Bolsheviks could already be in Paris. They continue to plunder the population and steal everything that falls into their hands. For more than a month these bandits have been talking about the retreat of the German army and the capture of cities:

Orel, Briansk, Kursk and others. In reality the front is where it was, and even the city of Yelets has been taken. The Bolshevik 61st Army was encircled at Yelets. All of this is simply a lie, as it has been for the past 24 years.

Filled with the ideal of fighting for freedom, honor and faith, during this period our brave soldiers and commanders have hit the hangmen hard at Tarasova Guta, Shemyakino Guta, Kholmechi, Igritskoye and Dubrovka. Our losses in the fighting were minimal and could have been even less if the commander at Shemyakino had performed better.

The bandits lost more than 200 men. They lost 80 men killed at Dubrovka. These figures do not include the wounded.

We have no desire to spill blood, but if we are attacked we reply with repeated heavy blows.

Those who fall into our hands carrying weapons will receive no mercy, but those who come to us voluntarily with or without weapons will be treated as our allies.

Police and commanders! I salute your victories and wish you further success in our struggle for a happy new life, for a new free Russia. Forwards to fresh victories!

Document 18

Appeal to the Population of the Lokot District
(formerly the Rayons of Brasovo, Navlya, Susemka and Komarichi)

For more than eight months the blood of the Russian people has been shed madly. Does our homeland need this blood? What do the Russian people have to defend? Nothing, and a thousand times nothing. This has been proved by the army, which comes from the people, and which has no desire to fight for various helmsmen. Entire companies, divisions and armies go into captivity. Stalin's so-called historic solutions do nothing to help the homeland, because they are not in keeping with the interests of the people and only benefit a small group of bloodsuckers like Stalin and his followers, who live well and want to suppress the Russian people.

Stalin and his cronies on that side of the front and the partisans here have sold our great homeland to the English and American capitalists. Now that they have lost everything, they want to save their situation with lies and betrayal. This lie is well known to the population. German soldiers have never put out eyes, cut off ears. The German Army is powerful, it is marching from victory to victory. It is bringing the Russian people liberation and giving it what matters most: the field and the horse. We have begun distributing land in the Rayon, where there are no partisans. The other Rayons must be freed of partisans so that the farmers can work their fields in peace.

Farmers! Liberation from these knaves and executioners is in your best interests! Spring is here! You ought to be providing for yourselves and your families. They are forcing you to go hungry, as it has been for 24 years. Everyone mobilize; remember, it is still not too late.

He who wishes to live well and happily must not go with the executioners. Destroy your enemies, only then will you be free and bring about work, well-being and the blossoming of our homeland.

Do not fear the police and the Germans! They know that you will be lost if you follow the Bolsheviks.

Those who do not oppose us, who come to us voluntarily, will save themselves and their families, they will have a fine life.

And those who oppose us with weapons in their hands will lose everything and will be cursed as traitors to the homeland.

Document 19

Open Letter from Captured Partisans from Lokot

Comrades, soldiers and commanders!

We former partisans from various battalions are well. Some of us were wounded, and even though we were captured with weapons, our lives were spared. They cared for our wounds and fed us. Some of us are working. No one has been shot, even though we have been prisoners for two months already. We regret that we previously followed you and believed the commissars who told us that they shoot the innocent here.

Here anyone can work if he truly wants to. Commissars who formerly operated in the Rayon are working here. They laid down their weapons. Our former partisans are working towards their diploma. Some, such as Vasinkov, member of the Rayon committee, Zovoks director Voropanov, Chupakov, and others have been given the opportunity to work and make up for their former mistakes.

We know why we are so powerful. We are heavily armed, our battalion is united, for it wants to fight, not for itself, but for the whole Russian people.

We were betrayed just like you. Now we know the truth. Tie up your commanders and commissars, bring them to Lokoty and come yourselves in groups of three to five. By doing so you will save your own lives and those of your families. Enough with the murder of peaceful civilians and plundering. Down with the commissars and political leaders who have stained your hands with innocent blood. Leave all that, take up the plow and the harrow and get ready for spring. You will be given land and horses, for here the distribution of land and horses has begun. Save your children and your wives, for it is not too late.

We are not being forced to write this letter, rather we do it willingly.

Signed by former partisans of the Susemka, Saburova, Kokorevka and Yanbulan Battalions.

Document 20

Another Letter to Partisans and Commanders

We have received your letters and we especially thank you for your reports, which clearly show that you and your commissars are poor fighters and liars. You can't even lie. If all the kilometers you have taken were added together, the Red Army would be in Paris and you would have the opportunity to govern as you have for the past 24 years.

Our account is more truthful than yours. Listen to it and pass it on to other people whom you have deceived.

1.) At the front, the Bolsheviks have only suffered defeats at the hands of the German Army. The cities of Livny and Yelets are not encircled, rather they have been taken by the Germans. The 61st Army has been encircled and captured.

2.) On our fronts we have repulsed every one of your attacks with heavy losses to you. At Kholmech', Kholmetzki Chutor, Barasovka, Shemyakino and Dubrovka you lost more than 200 men, plus many weapons and much ammunition. That is a true account. We also suffered some casualties in these battles, but they were only 10% of yours. You want to keep that secret, but it is impossible, the people know that, all those who have been mobilized know that. They have become demoralized as a result. You want to convince the people that we are traitors. In 24 years you have made the homeland foreign to us and levied various taxes on the people. Many millions have been killed or exiled. The people became ever poorer while you cried we are living in happiness and joy.

You bandits live well and happily for blood, tears and the suffering of millions, that is true. Name a single village where you have not plundered, where you haven't exiled innocent people. How can you betrayers talk about the homeland when you have sold it to American and English capitalists. What do the Russian workers and farmers have in common with the American capitalists?

Where is your honesty, if you previously called the English hard-headed? You are bankrupt everywhere!

No one will believe you, no one will follow you. If anyone is still with you, it is mobilized youths of 14 to 17 years and old men of 60 to 65. But even these people will run away, for their way is the other. They need horses and land; they are thinking about the year 1942 so that they and their families are not destroyed.

Our people have no fear, they know what they're fighting for and that is why they have suffered so many casualties. Put an end to the lies! You can't deceive the people any longer. The new life and the free homeland will be created.

We don't shoot anyone for nothing, and if we do it, we do it to people who are unwilling to let go of their past. Our prisoners are still alive. Sidorinko from the Saborov Battalion is still alive, as is Dugin from Susemka, Barenov, and others.

We shoot such people as Litvinov, commissar from the Kalino Battalion, Yanbulan, Sedakov, Ivashev, Chernobayev, those who tormented the people. You will suffer the same fate. Your own people will kill you.

If you manage to get away from the front, you will starve to death.

Document 21

Appeal to all Soldiers and Commanders Mobilized by the Partisans

After the many battles we have fought against you, you have realized that we are powerful and determined to create a new life. We demand that you and your commissars put an end to it! For 24 years you have lived in deprivation and misery, you have been burdened by heavy taxes and all eleven farms in the village were forced to feed the Stalinist overseers. The time has come to put an end to this monster, for the commissars are leading you to death.

In recent days you have lost 200 killed in the battles against us. Don't believe that we shoot all partisans. Your comrades are alive with us as prisoners: Sidorenko from the Saburov Battalion, Kubanski, Dugin from the Susemka Battalion, Parfenov and others from the Kokorevka Battalion and more. It is worth noting that we do not attack but instead defend ourselves, so as not to lose people. We have not shot the partisans who have voluntarily come to us.

Your leaders began mobilizing boys of 14 to 17 and old men of 60 to 65. Who needs that? This insane war needs only commissars and officers to extend its own life.

They are therefore able to destroy hundreds of innocent lives. They need the land and the horse, the agricultural equipment. If you didn't want to fight at the front, it makes no sense to fight now when the front is far away. This struggle is only necessary for your commissars, for without soldiers they could no longer exist. They say the front is near, but that is a blatant lie.

The Russian people have been without a homeland for 24 years. The homeland had only the Bolsheviks, and therefore you did not fight. The people do not want to fight for oppression, taxes and prisons. That should be done by the commissars and communists, for they are living in "well being and pleasure," as they put it. Some of these people have fled, the rest have hidden in the forests and plunder the peaceful population. It is impossible to get far with the lie. The Red Army has won no victories. The soldiers were poorly fed, they were inadequately clothed, the cavalry was sent against tanks and the infantry had just one rifle for every four soldiers.

In February the Bolsheviks attempted a breakthrough and as a result lost the 61st Army, which was encircled and captured. The German Army has taken Yelets and Livny. This is the truth and you have been deceived, as during the previous 24 years. Away with this monster! Come over to us!

By doing so, you will save your own lives and those of your families, and will create a new life in a new, great, free homeland.

Down with the commissars, those exploiters of the Russian people. Forwards for happiness, for a new homeland, with the friendly German people.

Document 22

Certificate of Obligation for Members of the People's Defense

1.) As a citizen of the new Russian Empire, I agree to be a fighter with the police battalion of the Lokoty District.

2.) I will bear this title honorably, closely study combat tactics, and maintain weapons and ammunition in good order.

3.) I promise to be highly disciplined and carry out all orders from the commander under the mayor of Lokoty.

4.) I promise to do everything that is useful to the new Russian Empire.

5.) I promise to join combat against the partisans as soon as the mayor gives the order.

6.) I promise to act in conjunction with the German armed services.

7.) Should I fail to live up to these obligations, I should be punished severely, even shot.

Document 23

Letter from Kaminski to the Headquarters of General Brand in Briansk
10 March 1942

I wish to report that, as a result of the fighting near Tarasovo Guta and Shemyakino on 9 March 1942, several houses were destroyed by our gunfire. Twelve houses near Kokorevka belonging to the forest administration were completely destroyed. A direct hit reduced the partisan headquarters in Kokorevka to rubble.

We suffered the following casualties: 1 dead, 1 wounded and 1 missing.

According to statements by prisoners, the enemy's losses were greater than previously reported.

The partisan battalion commander was killed and the senior commander severely wounded.

Request support with ammunition and aircraft and the destruction of the villages named in the report of 8 March 1942. The ammunition can be sent by rail via Lgov to Brasovo. Today a train arrived in Pogreby via Lgov.

Document 24

Report by the Foreign Office Liaison Officer attached to 2nd Army Headquarters, Rittmeister Graf Bossi Fedigotti, Concerning the National-Socialist Russian Battle Group Kaminski in Lokot near Navlya

Report No. 5

Since the conclusion of the autumn fighting, the huge area of forests which extends from south of Briansk to roughly the Konotop – Lygov – Kursk railway line, with a length of more than 150 km and a width of more than 50 km, has been a gathering point for thousands of partisans. Consisting in part of stragglers from Red Army units caught in the Briansk pocket and in part of communists, commissars and Red party members, the partisan groups have become an ever-growing threat to the rear army area. These partisan groups are gradually forming themselves into highly-disciplined fighting units, which are arming themselves with the thousands of rifles, machine-guns and heavy weapons left behind in the area of the former pocket and are hauling abandoned artillery pieces from the forests. They are now operating with such effect that significant portions of the rear army and army areas cannot be used for the passage of supplies because they have become operating areas for the partisans.

A particularly important rail line runs from Briansk south towards Lgov. The safeguarding and use of this line is a matter of life and death to the 2nd Army. Since the autumn, however, the 2nd Army's supplies have been rerouted through Gomel and Orel to Kursk. During the long winter months, however, it was not possible to route the 2nd Army's supplies down the Briansk–Lgov line to Kursk. The reason for this was the presence of about 7,000 partisans under the command of General Vasilyev and Colonels Sebastyanov and Silivyerstov occupying the entire forest region around the rail line. This partisan group called itself and still calls itself today: Third Red Army in the enemy rear. It is well-equipped, with light and heavy artillery, with radio equipment, tanks and every kind of modern weapon. Not only does it consist of the elements mentioned above, Russian troops trapped behind the lines and Red party members, rather the Russian officers regularly seize the entire male populations of every village they are able to reach, providing them a reliable source of replacements.

In January the restoration of the Briansk – Lgov railway line became increasingly vital. Though lacking sufficient troops to clear the forest, the Army Headquarters decided to reopen the rail line. An operational group of railroad pioneers was given the task of repairing the tracks, repairing the blown railroad bridges and guarding the line against the partisans at least for a width of a few kilometers. The railway pioneers who had been given this difficult task carried out their orders. It is not the purpose of this report to laud their efforts, it can only be mentioned that what the pioneers of Hauptmann Strobel's operational group achieved, especially when one takes into account the bitter winter cold and the constant pressure from the partisans, represents one of the most outstanding feats by our railroad pioneers. In their struggle with the partisans the pioneers were supported by scratch army battalions, but sometimes they had to hold their own while the bridges and tracks were being repaired. One day, however, just after they had reached the densest part of the forest, in an area where most important bridges had to be repaired, they suddenly encountered armed Russians wearing white armbands and large George Crosses. They turned out to be bitter foes of the Red Army and, under the command of a nationalist Russian officer, had already cleared the most important section of forest. Armed with weapons they had found in the surrounding forests—light and heavy machine-guns, mortars, mountain artillery pieces and heavy howitzers—these volunteers formed a corps of about 1,400 men. With unbelievable tenacity they had attacked the numerically-superior enemy, inflicted losses, in fact drove him from his forest positions, took his bunkers, and attacked the village in which he had dug in. In a word, they created all the conditions required to more quickly continue the repairs to the rail line. Asked about their officers, these militiamen declared that they owed their allegiance to just one officer. This officer is the head of the National-Socialist Russian Party, the engineer Bronislav Kaminski.

What was simply most inconceivable was that Kaminski's militia had achieved what the Hungarian troops committed for the same purpose, for example, had been unable to achieve, namely the destruction of the enemy. When one entered the headquarters, even in the hallways one got the impression that order reigned there. Each door bore a sign identifying the office. In the hallways were armed guards, who made a disciplined and military impression. On entering Kaminski's office one was favorably impressed by the simplicity and military austerity of the room. Surrounded by his closest staff, all outwardly plain looking men, his eyes provided another indication of an open nature, leading one to conclude that he is capable of being very tough and extraordinarily energetic. He has the plain exterior typical of many Russian personalities of stature. Kaminski also speaks some German.

Before returning to Kaminski's idea and his plans to build up his party, a brief description of his life.

Bronislav Kaminski is today 41 years old. He comes from Vitebsk. His father was Polish, his mother German. He studied in Leningrad and, after earning the money for college, became an engineer in the paint industry.

During his studies he associated mainly with the Bukharin group, which strongly opposed the introduction of the collective farm system. In 1929 Kaminski, along with others, signed a counter-declaration by the Bukharin group, expressing its opposition to Stalin's agrarian policies. Years later this signature came back to haunt him. In August 1935 he was suddenly arrested and accused of conspiring with German and Polish agents (§ 58, Point 6). After months in prison, it was demanded that he admit to dealings with foreign intelligence services. When he refused to do so, he was made to stand for 26 hours, until he collapsed. Several days later he was informed that he was being placed in the charge of the NKVD and had been sentenced to ten year's deportation for having signed the Bukharin declaration in 1929.

Kaminski was first taken to Butirka prison in Moscow and then was placed on a deportation train bound for the Urals. He subsequently arrived at the Nishin-Tagirski concentration camp in the Chelyabinsk region. Almost all of the inmates there were members of the intelligentsia who were working in the mines. They were mainly doctors, professors and engineers. There was an outstanding spirit among the exiles, and in particular the prisoners possessed great moral strength. The prisoners also included many members of the Bukharin group. They, but the other prisoners as well, saw the introduction of the collective farm system as a form of serfdom for the Russian people and were therefore strong opponents of the Red agrarian order in particular. During his imprisonment, Kaminski refused every opportunity to apply for a pardon. He did not feel guilty, as he had not broken any laws of the state, rather he had merely signed an internal political counterstatement. In Leningrad, meanwhile, Kaminski's mother had appealed for the release of her son. With the help of a close friend, she was able to have Kaminski's sentence reduced, and he was sent back to European Russia as a forced laborer. After five years in exile he arrived in Lokoty, where he was forced to settle and became chief engineer in the local refinery. Kaminski has lived in Lokoty since that time.

Kaminski took part in numerous political discussions while he was in the concentration camp. While there he also wrote down a national and social Russian ideal. The experiences that led him to develop this ideal had been gained mainly during his time in Leningrad, where he had read much banned literature. In Leningrad he had discussed National-Socialism, mainly with German engineers. In particular, an Engineer Schwarz working in the "Respublika Leningrad Ultramarine Paint Factory" told him much about the National-Socialist ideology and the pair debated the subject at length. In the engineer's club in Leningrad, where German, English and Finnish engineers socialized, the Russian was offered the opportunity to learn about events in the west. Kaminski and his friends had known nothing about a national Russian émigré movement, however. In Kaminski's words, *he and his friends developed the idea of creating a National-Socialist homeland largely as a result of comparing conditions in Russia with those abroad. Kaminski also revealed that, while in prison, he had learned from a judge that the formation of a National Russian Party had been uncovered in 1935. The members of this small group had been killed immediately. Concerning the emigration, Kaminski said that he rejected the tsarist emigration, but he would welcome all victims of bolshevism who had emigrated in recent years, because they would be necessary for the establishment of a national Russian organization.*

To return to the background of the rise of a National-Russian-Socialist ideal, it is important to recognize a person who played a leading role in the establishment of Kaminski's group. He was Ivan Konstantin Pavelich Voskoboynik (known as Lomashkov in Moscow), former head of the Moscow Office of Weights and Measures. Voskoboynik took part in the uprising on the Volga in 1921. Until 1931 he lived in Moscow under the name Lomashkov. One day he was exposed, arrested and sent to the concentration camp in Novosibirsk. There he spent three years as a prisoner. After his release he tried to find a position in the Ukraine. As he had been in a concentration camp, however, no one wanted to hire him. The political authorities approached him to become a member of the NKVD, but Voskoboynik refused. In order to find work, Voskoboynik finally falsified his papers and thus ended up in Lokoty. In the Novosibirsk concentration camp, Voskoboynik had been known under the name Engineer Zemlya. There, too, the camp population had included many members of the intelligentsia.

Voskoboynik should be seen as the actual founder and first leader of the Russian National-Socialist battle group. When, in the autumn of the previous year, the bulk of the Red Army left the area south of Briansk, Voskoboynik and Kaminski decided to act. Six men with the same idea got together. Basically, this idea encompassed the following three points:

1.) Destruction of the Stalinist and collective farm system.

2.) Creation of a National-Socialist Russian state with close contacts with the Axis. (Without these close contacts the creation of a new Russia is impossible.)

3.) Bearer of the new state's national ideal is the National-Socialist Russian Party.

As well, as part of the agricultural order, each farmer shall receive at least ten hectares of land. It is significant, however, that the land given to the farmers never becomes their property, but instead remains property of the state. The farmers are thus given the land as a sort of loan from the state.

The church shall be restored to its former position but will have no political influence.

The symbol of the new Russia is a black George Cross on a white field. The cross symbolizes the crusade by all well-meaning people against Bolshevism. St. George shall be the symbol of the Russian fatherland of tomorrow, for he slew the dragon of the World Revolution, and St. George is also an old Russian symbol.

Kaminski acknowledges that these points are only general foundations. In general he has not yet developed a party program, although he has put his reasoning down on paper in the attached appeals (see Appendices No. 8, 15, 16, 17).

In the rayon of Brasovo, 300 men responded immediately to Voskoboynik's appeal and declared themselves ready to fight for a better Russia. The first combats with left-behind elements of the Red Army resulted in the creation of a small battle group whose numbers grew slowly. In addition to officers and men of the Red Army, the greater number were Kulaks, which says a great deal. In December a representative of Voskoboynik and Kaminski, by the name of Mossin, approached the German authorities in Kromy.

Mossin requested that the G.F.P. and the military police check out the individual members of the new, small battle group. At about Christmas Mossin delivered the new group's records to the intelligence section of Headquarters, 2nd Army in Orel. On Voskoboynik's and Kaminski's behalf, Mossin asked for permission to found a national socialist Russian party. The intelligence section did not go into the question of founding a party; instead, it gave back the records pending the return of the V.A.A. Recognizing the military possibilities that Voskoboynik's officer entailed, however, the head of the intelligence section posed the following three questions to Mossin:

1.) What is Voskoboynik's attitude towards the partisans?
2.) Is Voskoboynik prepared to conduct propaganda against the partisans?
3.) Is Voskoboynik prepared to actively take part in the struggle against the partisans?

In the name of his superior, Mossin declared that his group was ready to take the sharpest action against the partisans. He also promised to immediately provide the materials required for the study of his superior's political intentions. Various documents were subsequently submitted and passed on by the V.A.A. (see Telex No. 7822 and subsequent submission of documents).

As the Lokoty area left the army area[55] *soon afterwards, the Voskoboynik matter was passed on to the 2nd Panzer Army, which subsequently worked with his battle group. With partisans beginning to flood the area, however, the cooperation between Battle Group Voskoboynik and the 2nd Panzer Army's rear area commander was more theoretical than practical.*

On 8 January a powerful force of partisans launched a surprise attack on Lokot. The partisans captured Voskoboynik and shot him. Voskoboynik distinguished himself through acts of bravery moments before he was captured. Kaminski, who fortunately was not in the camp, was warned in time and escaped. He swore to avenge Voskoboynik and to organize a proper fighting force. He began widespread appeals for men to join the "Otriyad". Following his manifest, he employed agitation, but he also sent his men into the forests to search for weapons and promised to fight hard against the partisans. From Voskoboynik's original group he created mobile combat battalions, which soon became the deadliest foe

---

[55] The army in question was the 2nd Army.

of the partisans, which were prepared for everything else. When they realized that they were facing a foe who fought with the same weapons and understood how to operate skillfully in the local terrain, they sent emissaries urging them to cross over and fight with them for the freedom of the Russian fatherland. Kaminski refused. The partisan leader subsequently put a price of 200,000 rubles on his head. This was the beginning of the most difficult time for Kaminski. It was the time of the hardest winter months, during which the German pioneers were more than 100 km away. Far to the south, they began working on the railway and were had no contacts in the north, toward Briansk. Although he had never been a soldier and his chief of staff Mironenko had never served, Kaminski understood how to earn the trust of his military subordinates. He organized his units into companies, took guns and heavy weapons from the partisans and thus equipped his units with heavy infantry support weapons. Employing an old Russian winter tactic of using sleighs to sweep through the forests toward the villages, he attacked the partisans wherever he found them and gave them no rest. In numerous battles and minor skirmishes he demonstrated his enthusiasm and his faithfulness to the ideas he had developed. The fiercest battle he won was the successful defense against an attack by 2,000 partisans in the Komarichi area, between 3rd and 11th March 1942. A large number of killed and wounded were proof of his troops' spirit. When our pioneers arrived, Kaminski's battalions joined up with the German units. Kaminski people in part assumed responsibility for defending the railroad pioneers as they worked on the tracks. The relationship between the German officers and Russian leaders was comradely and marked by their shared struggle.

Kaminski openly admitted that he was not about to transform his battle group into a political instrument without the approval of the German authorities. He was convinced that his tasks at that time were purely of a military nature. He was, however, passionately hopeful that he would also be granted political recognition. In assessing the basic ideas he had developed for the future, as with so many Russians, one finds few clear concepts. He had thus not yet fully developed the political and ideological structure of his ideas. What is important to realize, however, is that Kaminski was a skilled political leader committed to serving German interests in the reorganization of the eastern territories. This man would definitely be useful as a propagandist for a German new order in the east, provided that we take into account certain requirements of the Russian mentality. In addition, experience in the military realm has taught us that we will never be able to pacify the rear areas without the participation of units of the Russian militias who are native and familiar with the terrain. The units of our allies are inadequate, both qualitatively and quantitatively. On the contrast, as it has unfortunately turned out, the behavior of the Hungarian units in particular towards the civilian population has caused a rising bitterness in the latter. We should not forget that the national ideal is now also beginning to take hold in the Red Army. It cannot be denied that there are still men in Russia who, by means of the Red Army, can remove Stalin and his followers. Today the partisan groups in particular regard themselves as freedom fighters rather than red guerillas. The motto of General Vasilyev's 7,000-man group, for example, is: "For a free Russian fatherland! Never under the heel of the German *fascists!"* This slide towards nationalism, which generally speaking can be observed on the left and right, must be skillfully headed off by the German authorities, before hostility towards the Red Army and dissatisfaction with conditions and events in the occupied areas results in a nationalism that can become very dangerous to the fighting German army, through passive resistance alone. The employment of units like Kaminski's in the military realm forces men with political leadership abilities into the military obedience system. In this way it is easier to steer these men and their groups than if they are left to themselves or suddenly forbidden. In the interest of the fighting troops, therefore, it must always be remembered that:

1.) the use of foreign volunteer units is militarily necessary.

2.) the political leadership tries to engage the positive elements of these groups in its service.

If this is done in time, the leaders now opposing the Reds will become reliable instruments. Their use for conducting active propaganda among the enemy also appears to be extraordinarily effective. The soldier at the front is of the opinion that we must exploit every option for crippling the striking power of the Red Army. Experience has also shown our troops that the Russian soldier, who fights at his side against the Reds, is the only soldier equal to the German physically and in courage in the face of the enemy. As individual fighters, the German soldier values the Russian volunteers several times higher as the soldiers of some of our allies. It is clear, of course, that this cannot be brought to a common denominator with the political ambitions of the Reich. First and foremost, however, we should remember that because of their sacrifices the soldiers demand that we mobilize all available forces to strike the enemy where he is most vulnerable. And if Russians allied with the German Army fight the Red Army, it constitutes a decisive burden on the latter's structure.

Document 25

Translation of a Letter from Kaminski to Headquarters, 2nd Panzer Army
10 June 1942

Enclosing my requests for the supply of my battalion with arms and rations, plus uniforms and other equipment, I ask, Herr General, that you give special attention to my situation, which has become more acute, in part due to unfortunate actions by Hungarian units and also the present exhaustion of arms and other areas of supply. This becomes more understandable if one adds that I will shortly be taking the offensive, which of course will result in greatly increased consumption. If the figures contained in the request seem high, I ask that you not allow them to upset you and to give whatever you can. In particular, we are in need of ammunition. As well, many wounded are showing up in my hospital. As a result of this, we have had to cut all of the underclothing in my possession into bandages. I ask that you also give this your most serious attention.

As a result of the events of the nights of the 2nd to 3rd and 5th to 6th of June 1942, I can say with certainty that the partisans in our district have received reinforcements from other districts. I have never experienced such a desperate and numerically strong attack for as long as I have been fighting partisans. The attack was carried out along the entire line of front and the enemy tried to cut our battalions in the forward line. The only conclusion that can be drawn is that further fighting will develop in our sector of front. I therefore ask that you also help our partial sector by sending two or three companies of German troops. I am firmly convinced that it will then be all over for the partisans here. I also wish to report to you, Herr General, that all of the partisans have our white armbands with the black cross, which they can make very easily and which enables them to get close while we lose very many. This leads to the conclusion that, as quickly as possible, my men should be given uniforms that the partisans cannot copy.

Since the recent fighting I have had several losses in personnel, making the staffing of my battalions an extremely serious problem.

In addition to all I have said, I must report that I have only enough cartridges and other supplies for two days. If I am not supplied with ammunition very quickly, very unpleasant measures, possibly even a retreat, may become necessary.

I must also report that the Hungarians in Lokot offered little support in this fighting, indeed sometimes they even moved away. I have proof of this, which I can provide on request.

I am convinced, Herr General, that you will come to our aid in the immediate future. Please accept my sincerest request for forgiveness and my best wishes in the struggles with the most terrible monster the world has ever seen.

Document 26

From the Records of Headquarters, 2nd Panzer Army

Kaminski, leader of the self-governed district of Lokot, expressed the following wishes on 5 September:

1.) Incorporation of the Rayon of Mikhailovka into the self-governed district. The request is made to more effectively combat the partisans, as the partisans prefer to withdraw into the "neutral territory" of the large forests in Mikhailovka and from there attack the Rayons of Dmitrovsk and Dmitriyev. Major von Veltheim supports the incorporation, the army commander agrees with the incorporation.

2.) Despatch of 5 – 10 younger Soviet officer POWs to Lokot. After they have been checked out, they are to be employed as officers in the militia. None above captain's rank. The army commander agrees.

3.) The newspaper "Retsch" shall write more about the self-governed district of Lokot. Army commander has no reservations. Kaminski also suggests that "Retsch" can only expand its readership if it pays more attention to agricultural affairs, the concerns of farmers and tax questions. The rate of sales in the self-governed district is, however, consequently it seems to me questionable whether addressing these topics will not lead to a drop in deliveries in the rest of the area. (The Intelligence Officer is addressing Points 1 -3).

4.) Delivery of used German uniforms, including footwear, initially for 1,000 men. There is a tailor shop in Lokot to make repairs. The army commander has already issued appropriate directions to the quartermaster.

5.) Army commander has no reservations about delivery of rifles and machine-guns provided sufficient stocks are available.

6.) More fuel, as 8 tanks and 5 armored cars are on hand, for which the previous allotment was inadequate. I have already brought the delivery difficulties to Kaminski's attention. (I will bring Points 4 -6 to the attention of senior quartermaster Hauptmann Neumann.)

7.) The army commander agrees with the delivery of medicines and dressing material, provided they can be spared. I will discuss this with the medical officer, Armeeapotheker Dr. Mayer.

8.) Delivery of 70 tons of salt in return for promise to deliver to the army of an unspecified quantity of tinned tomatoes, pickles, etc. By order of the army commander I will speak with Wiko about this.

Document 27

Appeal to Partisans by the Mayor of Lokot

Partisans still holding out in the forests or in villages of the former rayons of Pavlinsk and Susemsk!

For the last time the entire population of the district of Lokot, likewise the district government (which today administers six former rayons) and its leaders, together with the German headquarters, turns to you. We are well informed about your inhuman life, which must be as meager as that of cavemen.

We know that there are only a few of you who are voluntarily living this vile, barbaric life, while the vast majority were forced to serve unwillingly, at gunpoint. We know that you were forced to leave your families and that the majority of these families left to their fate are without shelter, without bread, without clothing, condemned to death by you.

One wonders why you, your wives, your children, fathers, mothers and brothers and sisters, and other relatives, are forced to live such an inhuman, hungry and fratricidal life?

To fulfill the order given by Stalin on 1 May of this year? Is that not a lie then? Is it not total deception? Do you still believe this lie? After all, Stalin lied to us for 24 years and sucked all the strength from the Russian people with his Five Year Plans. During those 24 years we endured with you the most difficult, arduous life, which was little better than serfdom. An unprecedented terror in law and politics, insane prices for products and goods (and they were difficult to obtain), the slavery of the collective farms which turned our land into an enormous concentration camp—that is what Stalin gave his party and his people. Do you still believe in Stalin and his orders? In his order of 1 May, Stalin wrote that the Red Army is now stronger and its generals wiser than ten months ago and therefore the victory must be theirs. Yes? Victory will surely go to the German tanks! As it happened, is happening and will happen! In recent months the Red Army has lost more than one million killed and captured in the loss of the city of Kerch, in the fighting at the gates of Sevastopol, and at Kharkov, without mentioning the huge losses in equipment and ammunition. After such losses can one still think of a victory by the Red Army? Definitely not! We can assure you that the victorious German army under its supreme commander and leader of the NSDAP Adolf Hitler will achieve the final victory over Bolshevism. The war is already lost and the power of the Soviets will never rise again, even if your leaders, the Jewish commissars, have not yet admitted it. They wish to continue deceiving you because Stalin orders it.

Partisans, volunteers and those forced to serve! Your time has come to come over to us with your weapons and begin establishing a peaceful and happy life for you and your families.

For millions of people of the liberated Russia are breathing a sigh of relief and are beginning to work for themselves. Imagine that the dream of tens of millions of farmers is becoming a reality: the farmers have received land for their own use, on his plot the greenery is the hope of the future. Almost every farmer has his horse, cow and other agricultural inventory.

Though there is a war going on, the standard of living of the worker is also not bad. A place to live and heating are guaranteed. His average earnings are 3 – 4 loaves of bread and 300 to 400 rubles in cash, which is also gaining value, plus each worker is allocated one hectare of land for his own use. The fighting men are also paid, 2 loaves of bread and 250 rubles, plus 50 grams of butter, bread and other products as required. The fighting men have been given 10 hectares of land, which likewise is worked and planted with the assistance of the state.

Now compare how our people live and how you live.

We know about your situation, the situation of the wives, children, mothers and fathers of your former comrades who have come over to us. Is anything being sown on your side? And even if there is, we know how the Jews and commissars love peasant bread and of course will exploit the opportunity. The specter of starvation also hovers over you. We appeal to you in order to save your lives and those of your families and we hope that you will understand, will stop shedding the innocent blood of the Russian people and come to us like men. You will see for yourselves, how diligently and freely the farmers are working in the fields and also at the worktables (where industry has been restored).

Don't believe that prisoners or partisans who desert to us are shot or otherwise punished, that is a vile lie. All who honestly and voluntarily desert to us are given the basics of life and also work.

What we say is not unfounded. Your former active partisans are waiting to speak to you, even those who did not surrender voluntarily, but were captured during your attacks in January and February.

We hope that you understand the pointlessness of your resistance and will immediately do what we tell you. By doing so you will save the lives of yourselves and your families and can begin free and honest work.

Document 28

Report by Rear Area Commander 532

*"An abandonment of the clear line prescribed by the [German] master
position would be interpreted, not as accommodation, but as weakness."*

8 October 1942

Grievances against Kaminski:
1.) While the commander of the Imperial Hungarian Division and the other German and Hungarian officers in Lokot get about on foot, Kaminski has made a bad impression by driving around with a female companion (who has already been addressed as "Madam" by the German officers) in a motor vehicle (2 cars and trucks) bearing the legend "In the Service of the German Armed Forces" in large letters, and this despite the close proximity of the theater, cinema, etc. Often the passengers (women) clearly indicate that these trips are not official or vital to the war effort.

2.) Oberleutnant Buchholz, local commander in Navlya, complains about the often arrogant behavior of the militia, such as a recent case in which a mounted militiaman asked a German sentry for the password in a questioning tone. Major Müller, 14th Field Railroad Operating Battalion, reports of a German Feldwebel who was stopped by militiamen and asked for his papers.

From these incidents, which are only intended to serve as examples of the general attitude of Kaminski's militia toward the German military, it is clear that it is high time to make clear to every resident of the self-governed district of Lokot that the occupation troops must be given priority in every respect and that a reversal of this obvious relationship cannot be tolerated. As well, however, it is necessary that the required restraint be shown by all sides towards Kaminski while clearly advocating the master's point of view. Any deviation from this line would mean a diminishing of German stature in the psyche of the Pole Kaminski and the Russian population. An abandonment of the clear line prescribed by the [German] master position would be interpreted, not as accommodation, but as weakness.

1.) Several officers who are knowledgeable of the situation (Major v. Veltheim, Oberleutnant Buchholz) have independently made the same observation, that the population still reveres Kaminski's predecessor, who was shot by partisans, but hates Kaminski. They "tremble" before him and are only kept in line by fear.

Major von Veltheim reports that the despotic regime set up by Kaminski resembles that of an African chief, to whom any means are justified to somehow place everyone more or less in a state of major dependence. He even used this process on Major von Veltheim, who was forced to make a personal request to Kaminski for the smallest items, whether a few boards or workers, transport, a few eggs, or the like. Any attempt to procure directly was unsuccessful, obviously on Kaminski's order. Major von Veltheim reported that he [Kaminski] constantly threw up roadblocks in order to reaffirm his dependence and Kaminski's indispensability.

Kaminski's Militia Tanks

According to information from Major von Veltheim the tanks have never been used effectively in combat.

Kaminski's tank workshop, which has been praised to the skies, is in several opinions nothing more than a hastily-improvised facility which is only capable of ad hoc solutions.

Given the current supply situation, the release of fuel and ammunition for these tanks needs to be scrutinized most carefully. For the time being, no further allocations are to be made without the approval of the chief of staff.

As an example of irresponsible tank use and reckless wasting of fuel, Major Müller points to a drive made by Kaminski from Lokot to Navlya to make inquiries and carry out government business. This drive, during which Kaminski was himself in the tank, resulted in heavy damage to roads and bridges. Kaminski subsequently summoned those responsible for maintaining the roads and bridges and gave them 24 hours to fix the damage he had caused. He leant emphasis to this order with blows to the head and kicks to the backside and stomach.

Apart from wasting fuel and workers, such behavior by Kaminski is injurious to the image of the German military, under whose express protection and on whose behalf he operates.

Lokot Volunteer Battalion

3 companies of about 350 men each, 12 light machine-guns (German), 3 heavy machine-guns (Russian).

It is considered necessary to maintain an equipment of 10 light machine-guns and 3 light mortars per company.

1st and 2nd Companies completely uniformed. 3rd Company without uniforms and boots.

German instructors, presently 1 officer, 19 NCOs and enlisted men.

Six of these are army interpreters, 14 men from the 216th Inf.Div. As General von Gilsa (216th Inf.Div.) has been deployed elsewhere, withdrawal of the 14 instructors (including 1 officer) must be anticipated soon.

Oberleutnant Hemke is unsuitable and must therefore be relieved. In addition to a chief instructor, a battalion officer appears necessary.

Major von Veltheim has advised that Order 1267 (Secret) from the Operations Officer, Panzer Army Headquarters requires clarification.

The order states:

The Lokot Volunteer Battalion is to be established as per Order 1119/42 (Secret) from Headquarters, 2nd Army dated 21 June 1942:

1.) In addition to locally-stationed forces, a battalion-size unit (600 – 800 men) is to be formed from members of the Lokot militia. This unit will remain attached to Engineer Kaminski, who will also continue to be responsible for its welfare and supply.

2.) The battalion is to be concentrated and must be capable of action in the wider surroundings of Lokot.

3.) Headquarters Gilsa is to provide a training detachment of 1 officer and about 15 Feldwebeln or Unteroffizieren from attached elements of the 216th Inf.Div. for training, not command, until the situation permits a detachment from the corps area. Training is to begin immediately.

4. Matters of pay and rations will be addressed separately.
Headquarters, 2nd Panzer Army, Operations Officer, 1267/42 (Secret).
It must be made clear that the Lokot Volunteer Battalion will not be placed under Kaminski's command until the formation process is completed.

Document 29

Strengths and Weapons Complements of the People's Defense Battalions
in the Rear Army Area in the Self-Governed District of Lokot
31 December 1942

Btl. No.	Location	Strength	Rifles	Light MG	Heavy MG	Light Mortars	Heavy Mortars	Pistols	SMG	Guns AT Guns
H.Q.	Lokot	343	169	4	--	--	--	110	--	4
I	Tarasovka	680	523	25	16	7	5	18	2	5
II	Kholmetsky	720	595	29	19	10	3	37	8	6
III	Dubrovka	801	696	37	23	26	5	17	8	7
IV	Lokot	423	395	18	4	--	--	1	--	--
V	Navlya	984	862	19	15	5	2	41	10	6
VI	Igritskoye	582	504	14	13	3	--	--	2	2
VII	Seletchnya	718	644	27	14	--	--	--	1	3
VIII	Dmitrovsk	*undergoing reorganization and reformation*								
IX	Dmitriev	446	391	8	2	1	--	--	--	1
X	Sevsk	*undergoing reorganization and reformation*								
XI	Lokot	690	644	23	15	12	--	30	5	8
XII	Susemka	*undergoing reorganization and reformation*								
XIII	Mikhailovka	*undergoing reorganization and reformation*								
Total:		6,387	5,423	205	121	64	15	254	36	42

Document 30

Rear Area Commander 532 Interrogation Record

Loginov, Dmitri Vasilyevich, born 5 November 1923 and a resident of Ryasnik, rayon of Karachev, agricultural worker.
Turned himself in after the attack on Krasnye Dvoriki.
On 20 November 1942 I was drafted into the headquarters company in Karachev by Mamtshur, head of the People's Defense in Karachev. On 18 February 1943 I and 14 others were detached to Goshsht (25 km southwest of Karachev). We remained there until 25 February 1943. We then moved on to Tsarevo-Zaimishche (19 km west-southwest of Karachev). Eleven local People's Defense men joined our detachment. On the night of 28 February we were ambushed by more than 100 bandits, who carried off 25 members of our detachment. They left behind the bloody bodies of our machine-gunners. The bandits had with them 50 sleighs loaded with stolen food. We passed Revny on the way to the bandit camp. We rested there for a short time and at about 5 o'clock we moved out. We then passed a burnt-out village and at about 11:00-12:00 on 2 March 1943 we arrived in the bandit camp at Duka. The band was divided into four companies. I estimate its strength at 500-600 men. They were armed at least with rifles and semi-automatics, most bandits had automatics (70 rounds). There were plenty of light machine-guns. There were 7 heavy machine-guns in the 1st Company, to which I was assigned. I also saw several mortars and 2 45-mm anti-tank guns in the band's camp. The band lived in 30 earth huts, each capable of accommodating 30 men. Around the Duka camp there were other bands, which I did not know.
On 9 March 1943, 100 men armed with 15-20 rifles, 35-40 automatics, 20-25 semi-automatics, 15-20 light machine-guns and one 52-mm mortar on approximately 25 sleighs were sent out. We passed Revny, and during the night of 9-10 March 1943 arrived near Frolovka (19 km west-northwest of Karachev). Nothing could be done there, however, because German units were stationed in the village. The band then moved into the forest, approximately 5 km southwest of Frolovka (there were old earth huts there) and rested until about 07:00. We then continued on through the forest, on the way passing a larger burnt-out village, and at about 13:00 arrived at a forest camp in which there were about 200 bandits, armaments uncertain.
We stayed there until 13 March 1943. At about 12:00 the 200 men left. Where they went I do not know.
At 14:00 we moved away from the camp in a slow march with rest stops. We passed the burnt-out village again, then moved from Frolovka through the forest, somewhat to the left of our earlier route, and during the night came to Krasny Dvoriki (19 km west-northwest of Karachev). When we emerged from the forest we came under heavy fire, whereupon the band fled.

I hid in a barn until morning so that I would not have to march with the band any more. When it was light I took my semi-automatic and turned myself in to the Germans.

In the camp near Duka I was given 1 kg of bread for ten days. Twice a day there was a thin soup with a little horse meat. There were four captured Hungarians in the Duka camp. I overheard the partisans say that there was also a senior German officer there.

Document 31

Order by Headquarters, 2nd Panzer Army for Anti-Partisan Operations South of Briansk
22 March 1943

1.) *The situation requires the soonest-possible destruction of the bands in the forests south of Briansk that have been reinforced by members of the Red Army. As the weather and road conditions do not permit this mission to be carried out to completion at present, all means are to be used to drive them into the smallest possible remote area, surround them and, once the roads have dried, finish them off.*

2.) *Generalleutnant Bornemann is responsible for the execution of this mission.*

3.) *Placed under his command are:*

Headquarters, 442nd Special Purpose Division, which will be reinforced as per special order

707th Division
251st Division
Group Källner
Hunting Group Huzel
Battle Group Zehender

Headquarters Rübsam with People's Defense units from the self-governed district of Lokot after closer consultation with Oberst Rübsam.

102nd Hungarian Security Division

security forces of Rear Area Commander 532 on the Desna corresponding to their present sectors

security forces to be made available by XX Army Corps

Separate orders will be issued specifying timing of the attachment of forces. On 28 March 1943 XX Army Corps and XXXXVII Panzer Corps will report where the units to be released by them are located.

4.) *Mission:*

a) A concentric attack from the north, east and south is to drive the bands in the forests south of the Navlya – north of Seredina Buda – Gremyach together against the Desna and then destroy them. It is vital that we establish a secure link between our forces on the Navlya and the Desna as soon as possible, open the Navlya to Seredina Buda railway line and reach the line Susemka – Staraya Guta – Ulitsa River.

b) Following the destruction of the enemy forces south of the Navlya, the area between Briansk and the Navlya is to be cleared of the enemy.

5.) Generalleutnant Bornemann and his headquarters are to move into the combat zone as soon as possible. Advance detachments to be dispatched immediately. Scouting and attack preparations to begin immediately. Intended plan of action, deployment of forces and schedule are to be reported to the army. This shall include timing requests for the attachment of individual units and their preparation, as well as requests for support from the air force and intelligence service and for signals communications.

6.) Separate orders will be issued for assumption of command by Gen.Lt. Bornemann.

7.) Until the order for the assembly of forces for the anti-partisan operation under Gen.Lt. Bornemann takes effect, XX Army Corps and XXXXVII Panzer Corps are to reach the following objectives:
   a) XX Army Corps line Susemka – Staraya Guta – Ulitsa River line
   b) XXXXVII Panzer Corps Altukhovo and contact with the Hungarian forces north of the Navlya, further Kokorevka – Kholmechi – Gavrilovo Guta.

8.) At 20:00 on 23 March 1943, Generalleutnant Bornemann will pass his duties as commander of the Army Traffic Control Headquarters to Major Kühnert.

Document 32

Assessment of the Partisan Situation in the Briansk Forest
by Headquarters, XX Army Corps
25 March 1943

While in the past the bandit situation in the Briansk Forest has had an extraordinary influence on the conduct of operations in the sector there, it has now become of decisive importance to current and future operations. The partisans have realized this and have strengthened their forces in the bandit area, previously estimated at 6,000 to 8,000 men. Through direct contact with the Russian front, they have been able to fundamentally augment their organization, equipment and signals command network based on previous experience. The bandits' morale has been greatly bolstered by the success of the Russians, their clever propaganda and reports of their military importance in Stalin's speeches, etc. It must be assumed that the same applies to the civilian population living in the bandit area. Elements of the population that do not agree with the partisans have moved away. Those that remain are either active [partisans] or equally-dangerous supporters. There is proof of this. Whereas it is long past time to put a clear end to this bandit presence, the sole limiting factor has been the shortage of forces.

Barely 30 km of area near the front separates our front line from the bandit area. While XX Army Corps' rapid advance toward Sevsk, which took the partisans by surprise, has resulted in operational benefits by closing the gap in the front and shortening our lines, the presence of partisan masses in our rear and deep flank poses an extraordinary threat to all subsequent operational measures. It would be a mistake to economize with forces in this situation. XX Army Corps' communications corridor with the rear leads past two bandit-held forests over a length of almost 100 km. The bandit-held forests narrow this corridor to a width of 18 kilometers at its most vital spot, specifically in the Seredina Buda – Chernetskoye area. Unfortunately almost all of the lines of communication run towards the Seredina Buda traffic net, which is exactly where the traffic net is interrupted by the Snobovka and Tara Rivers.

The rapid execution of our operations is due to the relative lack of activity by the partisans so far. Now, however, all intelligence suggests that the bandit leadership already has clear directives and intentions. These will undoubtedly be concentrated in the above-described area. Only there can they achieve decisive effects against our future operations, especially as the coming muddy period will restrict communications to a few lines. The tough stand by the enemy at Sevsk and the pressure from bands in our rear against our communications leading there, which is already perceptible, are clear indications of an enemy command acting according to a plan.

Provisional countermeasures:

1.) Creation of a dead zone between our forward lines of security and the southern edge of the inhospitable section of the Briansk Forest through the following measures:

    a) Burning down of the villages situated between the two positions, evacuation of the hostile population thus rendered homeless. All operations must achieve surprise and have a lasting effect.

    Sequence: Susemka – Avangard – Nikolskiy, later Staraya Guta; simultaneous with above operations Nov. Vasilyevskiy – Kornakhovka – Belye Bereski, then settlement region in the area between Susemka and Staraya Guta, then the villages forward of the line of security in the area west of Staraya Guta.

    The evacuation is to extend the length of the Novgorod Severks – Seredina Buda – Sevask road, possibly sparing absolutely reliable elements in the main villages on the road.

    For removal and disposition of the evacuees see Qu. Proposal.

    b) Creation of effective obstacles by flooding and mining of the area in front of our line of security. Proposal by Pioneer Operations Officer.

    c) Continued disruption of enemy plans through regular patrol operations and provoking enemy patrol activity in the more open intervening terrain.

    d) Thorough reconnoitering of the bandit area.

    e) Continued air operations to harass the enemy.

    f) Immediate employment of the harshest measures against elements of the population which actively or passively support the bandits.

2.) All troop billeting areas in the threatened area, especially along the main road, are to be fortified strongpoint-style. Clear conditions of command are to be created by setting up local garrison headquarters, creating of alert units, guarding lines of communication between all strongpoints, and implementation of measures for more rapid provision of mutual assistance.

Creation of an intelligence system among the population, exchange of reconnaissance information and experiences, scheduling and practicing of all alert measures, reinforced bridge guard details, combing of the wooded areas, especially [astride] the main road, fire lookouts, air defense organization.

3.) The above measures are to be carried out as required along the Seredina Buda – Yampol railway line.

4.) Line of security to remain as is for the present, change after reconnaissance and suggestions from the units.

Document 33

Extracts from the Daily Activity Reports by Secret Military Police Group 639, Attached to Headquarters, 2nd Panzer Army, Concerning Partisan Activity, for the Month of March 1943
30 March 1943

On 24/2/43 the 2nd Company of the Karachev Russian People's Defense left its strongpoints in Malye Luki, Osinova, Tserovo Zaymishsht and Pryutovka and moved into the nearby forests to join the bandits there. On 26 and 27/2 almost all members of the company returned, except for a few people who remained with the bandits in the forests. Based on interrogations by the Karachev field detachment and inquiries by Rear Area Commander 532, the 7 ringleaders were sentenced to death by shooting. The sentence was carried out on 12/3/43.

The investigation revealed that the platoon leader of the Abramov People's Defense was a ringleader. A. was also sentenced to death by Rear Area Commander 532. This sentence was also carried out.

Interrogations associated with this incident clearly revealed that the civilians aligned with the bandits took part in the conversations that preceded the desertion. The three Russians Arasazev, Gukov and Kosatch were thus identified and arrested. They were also shot. Also arrested were two women sent by the partisans to Briansk to serve as agents. They were to first recruit reliable people who could later serve as runners. Both women had received their orders from the Ponorovski Brigade, which is located roughly in the Yurkovo Polye, Dumsch Orlinka area—approximately 50 km south-southwest of Briansk. Three other persons with contacts with these agents were also arrested. The inquiries have not yet been completed.

Summary of Bandit Attacks Carried Out:
During this reporting period a total of nine attacks were made on roads or strongpoints on the Briansk – Orel road. Most were carried out by groups of bandits several hundred men strong. All cattle found were taken away. Militia and People's Defense men were taken away. Our losses were 9 killed and 3 wounded. Only 1 dead bandit was recovered, as they almost always carry off their dead and wounded.

A total of four rail demolitions were carried out. Three of these took place on the Belye – Karachev section, all between Kilometers 105 and 107. A total of 96 mines have so far been disarmed on this section. One soldier was killed and 5 wounded in the explosions or removal of mines. Five Russian civilians were also killed and 5 wounded. Another track demolition was prepared on the Lyudinovo – Sukreml section (north of Shisdra). This operation was, however, detected in time and 24 explosive charges were disarmed.

Another attack was made on a patrol from the Hunting Detachment, near Dvoriki, where it was ambushed by about 100 partisans. The bandits wore the identification symbol of the day ordered by the German side, enabling them to carry out their ambush. Eleven German soldiers fell into the bandits' hands. They were stripped naked and murdered, some in bestial fashion.

Bands attacked three strongpoints on the Briansk – Karachev road manned by Russian militia soldiers. No indications of fighting were found, however, the militiamen disappeared with all their weapons and equipment. It is assumed in this case that the militia members and the bandits had worked out an agreement. The strongpoint was subsequently occupied by SS men.

Bandit Areas:
Area north and south of the Briansk – Karachev rail line.
Area north of Briansk in the region Ordzhonikidzegrad – Bytosh – Lyudinovo – Zhukovka – Dyatkovo.
Wooded area south of Briansk.
Wooded area west of Desna – north of Nevlya (south of Briansk).
From Lokot was reported: On 20/3 a group of 850 persons evacuated from the front (women, elderly and children) passed through Lokot. The weary women and children, who had marched 40 kilometers, cried and evoked the strong sympathy of the population. An unfavorable impression was made by the escort of German soldiers, which carried clubs as well as weapons. The women related that several children had died during transport. The escorts stated that they had killed those who collapsed during the march, and that the transport had numbered more than 1,000 persons when they took charge of it. The affair produced outrage among the population. Kaminski was also critical and complained about the mistreatment of the evacuees, who included relatives of People's Defense members.

As also reported from Lokot, with the help of a captured bandit Kaminski exposed a resistance movement. So far 40 men have been arrested. The head of the band may be the leader of Kaminski's mobilization department. His wife—a dentist—admitted that they wanted to poison Kaminski. Prior to a planned concentric attack on Lokot, the band planned to set the fuel dump on fire and induce general chaos by shooting leading German and Russian personalities and other acts of terror. Military secrets were played into the hands of the bands.

Document 34

Order by Headquarters, 2nd Panzer Army for the Destruction of the Enemy Forces in the Wooded Area south of Briansk
9 May 1943

1.) Enemy situation will be discussed separately.

2.) The XXXXVII Panzer Corps is to destroy the enemy forces in the wooded area south of Briansk between the Briansk – Lokot rail line, the Ulitsa and the Desna through a concentric attack, mop up the area and pacify it.

The operation is codenamed "Gypsy Baron".

Operational Requirements:

a) Departure of the units attached as per Para. 3 from their current quartering areas and their concentration for "Operation Gypsy Baron" are to be carefully concealed.

b) The operation itself is to be initiated as soon and as abruptly as possible, and is to be carried out with all vigor and maximum pace.

3.) Effective 8/5 at 12:00 hours, the following units are attached to Headquarters, XXXXVII Army Corps, tactically, and on the arrival of forces in the concentration area, in matters of supply:

4th Panzer Division
18th Panzer Division
10th Jäger Division (motorized)
292nd Jäger Division
7th Jäger Division
Mountain Pioneer Battalion 85
Bridging Battalion 593
102nd Hungarian Light Security Division
all security forces of the commander of Rear Army Area 532 in the combat zone east of the Desna and positioned on the west bank of the Desna.

4.) The divisions attached to Group Weiss as per Para. 3 are to move up shortly with division H.Q., division signals battalion, all infantry and pioneers, one light artillery battalion each, one heavy battery each, anti-tank battalions (medium anti-tank guns only and one platoon of heavy anti-tank guns) and all available Panzer IIIs. All remaining elements, plus all not required by the operation, are to be left behind in the present quartering areas. Separate orders to be issued concerning supply units to accompany the divisions (see Para. 10 c).

5.) "Operation Gypsy Baron" must be concluded by 2 June at the latest, so that participating units can march or be transported back to Group Weiss.

During the course of the operation, 10th Jäger Division is to be pulled out at the earliest opportunity so that it can assemble in Ordzhonikidzegrad at the disposal of the army. Efforts are to be made to complete this assembly by the evening of 24 May.

After the conclusion of the operation, Rear Area Commander 532 is to take over the mopped-up area, occupy it with security forces strongpoint-style and carry out its ultimate pacification.

6.) Approach and Transport Out of Formations and Units:
a) Assigned road movements:
4th Panzer Division (less tracked elements) via Karachev - Briansk
7th Jäger Division via Dmitrovsk into the area around Lokot
10th JGD (motorized) via Orel – Karachev into the Briansk area
18th Panzer Division with wheeled elements via Orel – Karachev into the area NE of Navlya
All overland movements are to be carried out by night.
Movements by the 7th JGD are to be closely coordinated with Group Weiss.
b) Assigned rail movements:
Tracked elements of the 4th Panzer Division to Pochep, the tanks to Navlya
292nd Infantry Division to Komarichi and Novgorod Severskiy, if possible also Seredina Buda.

7.) Headquarters. 2nd Panzer Army will arrange traffic control in Orel and on the Orel – Briansk road through Army Traffic Control Headquarters.

8.) A separate directive will be issued for support of the operation by the air force.

9.) Group Weiss is asked to immediately issue orders for the temporary attachment of the elements of Headquarters, XXXXVII Panzer Corps remaining in the present quartering areas and the units attached to it as per Para. 3, as well as the release of these units remaining behind as part of "Citadel".

10.) Special directions will follow for:

a) for intelligence/reconnaissance by organs of the Abwehr and the air force.

b) for signals communications. Radio silence to be maintained until the start of the operation.

c) for supply.

11.) Preparations for "Gypsy Baron" are to begin immediately so that road movements can begin in darkness on 8 May, rail transports on the morning of 9 May.

12.) Headquarters, XXXXVII Panzer Corps to report:

a) Immediately, on 1:100,000 map, detailed plans for employment of forces, timetable, road and rail movements. As well, for rail movements, the XXXXX is to be advised immediately of the desired sequence of transports, the entraining and detraining stations, when the formations/units will be ready to entrain, and transport sizes.

b) Soonest possible requests for reconnaissance and air support.

c) Soonest possible first command posts of corps and division headquarters and desired signals communications which cannot be provided with own resources.

d) Continuously during the buildup and operation, as per current general orders, the morning report, pre-orientation and daily report.

On 20 May Rear Area Commander 532 to report to the army how and with which forces the area is to be secured and pacified after conclusion of the operation.

13.) Secrecy: (also see Para. 2)

The following measures are ordered to maintain absolute secrecy concerning "Operation Gypsy Baron" and the departure of Group Weiss' forces:

a) It is expressly forbidden to speak of anti-partisan combat or operations. The operation is to be characterized as a front-line action in any case. The enemy forces are therefore not to be characterized as "bands", even in written orders.

b) Phone calls that might reveal the departure of a unit, the new plan, organization of forces or dates and times, are forbidden.

c) The contents of this army order are not to be passed on. The number of personnel assigned to the overall planning is to be limited to the utmost.

Document 35

Letter from the Commander of the 5th People's Defense Regiment to Kaminski
8 May 1943

This letter is to inform you about my trip to the city of Dmitrovsk on 4/5/43.

I received Brigade Commander Kaminski's order concerning the transfer of the 8th Battalion of the 5th Rifle Regiment from the city of Dmitrovsk. After I arrived in Dmitrovsk, the German local commander issued an order stating that his men need not answer to the government of Lokot or follow Engineer Kaminski's orders. The German commander made a number of such statements in the territory of the rayon of Dmitrovsk, though I cannot remember all of them.

The order about not subordinating themselves to the administration of the Lokot district was sent by the local commander and military police to the village elders on one day—6 May 1943. The members of the 8th Battalion were told that Lokot was no longer responsible for the rayon of Dmitrovsk.

Approximately 200 members of the 1st and 3rd Companies refused to carry out the order for the transfer of the battalion and departure for Lokot, meaning they deserted. And 70 men had run away even before the departure, the fault of the battalion commander.

When I learned of this, I went to the war commander and military police and asked for their support. I was determined to assemble the men.

Then I was told: rounding up and assembling the deserters of the self-governed district of Lokot is forbidden in the territory of the rayon of Dmitrovsk.

Conclusion:

Some units of the German military situated in the territory of the rayon of Dmitrovsk are contributing to the breakup of the Russian People's Defense, and if this should continue it will result in the creation of new [partisan] bands in the territory.

I ask you, brigade commander, to bring about the complete return of all deserters from the 8th Battalion, 5th Rifle Regiment, so that the battalion can be at full strength. There are many people in the rayon of Dmitrovsk who could serve as replacements for the regiment.

I also ask, brigade commander, for an order that the deserters be severely punished so that no more such incidents take place in the Russian People's Defense.

Document 36

Report on the VIII People's Defense Battalion by the Rübsam Group
11 May 1943

The VIII People's Defense Battalion of the Kaminski People's Defense Brigade was formerly stationed in the Dmitrovsk district. When the front around Dmitrovsk was created, it was attached to the German troops there. This subordination lasted until 5/5/43. Initially employed in the reconnaissance role, the battalion was later taken out of the line and used for entrenching work.

With the approval of the XX Army Corps, the battalion was supposed to be transferred to Lokot on 6/5. The regimental commander of the 5th People's Defense Regiment, Turkalov, was put in charge of the move. At the instigation of the group, he received the necessary orders from Mr. Kaminski. As well, he received documents from the group which clearly stated that he had been tasked with the relocation of the VIII Battalion.

On 5/5 the battalion was moved from where it was working to Dmitrovsk. Departure for Lokot was scheduled for 11:00 hours on 6/5.

Prior to the time of departure, but mainly during the final preparations for the move and then during the march, 200 men left the battalion and fled home.

On Easter, when all of the company and platoon commanders and senior sergeants went on leave, the men went home too, without permission.

While all of the officers, with the exception of one platoon commander, returned after Easter, about 70 men failed to return. Thus, on 7/5, just 74 of the battalion's 546 men arrived at Gorodischche near Lokot.

The group was informed of this on the evening of 8/5, and simultaneously the report by regimental commander Turkalov was sent to Mr. Kaminski. On 9/5 Hptm. Köneke, the army's liaison officer in Kaminski's headquarters, and Hptm. Seckler, group adjutant representing Oberst Rübsam, drove to Dmitrovsk to investigate the incident on the spot after regimental commander Turkalov reported that the local military commander had intervened.

Neither the local commander nor Sonderführer Thielen could be found. After consultation with the 72nd Jäger Division, to which the battalion had been attached, it was learned that, while the division had regretted the transfer of the battalion, it had done nothing to impede the move and regimental commander Turkalov had received only support. A request by Sonderführer Thielen for permission to try and have the battalion remain in Dmitrovsk was rejected by the division. The battalion was handed over to the People's Defense regimental commander at its work site.

Interrogations and questioning revealed the following reasons for the desertion of the People's Defense men.

1.) Because of an order from the 2nd Panzer Army, allegedly made public by the local military commander, stating that Mr. Kaminski was no longer authorized to issue orders in the Dmitrovsk district, the men concluded that Mr. Kaminski no longer had any command over them and they therefore refused to follow the order to move to Lokot.

2.) They preferred to remain under German orders, mainly because they received better food there. (72nd Jäger Division stated that it was very satisfied with the battalion.)

3.) Most of all, the men wanted to stay in the Dmitrovsk district because it was their home and they thus could go home to work.

4.) In general there was the urge to go home.

On 9/5 Hptm. Seckler asked the 72nd Jäger Division, as commanding division in the Dmitrovsk district, to issue an order giving the People's Defense men who had run away until a certain time to return to duty with their weapons. Those who did not report by then would be considered deserters and hunted down.

The commander of the VIII Battalion was ordered back to Dmitrovsk in order to work exclusively under the direction of the division and reassemble his battalion.

The prevailing opinion is that the People's Defense men who ran away will respond to the German appeal without hesitation.

The fact that the men no longer want to remain under Kaminski's orders, but instead prefer to remain under German orders, gives cause to consider either attaching the battalion—once it has been reassembled—to the German unit in the Dmitrovsk district as an eastern unit, or disarming the men and employing them as foreign auxiliaries.

Even considering the point in Para. 1, the People's Defense men who deserted, especially the officers, have breached all military discipline and order and are guilty of severe lack of discipline. The guilty must be made to answer for their actions, in order to avoid threatening and undermining discipline and order in the rest of the People's Defense.

It is therefore necessary that the battalion, once it has been reassembled, make the deserters available to Mr. Kaminski so that he can conduct the investigation and punish the guilty. Leaving the deserted officers and men in the Dmitrovsk district and failing to take decisive action would only encourage lack of discipline in the rest of the People's Defense.

Mr. Kaminski has no objections to later returning the battalion to the Dmitrovsk district and letting it go if the Dmitrovsk district should later fall outside the self-governed district.

Document 37

Letter from Refitting Staff 3 Concerning the Self-governed District of Lokot
and the People's Defense There
13/5/1943

The divisions' formation area south of the Briansk – Karachev road east of the Briansk – Lokot rail line to the Nerussa is part of the self-governed district of Lokot.

The self-governed district of Lokot is an area which, by decree of the Führer and Supreme Commander, is self-governed under the leadership of Engineer Kaminski. For a long time the administration has successfully waged war against the enemy groups in the Briansk Forest without significant support from the German military. During the winter fighting of early 1943, which saw part of the self-governed district fall into Russian hands, the administration of the district distinguished itself, as did, with a few exceptions, the Lokot militia, effectively supporting the German troops fighting there in every respect.

It is obvious that the self-governed district will support "Operation Gypsy Baron" with all its resources, as it will eliminate a constant threat to the self-governed district.

To have smooth cooperation with the self-governed district, however, the German forces must behave correctly toward the population and the institutions of the self-governed district.

The self-governed district has an armed militia (Lokot People's Defense), the bulk of which is deployed in the forest front facing west on security duties.

Strength is approximately 12 battalions with heavy weapons and some tanks (Russian models). The People's Defense is organized in battalions and is under the command of the head of the self-governed district in his capacity as brigade commander. The People's Defense Brigade is subordinate in all respects to Headquarters, 442nd Special Division in Lokot, commanded by Gen.Lt. Bornemann. To ensure trouble-free interaction with the elements of the People's Defense in the divisions' sectors, the divisions are to immediately contact Gen.Lt. Bornemann, who is to obtain the cooperation of the local People's Defense commanders. The men are to be briefed on the special nature of the People's Defense, especially that the People's Defense has extraordinary clothing problems, as it has not been possible to completely outfit it with German uniforms.

I require that it be made absolutely clear to the troops that the self-governed district and its institutions exist by order of the Führer, and that excesses by the troops against the self-governed district represent a breach of a Führer decree. I will therefore severely punish any excesses without regard to person.

Document 38

Letter from Rear Area Commander 532 to Headquarters, 2nd Panzer Army Concerning the Kaminski People's Defense Brigade
19 May 1943

Attached is a report by the Rübsam Group concerning the unauthorized return of People's Defense Battalion 8 of the Kaminski People's Defense Brigade to Lokot.

The root cause of the entire incident is that People's Defense Battalion 8 was employed in a way that contradicted the People's Defense's "ties to the Rayon". It is a fact that the members of the People's Defense joined the force on the condition that they would defend their immediate home, meaning their house, their village and, if necessary, their rayon, against bandit attacks. If we move a People's Defense unit to a completely other district, we are assigning it a task that it does not feel obligated to carry out.

The claim made on Page 1 under Paragraph 1, that the local commander in Dmitrovsk made public an order from the 2nd Panzer Army stating that commander of the People's Defense Brigade Kaminski had been relieved of authority in the district of Dmitrovsk, requires clarification.

Handwritten addition by Headquarters, 2nd Panzer Army:
Why is an exchange of letters necessary? Rübsam Group should instead see to it that the battalion reassembles.
Suggested Course of Action:
1. Appeal by us through Group Weiss in the Dmitrovsk district that members of the battalion have until ... to report, otherwise they will be held responsible (as deserters).
2. Restoration of the battalion to full strength in Lokot and then transfer back to Dmitrovsk.
3. Punishment of the guilty.

Document 39

Telex from Group Weiss to Headquarters, 2nd Panzer Army Concerning the VIII People's Defense Battalion
19 May 1943

The 72nd Infantry Division is to see to it that an appeal is made and that all members of the VIII People's Defense Battalion are assembled and held. These people are to be brought to Lokot and handed over to the Kaminski Group.
Completion report to Group Weiss via Headquarters by 1/6.

Document 40

Report by Rear Area Commander 532 on the Successes Achieved by the People's Defense during the Period from 1 November 1942 to 30 April 1943

5/11. Powerful attack on Kokushino (30 km SW of Lokot) repulsed. 50 enemy dead counted, 5 prisoners with just 2 own dead and 2 wounded.

18/11. Large camp destroyed in forest east of Nevar (40 km SE of Lokot). Just 5 own wounded, but 48 enemy dead counted, 37 prisoners. Captured: 70 cows, 52 horses, 100 sheep, 39 rifles, 3,000 rounds of small arms ammunition.

5/12. Allegedly 800-man-strong band put to flight in Kurganka (15 km SW of Sevsk). 18 enemy dead. Just 12 own wounded.

14/12. 300-man-strong band which had attacked Komarichi station, forced to retreat near Tritskoye (27 km SW of Lokot). 39 enemy dead, 5 prisoners. Numerous wounded hauled away by the enemy. 1 anti-tank gun, 11 horses with loaded sleighs, 1 light machine-gun, 25 rifles and large quantities of ammunition captured. People's Defense losses: 2 killed, 6 wounded. (In the fight at Komarichi railway station 2 enemy dead, but also 2 German dead and 4 wounded and 2 Hungarian dead and 2 wounded.)

18/12. With the support of a platoon from 4th Company, 313th Security Battalion, a powerful band that entered Ostapovo (4 km NE of Mikhailovka) was driven back. 43 enemy dead, including the band leader. 23 rifles, 1 heavy machine-gun, 3 light machine-guns captured. People's Defense losses: 11 killed, 7 wounded.

21/12. After fierce fighting, the People's Defense garrison of Trostnaya (30 km SSW of Lokot) repulsed enemy forces that had entered the town. 5 dead, 4 prisoners. Captured 25 rifles, 3 light machine-guns, 1 heavy mortar, 1 submachine-gun.

26/12. After Butre (30 km SE of Briansk) was plundered, a PD company from Navlya blocked the enemy band's retreat and seized the stolen goods. 11 bandits were shot. 6 own wounded.

29/12. Near Orliya (15 km W of Sevsk), a People's Defense company ambushed a bandit supply column and captured 80 hundredweight of grain, 30 horses, 12 cows.

31/12. A People's Defense company from Navlya captured a forest camp 14 km NNE of Sineserki, from which the enemy was able to flee in time, seizing 600 rounds of 82-mm mortar ammunition, 85 76.2-mm shells, 50 rounds of 45-mm mortar ammunition and several cases of rifle ammunition.

1943

8/1. Fierce battle at Kurganka (15 km SW of Sevsk) with about 500 bandits. 12 enemy dead, including 1 political commissar, 1 lieutenant and the chief of staff of the Sevsk bandit battalion. 4 own wounded.

4/4. Attack by a reinforced patrol of People's Defense Battalion XII on a camp containing about 200 bandits at the eastern edge of the Ramasukha Forest, in which the enemy was driven into the forest. Enemy losses undetermined, although numerous blood trails were found. Own losses: 5 People's Defense men killed.

Document 41

Report by Senior Military Administrator Dr. Günzel
Concerning the Self-governed District of Lokot
25 May 1943

By order of the commander-in-chief of Group Weiss, from 16 – 20 May 1943 I visited Lokot to study the self-governed district, its institutions and working practices. During my visit I had the opportunity to get to know the head of the SGD [self-governed district], Mayor Kaminski, personally and observe negotiations with German offices. I inspected various SGD installations in Lokot and the rayon administration in Brasovo. Through the liaison staff of Headquarters, 2nd Panzer Army in Lokot I gained an insight into the work of the German offices there and their files. The following report is based on personal impressions gained in Lokot and discussions with German offices familiar with conditions there.

1) The SGD of Lokot was created by order of the commander-in-chief of the 2nd Panzer Army on 19 July 1942. It then encompassed the rayons of Navlya, Brasovo, Susemka, Dmitrovsk, Dimitriyev, and Komarichi ,and in October 1942 was also assigned the rayon of Mikhailovka. As a result of the Russian advance in February-March of this year and the resulting changes in the military situation, the activities of the Lokot SGD are limited to the two rayons of Navlya and Brasovo with a combined total of 80,000 inhabitants (including 6,575 evacuees). The rayons of Sevsk (eastern part) and Dmitriyev are in Russian hands; the rayons of Komarichi, Dmitrovsk and Mikhailovka are combat zones; the rayon of Susemka is a partisan area (clearing operations currently under way there).

The founding order awarded the head of the SGD, Mayor Kaminski, the title "Lord Mayor". He was placed in charge of the administration in the self-governed district of Lokot and was simultaneously placed in command of the People's Defense in the area with the rank of brigade commander. The German side stationed a staff in Lokot to lend support in training of the People's Defense and administrative matters. In the intervening period the staff's composition has changed a number of times, and today it consists of an officer from Headquarters, 2nd Panzer Army (Hauptmann Könneke), who serves as liaison officer to the head of the SGD, a military administrator (Kriegsverwaltungsrat Kraushaar) and the Rübsam Staff, which is responsible for providing military training to the People's Defense. There is also an O.F.K. in Lokot; its activities are restricted to military matters. Kriegsverwaltungsrat Kraushaar is officially attached to it as Department VII [Translator's Note: Investigation of Records and Indexes].

The head of the SGD, Kaminski (born 16 June 1889 in Vitebsk) is Polish by nationality; his mother was an ethnic German. He speaks German, but with a Russian accent. Kaminski has twice been sentenced by the Bolsheviks, once to five years imprisonment, for which he was later granted amnesty, the second time to 10 years banishment, of which he served five years in Siberia. When the war broke out, Kaminski was an engineer in Lokot in the local refinery. After the arrival of German forces he took part in operations against the bandits and became secretary to the then mayor of Lokot, Konstantin Pavlovich Voskoboynik, who was killed by bandits on 8 January 1942. After his death Kaminski took over his post, improved his position with the German military by vigorously battling the bandits and extended his influence to other areas. As a reward for his activities on the German side, in July of last year he was placed in charge of a self-governed district encompassing seven, later eight rayons. Kaminski is not only active in the field of administration, but also in military and political areas. The SGD of Lokot should therefore be examined from these three sides.

2) Kaminski's military instrument is the People's Defense, whose commander he is, and which in 1942 he built up to a strength of more than 9,000 men. With this unit he mainly fought bandits; most of his equipment was obtained in these battles, in which he provided the German military with a force almost equivalent to a security division. In the spring of this year the People's Defense also took part in fighting against the Red Army and suffered considerable losses. The battalion deployed in Sevsk performed particularly well, while another deployed elsewhere was a flop. On 1 April 1943 the strength of the People's Defense was 7,096 men; it is organized in 13 battalions and 4 regiments. Its heavy infantry weapons consist of:

209 light and 146 heavy machine-guns
82 light, 7 medium and 7 heavy mortars
24 anti-tank guns (45-mm)
Artillery weapons:
21 guns 76-mm
8 guns 126-mm
1 37-mm anti-aircraft gun
1 88-mm anti-aircraft gun

The People's Defense also has 12 tanks, 3 armored cars, 27 trucks, 8 cars and 440 horses. It is currently outfitted with German uniforms, and the members of the People's Defense wear a white band on the left arm bearing an Iron Cross. Officers wear Russian uniforms without insignia.

Until the first quarter of this year the soldiers were paid by the SGD. This cost three to four million rubles per month. After the SGD was reduced to two rayons, this heavy burden placed the SGD in serious financial difficulties, and so on 1 April of this year the People's Defense was paid by the Wehrmacht. Likewise, as of 1 April soap and cleaning materials, and supplies of salt and sugar were delivered by the Wehrmacht, while provision of the rest of their rations remains Kaminski's responsibility.

The human material serving in the People's Defense is good, mainly strong young men. Provided they are dressed in German uniforms, the impression made by the massed battalions is not bad. Discipline is strict; regulations are strongly enforced and the death penalty is often employed. In general the People's Defense is loyal to Kaminski, even if *there are plots against him now and then. So far all have been uncovered in time by his efficient intelligence service. Kaminski himself has great interest in the People's Defense, often more than in administrative affairs; he is personally brave, wears the Wound Badge in Black and has achieved his respected position within the People's Defense by actively taking part in operations against the bandits. He has led each of his battalions in action at least once. On 4 April 1943 the XXXXVII Panzer Corps declared in an evaluation of Kaminski that the People's Defense had performed effectively in the security tasks assigned by the corps and that cooperation between the Wehrmacht and the People's Defense was generally good.*

3) In the area of administration, in 1942 Kaminski was given a free hand by Headquarters, 2nd Panzer Army. On 19 July he was given the task of setting up the administration in the self-governed district and he carried out this task in his way.

To carry out his administration he employed so-called "Kaminski orders", which were issued as required and which, in addition to trivial matters, also dealt with fundamental issues in all areas of administration. At certain intervals the orders were published in the Russian "Bulletin", a sort of official newspaper printed in Lokot.

Recently, the German military administrators stationed in Lokot have been working on a project to bring the SGD's laws more into line with the administrative laws in the rest of Army Group Center's area, as the decrees issued by Kaminski for the self-governed district often differ not inconsiderably from those issued by the German side. As direct contact between the troops and offices of the SGD often led to disagreements, 2nd Panzer Army has ordered that all contacts are to go through the army's liaison officer in Lokot. Since then there have been fewer cases of friction.

In general it can be said that Kaminski honestly desires to cooperate with the German military. He does, however, watch jealously over his rights, and negotiations with him often demand considerable adroitness, as he sometimes goes too far in his self-confidence.

a) Internal Administration

As in the rest of the army's area, in the SGD the country is divided into rayons, standard municipalities and villages; they are administered by the corresponding organs. Above them all as the central authority is the district administration in Lokot, which in Russian style is heavily sub-divided and therefore requires a large bureaucracy. Thus, according to the table of organization order and the district administration register of 12 October 1942, the district administration alone consists of 20 departments with about 500 bureaucrats and employees, with an associated cost of 3,000,000 rubles per month. Then there are the salaries of the employees of the rayon administration, municipalities and villages, which were also set by orders and amount to considerable sums. The self-governed district was only able to bear this heavy financial burden when it encompassed eight rayons and its income from taxation was considerable. After the SGD was reduced to two rayons, therefore, Kaminski decided to streamline the administration, and in the months of February and March of this year various orders were issued for economization measures and closure of departments in the district and rayon administrations. Nevertheless, the size of the bureaucracy was still very large, in keeping with the Russian style of administration.

The bureaucracy itself complained that, as is usual in the eastern territories, there was a shortage of skilled Russian personnel, and that the administrative work had to be carried out with men and women who lacked any specialized training. Kaminski nevertheless tried to increase the quality of his staff, educate them, and weed out unsavory elements. On 22 December 1942 Kaminski issued an order requiring all of his clerical staff to fill out a lengthy questionnaire and a self-written curriculum vitae. He also frequently employed the state control commission set up by the self-governed district to scrutinize the individual administration offices, mayors, state property, etc. If, as unfortunately was often the case, irregularities were found, he imposed penalties which were published in the Bulletin. Kaminski knew that his bureaucracy needed even more training and monitoring; he therefore reserved to himself the decision in as many matters as possible. As a result of this far too many ordinary matters had to be brought to him and he was forced to split his work time, but the department heads of the SGD were never trained to achieve a certain degree of independence. A change in this situation will not be possible until the bureaucracy acquires more experience in its areas of specialization.

In the political sphere it should be noted that an order issued on 15 September 1942 forbids moving about in the forest without a pressing reason or accompaniment by the police and is punishable as collusion with the bandits. Strict rules have also been issued against the production of homemade spirits and drunkenness. There is an air defense organization, and there is also an order to surrender weapons and equipment; anyone who wants to carry a weapon must receive a permit. To go into other political decrees would take up too much space.

An S.D. Einsatzkommando is stationed in Lokot and is concerned mainly with state and criminal police matters.

b) Budgetary and Financial Affairs

As already described, financially the SGD is very heavily burdened because of the high cost of the People's Defense and its huge bureaucratic apparatus; it already has a debt load of six to seven million rubles. The SGD has gained some financial relief from the Wehrmacht's assumption of responsibility for paying the People's Defense as of 1 April 1943 and reductions in the bureaucracy, however, the financial situation will remain strained as long as the self-governed district has only two rayons.

Separation of the SGD's finances from those of the rayons was not carried out in 1942; it is supposed to take place this year. The budget plan, which was set up for 1943 and concludes in a final total of 138,000,000 rubles, has been overtaken by military events and must be revised. Of the taxes collected by the self-governed district, 25% are to be retained by the rayon administration for its expenses, while 75% must be diverted into the coffers of the SGD. The municipalities will be funded from the monies assigned to the rayon administrations.

In the area of tax legislation, Kaminski has gone completely his own way in the SGD; it therefore differs considerably from the regulations in the rest of Army Group Center's area. Kaminski and his advisors have proceeded on the conclusion that, at present, the farmers are in the best position to pay taxes, while the income and wages of bureaucrats, government employees and workers are meager because of the fallen purchasing power of the currency. Consequently an income tax was not adopted; moreover, it was rejected as "bolshevist". Instead a so-called "household tax" was introduced, which essentially taxed the farmers. The taxes imposed for 1943 are quite high. For example, for a household of up to five persons, of whom three or more are capable of working, the tax is 2,400 rubles per year, for a household of more than five persons 1,900 rubles per year. As well there is an annual tax of 100 rubles per horse, 10 rubles per fruit tree, 100 rubles per beehive. For garden land and smaller vegetable gardens the taxes are much lower (300 – 1,000 rubles per year). Considerable tax reductions for social reasons are also planned. Those awarded German military decorations receive a 50% discount; families whose head has been killed in action against the bandits will not have to pay any tax.

Taxes are collected quarterly and, despite their relatively high levels, are paid willingly and on time. The farmers quickly raised the money to pay their taxes by selling food at the market in free trade…

Document 42

Records of Two Prisoner Interrogations by the 492nd Infantry Division
26 May 1943

Michael Briantsev was captured during the taking of Susyenka on 23/5/1943.

Personal information: Michael Briantsev, born 25/9/1925 in Chelmych, rayon of Sevsk. B. was with the 1st Company, 10th Battalion of the Russian Kaminski Brigade from September 1942 to March 1943. He was taken prisoner in March during the taking of Sevsk. Held in prison in Smelish for one month and then assigned to the Otriyad Rudinev. Otriyad Rudinev: base Susyemka, strength 2 companies of 45 – 50 men plus headquarters = 130 men.

Chief-of-staff: Panchenko

Commander 1st Company: Komylyakhin (Yamnoye), 2nd Company: Starodubtsev (Gerasimovka).

Weapons: 2 heavy M.G., 12 light M.G., 1 anti-tank rifle, 12 submachine-guns.

The commander fled in an armored car (English).

The brigade "For the Power of the Soviets"

1.) Otriyad Rudinev, 2.) Dzherzhinski, 3.) Pugachev, 4.) Budyenny, 5.) For the Power of the Soviets

Strength of the individual otriyade 100 – 300 men

Locations:

Dzherzhinski: Avangard

Budyenny: Susyemka

Rudinev: Susyemka

For the Power of the Soviets: forest northeast of railway, north of Avangard

The Otriyad Schkatov is believed to be in Chernya or Krasnaya Sloboda.

2nd Interrogation

Prisoner Viktor Prozenkao (see prisoner interrogation record of 25/5/43)

P. is an active military technician in the Red Army. After the destruction of the 72nd Independent Searchlight Battalion near Kursk he fled into the Briansk Forest, and since the beginning of May he has been an aide to the chief-of-staff of the Otriyad "25th Anniversary".

Brigade: "Voroshilov I" is to be moved to the Ukraine

Brigade: "Voroshilov II"

1.) 1st Otriyad (Btl.) "Voroshilov II"

2.) 2nd Otriyad (Btl.) "Voroshilov II"

3.) 3rd Otriyad (Btl.) "Voroshilov II"

The artillery battalion has attached to the brigade four 45-mm anti-tank guns and two 76-mm field guns.

Tactically attached:

4.) Otriyad "25th Anniversary"

5.) Otriyad "Seredina Buda"

Commander of the brigade: Lt.Col. Dudtsenko.

Strength: 1,200 – 1,500 men.

The brigade, as well as each Otriyad, has a radio section. In some cases there are also telephone communications.

Important orders are sent by runner in sealed envelopes.

The brigade has two trucks and three motorcycles in Smelish.

The Voroshilov II Brigade has: 1 mine-laying platoon + 15 men, 1 signals platoon = 20 – 30 men.

The combined Sumy headquarters is in Smelish.

Its commander is the secretary of the regional committee of Sumy – Kumanyok.

Chief-of-staff: Yimlyutin.

The staff has radio communications with all otriyads, in some cases also telephone links and runners.

Passwords are issued every seven days by the headquarters in Smelish and are valid for the entire Briansk Forest.

The main headquarters is in Moscow and is called: "Special Headquarters of Unit 00131".

Commander is Commissar 3rd Class for State Security Strokich. He is also chief-of-staff.

The Voroshilov II brigade was under orders to move through the Yampol Forest to the Ukraine (Kiev Forest) during May. The Otriyad "25th Anniversary" had already made a failed attempt. Supposedly there is a plan to move all bandit units from the Briansk Forest to the Ukraine. Total bandit strength is estimated at 15,000 to 20,000 men. After the move, the combined headquarters is to be houses in the rayon of Nishino.

No direction of retreat has been specified in the event of attack by German troops.

The most heavily occupied areas are Smelish and Nerussa.

The combined headquarters in Smelish has 3 medium tanks plus autos, trucks and motorcycles.

The Chapayev Brigade (Koshelev) is to be pulled out in the direction of Trubchevsk. It is powerful and well-trained.

Addendum:

The Gerasimovka – Yamnoye road is easily passable. In the spring of 1943 a road was laid from Yamnoye to Smelish with a branch to Chukhray. A bridge was also built over the Nerussa, which is restricted to horse-drawn vehicles. The Yamnoye – Zakharosna road is marshy and can only be used by pedestrians. The Konski Marsh begins north of the road. The road from Yamnoye to St. Novenkiy is in good shape.

Document 43

Letter from Headquarters, 2nd Panzer Army to Group Weiss regarding
Events Surrounding the VIII People's Defense Battalion
26 May 1943

The army cannot agree with the opinion put forward in the letter in question. The behavior of the People's Defense members represents a clear refusal to obey orders from German and Russian superiors and cannot under any circumstances be tolerated. What is more, it is imperative that the authority of German offices and likewise of brigade commander Kaminski be emphasized and that every attempt by members of the People's Defense to avoid an assignment or order they find uncomfortable be stopped. It is therefore again requested that the members of the VIII Battalion who deserted be rounded up by appeal and calling-up order, and if necessary by the use of coercive means, and the battalion delivered to brigade commander Kaminski in Lokot. It is to be pointed out to the People's Defense members that, once the battalion has been reorganized, men from Dmitrovsk and the surrounding area will to be employed in their district, but that anyone who fails to obey the calling-up order will face charges under the rules of war. Furthermore, it is essential that members of the VIII People's Defense Battalion currently serving as foreign auxiliaries in Group Weiss be returned to the battalion immediately. The army requests that they be made aware of this order.

Document 44

Letter from Headquarters, LV Army Corps to Headquarters, 2nd Panzer Army
regarding "Operation Freischütz"
1,459 Enemy Dead Were Counted against 27 of Our Own Killed!
12 June 1943

1st Assignment, Organization of Forces
The corps' assignment was to destroy the enemy forces in the army area between the Bolva and the Briansk – Zhukovka railway, in the wooded country northwest of Briansk and the open country on either side of the Vetma through a concentric attack, mop up the area and pacify it.
The enemy forces comprised the following:
a) the 3rd Partisan Division
b) the Orlow Brigade
c) the Solotukhin Brigade
d) various smaller bands

Prior to the start of the operation the enemy forces were estimated at 4,000 to 6,000 men, however statements by deserters and prisoners revealed that the enemy strength in the area of operations was at most 3,000 men.

Available to the corps for the operation were the following forces:
a) 5th Panzer Division
b) 6th Infantry Division (with arrival in the concentration area)
c) forces of the commander of the rear army area
d) 455th Special East Staff
Also promised were:
10th Motorized Infantry Division and
1 reinforced grenadier regiment of the 31st Infantry Division
These units were not attached, however, because of commitments elsewhere.
A total of four battle groups were formed from the available forces:
1.) 6th Infantry Division (commander: C.O. of the 6th Inf.Div.)
Headquarters, 6th Infantry Division
18th Grenadier Regiment
37th Grenadier Regiment
58th Grenadier Regiment
6th Reconnaissance Battalion
I Battalion, 6th Artillery Regiment
III Battalion, 6th Artillery Regiment
I Battalion, 42nd Artillery Regiment
6th Pioneer Battalion
6th Signals Battalion
six Panzer IIIs of the 31st Panzer Regiment (5th Panzer Division)
630th Pioneer Battalion (less 1st Comp.) (LV Army Corps)
I People's Defense Battalion (Rear Area Commander 532)
II People's Defense Battalion (Rear Area Commander 532)
2.) 5th Panzer Division (commander: C.O. 5th Panzer Division)
Headquarters, 5th Panzer Division
four command tanks from 31st Panzer Regiment
two Panzer IVs from 31st Panzer Regiment
13th Panzer Grenadier Regiment
14th Panzer Grenadier Regiment
53rd Anti-Tank Battalion (less two self-propelled guns)
Alert Battalion/116th Panzer Artillery Regiment
89th Panzer Pioneer Battalion
77th Armored Signals Battalion
3.) 455th Special East Staff (commander: C.O. 455th Special East Staff)
455th Special East Staff

455th Special Signals Platoon
2nd Company, 134th Division Fusilier Battalion
339th East Battalion
44th East Battalion II
Armenian Battalion I/125
1st Company, East Battalion I/447
East Company 110
East Cavalry Troop 1/447
East Cavalry Troop 2/447
4.) Security Group South (commander: C.O. 747th Grenadier Regiment)
747th Grenadier Regiment (707th Inf.Div.)
Armored Train 4   (Rear Area Commander 532)
587th Security Battalion   (Rear Area Commander 532)
791st Security Battalion   (Rear Area Commander 532)
XI People's Defense Battalion (Rear Area Commander 532)
Azerbaidzhaini Battalion 807   (Rear Area Commander 532)
II. Planned Execution of "Operation Freischütz"
Extract from Corps Order No. 1270/43 secret command matter of 15/5/43
Map 1:100,000 (Appendix I)
1.) Preparation of Forces:

6th Infantry Division (less one reinforced regiment) to assemble west of the Desna in the Peklina – Berestok – Voron'ovo – Pyatnitskoye – Rognedino – Dubrovka – Ryabshchitschi area, one reinforced regimental group east of the Desna in the Podkovka – Vetmitsa – Betlitsa Station – Noviki – Malaya Lutnya area.

The division will conceal the purpose of its concentration by spreading the rumor that it will be remaining in this area for some time to rest and refit.

Any enemy personnel that are found in the quartering areas are to be dealt with ruthlessly. Passive behavior requested against the enemy forces reported opposite the southern quartering group east of the Desna. Neither reconnaissance patrols nor operations are to be conducted to the east prior to the start of the [main] operation.

Beginning 17/5/43, Desna crossing sites in the Zhukovka – Zhukova sector to be located inauspiciously and crossing assets to be prepared and positioned.

455th Special East Staff will clear smaller enemy groups from the wooded area around Seltso – Stary Dyatkovo – Bytosh, after which it will immediately occupy step by step the blocking line in the Bazkino – Sneber sector. There is to be no increase in reconnaissance activity in the large wooded area to the southwest, rather it is to continue only on its previous scale.

5th Panzer Division will leave the units taking part in the operation in their current quartering areas. The strongpoints in the O'grad to Dyatkino main road are to be expanded and strengthened. No increase in reconnaissance activity.

Security Group South, with the 747th Grenadier Regiment, Azerbaidzhaini Battalion 807 and Armored Train 4 will continue to guard the rail line in the O'grad – left army border sector as before, People's Defense Battalion III is to be concentrated in Zhukova, People's Defense Battalion XI in Seltso. Security Battalion 587 to assemble in Briansk, Security Battalion 791 in O'grad.

2.) Manning of the Blocking Line.

The blocking line (see accompanying map) is to be manned abruptly on a broad font during the night before X-Day. The units are to be moved out as late as possible, but in such a way that the line is completely occupied by 02:30 on X Day.

6th Infantry Division will advance with its right wing close south of Zhukova. Advancing from the area southwest of Betlitsa Station, the reinforced regiment will comb the wooded area between Desna and Vetma and occupy the blocking line with its left wing in close contact with 455th Special East Staff in the area north of Bazkino.

455th Special East Staff will feed all still available forces into the blocking line.

5th Panzer Division will occupy the blocking line with its right wing in close contact with the left wing of 455th Special East Staff east of Sneber and its left wing in the area north of O'grad.

As before, Security Group South will continue to guard the railway in the sector O'grad – left army border with Grenadier Regiment 47 and Azerbaidzhaini Battalion 807. On the evening of D-Day minus 1 the 587th and 791st Security Battalions will be brought in by rail to Trosna and Rzhanitsa, respectively. Together with People's Defense Battalions III and XI, they are to be deployed in the blocking line in the O'grad – Zhukova sector with the focal point between Rzhanitsa and Zhukova.

Once the blocking line is manned, no civilians are to be permitted to leave the surrounded enemy territory, regardless of whether they hold a pass or not. Likewise no civilians may enter enemy territory from outside. Any such attempt, even by women or children, is to be stopped by force of arms.

3.) Concentric Attack

The concentric attack will begin according to plan on the accompanying map at 02:30 hours on X-Day.

The 6th Infantry Division will advance with its right wing along the Zhukova – O'grad rail line. The forces of Security Group South deployed in the outer blocking line (with the exception of the 747th Grenadier Regiment) will join the attack as soon as the right wing of the 6th Infantry Division have reached its areas of operation in the blocking line. From that point on it will be attached to the 6th Infantry Division.

455th Special East Staff: the advance by the left wing of the 6th Infantry Division is of vital importance to the attack by 455th Special East Staff. It will dictate the movements by the East Staff. Contact must be maintained at this place.

5th Panzer Division: the left wing will advance along the O'grad railway line. The forces of Security Group South deployed in the blocking line (with the exception of the

747th Grenadier Regiment) will join the attack as soon as the left wing of the 5th Panzer Division has reached its operational positions in the blocking line. From that point on they will be attached to the 5th Panzer Division.

During the attack, Security Group South will prevent enemy forces from breaking out or filtering through the line. Guarding of the railway must not be weakened through the release of units to the 6th Infantry Division and 5th Panzer Division during the course of the attack.

The units will advance on a broad front in their sectors and comb forests, villages and even poorly-accessible areas. In general the advance will be made in platoon strength, in exceptional cases in company strength. The heavy infantry weapons and artillery are to be as widely distributed as possible.

It is to be made clear to all unit commanders that an action involving the concentration of forces, the rule in a normal attack, is unlikely to bring success in this type of operation. The enemy, who will repeatedly attempt to avoid battle and endeavor to escape the pocket by breaking up into small groups, sometimes dressed in civilian clothes, must be encircled as tightly as possible. The objective of the attack is to destroy the enemy, not put him to flight. In the face of enemy resistance, an immediate attack promises the greatest success. If this requires the moving in of neighboring units, care must be taken in the vacated areas to prevent the enemy from breaking out there.

The daily objectives (blocking lines) may be seen on the accompanying map (colored lines). They are binding for all units and also must not be crossed, even if the enemy retreats. It is vital that, after thorough mopping-up in the area combed during the day, that all available forces are in the blocking line by nightfall so that, by maintaining close and constant communication with the next units, the enemy is prevented from breaking out during the night.

If terrain conditions require changes to the blocking line, care must be taken to ensure that contact is not broken with the units on the left and right.

All units, even the smallest, are directed to employ every available means of communications to maintain contact.

4.) Air Force

The air force will support the operation through:

a) continuous reconnaissance

b) attacks with bombs and guns, and

c) leaflet dropping

Operational orders to follow as well as recognition signals and passwords.

    Execution of the Operation (see accompanying map. Appendix 2)

1.) Preparation of Forces

During preparations for the attack it is absolutely vital that the buildup for the operation be carefully concealed to avoid jeopardizing its success before it begins. This can be accomplished without difficulty by 455th Special East Staff, the 5th Panzer Division and

Security Group South, as their assembly and quartering areas coincide. The 6th Infantry Division, which is being brought in from the area around Smolensk for the operation, will assemble without one reinforced regiment west of the Desna in the area Peklina – Berestok – Voron'ovo – Pyatnitskoye – Rognedino – Ryachichi.

One reinforced regiment east of the Desna in the area Podkovka – Vetna – Betlitsa Station – Noviki – Malaya Lutna.

455th Special East Staff will initially clear smaller bandit groups from the wooded area around Selzo – Stary Dyatkovo – Bytosh and then move step by step into the blocking line in the Bazkino – Sneber sector.

5th Panzer Division will initially leave the units taking part in the operation in their present quartering areas.

Security Group South will continue to guard the railway in the sector O'grad – left army border with Grenadier Regiment 47, Azerbaidzhaini Battalion 807 and Armored Train 4.

All groups of forces will restrict reconnaissance to their present areas.

The blocking line (see attached map) was occupied swiftly on the night before X-Day (21/5).

2.) Execution of the Attack

At 02:30 on 21/5 the troops launched a concentric attack (black) from the blocking line. The day's objective (green line) was reached with little enemy contact.

The population of Pogorovka (14 km NW of Lyubegoshch) resisted a search of their village and were shot down (59 persons). The village was burned to the ground.

Bombers flew 65 sorties, attacking fortified positions near Novo Nikolayevka and the camp in the source area of the Tereben (10 km W of Star) and southeast of Konshina (12 km W of Star). The attacks produced explosions and fires in Sadorye (6 km SW of Lyubegoshch). In addition to machine-gun fire, during its operations the air force came under anti-aircraft fire (20-mm) from the area south of Sadorye.

On 22/5 the continuing heavy rains hampered our movements considerably. There was also heavy mining, especially in the area between Ovechkino and Lipovo, in the Maleshino, Moshel and Sbrody area. Almost all were improvised mines created from artillery and mortar shells. Several abandoned camps were destroyed. The day's objective (yellow line) was achieved everywhere with minimal enemy contact.

At various times on 23/5 there were skirmishes with isolated enemy groups, which in general were driven back towards the center of the encircling ring. The 6th Infantry Division came upon a camp 2 km SE of Sadorye, which was taken and destroyed. The other groups discovered only abandoned camps. The day's objective (blue line) was reached everywhere.

The air force flew 67 sorties, attacking camps and villages in the area around Umyslichi.

The early morning hours of 24/5 witnessed the operation's first serious encounters with the enemy, who in places put up stiff resistance.

In the area 7 km south of Lyubegoshch, 455th Special East Staff repulsed a company-strength breakout attempt by the enemy. The enemy was counterattacked, driven south and 15 bunkers captured.

The 6th Infantry Division, too, was engaged throughout the day with, in some cases, larger enemy groupings. Heavy losses were inflicted on the enemy. One permanent camp was taken and destroyed. A number of abandoned camps, some heavily fortified, also fell into our hands. Aerial reconnaissance discovered fresh entrenching work near Domashova, Novo Nikolayevka and Umyslichi. Ten sorties were flown against these villages, which were attacked with bombs and guns.

The heavy continuous rain and the marshy terrain, some wooded, made the going very difficult for the troops. As well, combat operations were again complicated by numerous mines, which inflicted a number of casualties. Despite all the difficulties, by evening the units had reached their assigned objectives (red line).

During the night of 25/5 the 455th Special East Staff repulsed two breakout attempts with heavy losses to the enemy. In response to our light signals, Russian aircraft dropped four parachute canisters containing rifle and submachine-gun ammunition, mail and newspapers. The day itself saw little action by 455th Special East Staff and the 6th Infantry Division's left wing. The 6th Infantry Division took a forest camp with a garrison of about 40 men. The bulk of these escaped, however. Also on this day, a number of abandoned camps were destroyed and large quantities of ammunition of all kinds were captured.

Our reconnaissance and statements by deserters and prisoners revealed a massing of enemy forces in the area around Umyslichi. Consequently, after reaching the railway embankment north of Umyslichi the 455th Special East Staff was halted and ordered to go over to the defensive there. For the following reasons, the final line of encirclement (black line), which originally ran in the area Novo Nikolayevka – Domasheva, was moved north into the area surrounding Umyslichi (map: 1:100,000, App. 2).

During the fighting it turned out that the enemy's breakout attempts were directed mainly against the 455th Special East Staff which—because of its composition and weaponry—possessed a lesser combat value than the other groups. The 455th Special East Staff's forces were too weak for an attack against the now tightly compressed enemy. It had to bear the main burden of the fighting in difficult terrain. The danger arose that elements, at least, of the enemy would break out to the north there or filter through.

On the other hand, the railway embankment north of Umyslichi proved ideally suited to the defense, consequently the forces of the 455th Special East Staff were able to prevent the enemy from breaking out.

On the evening of 25/5 the enemy was encircled within the orange-colored line.

During the course of 26/5, in at times heavy fighting, the enemy was squeezed together in the area surrounding Umyslichi (black blocking line). A large fortified camp complex 1 square kilometer in area was discovered one kilometer north-northeast of Umyslichi. It comprised 30 closed camps, about 300 living bunkers and 100 fighting bunkers, 200 open field positions and three lines of infantry trenches. To all appearances it is the headquarters of the bandit leader Orlov and was hastily abandoned. A large number of enemy dead was found in the camp itself, some killed by air force bombs that scored direct hits.

On 27/5 the troops launched the final concentric attack against the mass of the enemy squeezed into a small area. In heavy fighting, during which repeated enemy breakout attempts had to be repulsed, by the evening of 27/5 the bulk of the enemy was destroyed and much booty captured.

As smaller enemy groupings had succeeded in breaking through or slipping away, mopping up of the wooded area surrounding Umyslichi was continued on 28/5. On 28 and 29/5 this final mopping up was extended to the entire wooded area northwest of Briansk between Bolva and the O'grad – Zhukova railway line.

"Operation Freischütz" concluded on the evening of 30/5.

IV. Results

The bulk of the enemy forces were destroyed, even though—because of the small size of our forces and the swampy terrain with old-growth forest—some enemy groupings succeeded in breaking or slipping through the ring of encirclement.

Enemy personnel and equipment losses during the entire operation:

1.) Deserters   6
2.) Prisoners   420
3.) Enemy dead   1,459
4.) Evacuated   2,392

5.) Captured: 5 heavy M.g., 12 light M.g., 193 rifles, 33 automatic rifles, 10 pistols, 4 flare pistols, 20 submachine-guns, 1 anti-tank rifle, 4 pairs of binoculars, 59,850 rounds of small arms ammunition, 53 hand grenades, 1 field telephone, 2 radio sets, 1 radio, 2 bicycles, 1 printing press (wrecked), 7 parachutes, 11 panye wagons, 78 axes, saws and shovels, 14 horses, 8 cows, 75 kg of explosives, 30 105-mm shells, 12 76.2-mm shells, 42 50-mm shells, 1,000 rounds of mortar ammunition, 140 anti-tank rifle shells, 51 explosive charges.

74 camps with 360 living bunkers and 157 fighting bunkers destroyed.

Own losses:
a) German personnel
Officers: 1 killed, 5 (1*) wounded;
NCOs and men 21 killed, 65 (4*) wounded, 1 missing
b) Native personnel
NCOs and men 5 killed, 14 wounded, 1 missing
(*remained with unit)

V. Lessons

a.) The lessons contained in the "Battle Directive for Anti-Partisan Warfare in the East" of 11/11/42 issued by the OKW were completely and fully validated in this operation.

The area of operations itself consists for the most part of old-growth forest which is almost all swampy. In places these forest areas can only be entered with the assistance of residents with knowledge of the area. A thorough "combing" of the area was often impossible. Taking into account the size of the area to be cleared and the difficult terrain conditions, the forces committed proved insufficient to achieve the complete destruction of the enemy.

The total clearance of such an area can only be achieved if sufficiently strong forces establish the densest possible encircling ring, reduce it in short daily steps (maximum 4 to 5 km) and thoroughly search the intervening terrain to prevent any breakout attempt by the enemy. The clearing itself should be carried out by powerful assault teams, which can eliminate the camps one after another with the help of locals.

b.) Details
1.) Enemy Conduct

According to information provided by deserters and prisoners, our activities took the bands completely by surprise. Not until the operation was under way did they realize that they were surrounded and being attacked from all sides. This explains why the bands initially avoided combat and allowed themselves to be forced back towards the center of the encirclement.

The battle tactics employed by the enemy were as expected. Tree snipers, partisan traps, concealed hideouts and the like were encountered. The enemy frequently used animal noises as a means of communication between sentries and groups.

There was no place for leniency with this enemy. Every captured enemy claimed to be innocent in every way, had been pressed into serving with the bands, etc. On the other hand, we have statements from members of the People's Defense who took part in the operation and who have personally seen these bandits taking part in partisan operations.

A soldier who fell into the hands of the partisans was murdered and was found horribly mutilated.

2.) Combat Tactics

The combat lanes must match the strength of the forces committed. In terrain such as was encountered in "Operation Freischütz", a man can scan at most 3 meters while advancing.

If sufficient forces are available, it is recommended that rear blocking lines be established.

The establishment of contact lines between the units and to neighboring units proved effective. "Maintaining contact" is one of the most important conditions for success in an operation such as this. Checking to ensure that contact exists and confirming the direction of march are constantly necessary.

The use of boundary detachments proved useful in maintaining contact between the units. Our troops found that whistling pyrotechnic cartridges provided an effective means of identification. Connecting points, daily objectives and boundaries should be assigned with reference to prominent straight-line terrain features (rail lines, roads, streams), as otherwise they are almost impossible to find.

Borders and boundary lines are to be made straight whenever possible. Changes of direction are impossible in dense forest.

In deploying and supplying the troops, the simplest organization is most effective in the difficult terrain associated with war against the partisans. The area to be combed in a day must have interval lines, where halts can be scheduled for the purpose of ensuring that contact has been maintained and for scouring especially-difficult areas of terrain. When faced with swampy areas that cannot be waded in line, it is recommended that these be encircled and then searched by assault teams (equipped with rubber boots).

It is advisable to have special detachments follow close behind the front line to inspect enemy living and fighting bunkers (aerial photos and maps provide clues to the probable need to employ these).

The dropping off of reserves behind the entire line is absolutely necessary, in order to be able to respond to sudden breakout attempts by the enemy.

It is advisable that the advance through wooded and marshy terrain be halted during rainy weather, as "bunching up" of the troops becomes unavoidable and the enemy finds numerous gaps (a lesson learned in any hunting activity).

The use of heavy weapons and artillery is extremely difficult in this terrain. It is most effective for battalions to move their heavy mortars, heavy machine-guns and infantry guns on a single road and only commit them when battle is joined. Experience has shown that it is not possible to have the weapons, even when loaded on pack horses, accompany the platoons. The troops become too exhausted from carrying the weapons for hours or days through marshes and forests.

Tanks with light covering infantry have proved very effective in blocking cross-roads and taking out bunker positions.

If the conditions permit, supply should be carried out using several different roads, for otherwise the roads soon become completely unusable through overuse.

Good road marking is necessary everywhere!

As the appearance of groups of infiltrators or single partisans must be expected anywhere at any time, the trains must follow up in the closest possible groupings, taking the necessary security measures. Stay together!

The advance by the troops was hampered to a significant degree by the presence of numerous mines. In some cases branches and sticks laid out on a road revealed the presence of mines. In several cases guard dogs were used successfully to sniff out bandits.

As the bandits sometimes pretend to be dead or wounded, when the fighting is over it is necessary to check the enemy dead and wounded.

Until the enemy is completely encircled, the lighting of camp and other fires is not recommended, otherwise the enemy's aerial reconnaissance can follow the intentions and movements of our troops and inform the bandits accordingly. No matter what the circumstances, all fires are to be extinguished before nightfall.

The heightened state of watchfulness during the night places very high demands on the troops. Consequently, whenever possible daily objectives are to be chosen which can be reached before noon, so that the troops can be given the opportunity to rest during the afternoon.

With a tight encirclement there is the unavoidable danger of firing at one's own people; it is therefore absolutely essential that the troops dig in deeply enough. In doing so it must be kept in mind that the riflemen must be able to get out of their holes quickly to engage in close combat should the enemy attempt to break out.

As the bandits frequently employ tree snipers, when searching a heavily treed area spraying the treetops with machine-gun fire has proved effective.

Finding weapons and materiel is extremely difficult, as most of the hiding places are in swamps under water. Here prisoners and deserters have proved most effective as guides. Extreme caution is required, however, as these "guides" often lure the troops into traps.

Several times the encircled bandits charged the encircling ring, screaming their battle cry, and attempted to break through. Our troops immediately screamed back and opened up a rapid fire from all weapons (aiming low even when the enemy could not be seen), which proved most effective.

3.) Operations by the Air Force

The following units were employed:

KG 51 (Ju 88 and Go 145) with 172 sorties in which about 1,200 bombs of every caliber were dropped.

1./(H) 11 (Fw 189): with 35 sorties (120 bombs and 500,000 leaflets. This does not include the photo reconnaissance flights used in preparations for the operation.

Camps and fixed positions were attacked with good effect. As well, the effect on the morale of the bands was very great, as statements by prisoners revealed. The air force must not be committed too early, for otherwise it will reveal to the enemy that a large-scale operation is under way against him.

Cooperation with the reconnaissance crews was very good. They provided reliable intelligence on the enemy and kept the command informed of the position of the front line.

4.) Equipment

All types of equipment must be as light as possible to ensure that the units and individual soldiers are as mobile as possible.

The troops must be generously provided with compasses, maps and aerial photos.

Good rubber boots or waterproof leather boots must be provided. The rubber overboots are not suitable.

Submachine-guns, machine-guns, rifle grenades and flare pistol H.E. rounds performed well.

Whenever possible, the heavy weapons (anti-tank guns) are to be pulled by horses, with the tandem team as the preferable mode.

5.) Signals

Despite many difficulties, the Type G backpack radio performed better than a description of the conditions led us to expect. (Basically there should be radio communication with all units down to the company level.) As before, however, field telephones remained the best and most reliable means of command. Because of the vast spaces and poor roads, forward-looking planning of the net structure is required.

Caution when using communications. On one occasion the enemy broke into the radio traffic of the G-lines.

The allocation of a Storch aircraft is absolutely necessary for command and the transmission of orders, for otherwise command is too tied to the command post on account of the excessive loss of time and the poor roads. This is the only way to ensure fast, personal influence on the units.

6.) Performance of the Eastern Units

Alongside the German units, the eastern troops fought well. Their confidence was considerably heightened by the actions of the air force, the presence of tanks and the cooperation with German units.

7.) Propaganda

Statements by deserters have revealed that the leaflets dropped were ineffective, as they were too general and did not take into account the special circumstances. They in no way got into the psyche of the bandits. As well, no deserter passes (with stamp) were attached.

8.) Intelligence

The intelligence information required for the execution of such an operation must be made available to the units early on.

The corps carried out the operation outside the corps battle area. The available intelligence information was very general; there was no time for further intelligence gathering. The special officer tasked with this mission a year ago did not contact the corps until just prior to the start of the operation, consequently there was no time to assess his information.

It is therefore necessary that all organs responsible for gathering intelligence on the bandits in the area in question be attached at the proper time to the command agencies responsible for conducting the operation.

9.) Population

Evacuation proved effective, however it was extended beyond the area of operations to a certain distance into the area allegedly already "pacified". According to statements by the People's Defense, this very population (for example on the Desna east of Rognedino) is closely tied, related to or related by marriage to the bands.

It is necessary that the evacuated villages not occupied by members of the People's Defense be destroyed to prevent them being used as shelter by new bandits.

The papers of the civilians must be checked regularly and stamped, as these are often sold, stolen or lost.

10.) Unified Command

There must be clear conditions of command in the entire area affected by an operation such as this. It is totally incomprehensible that units of another branch of the Wehrmacht (air force), which have been engaged in operations against the partisan bands in the same area for a long time, do not actively take part in the operation but instead are directed to "cooperate".

Such circumstances are difficult for the troops to understand and in no way correspond to the issued guidelines.

Document 45

Report by Headquarters, LV Army Corps to Headquarters, 2nd Panzer Army
29 June 1943

1.) No resident partisan bands were identified in the LV Army Corps' area during this reporting period.

2.) More sharply split into civilian and military groups than before, the remnants of the bands smashed in "Operation Freischütz", which were supplied with food, weapons and ammunition from the air, are trying to reorganize west and southwest of the corps area (see partisan band map).

3.) The activities of the bands, which avoid combat and change positions once or twice daily, are largely limited to attacks on the smallest groups for the purpose of procuring food.

4.) Successes and losses to the enemy and our own troops (including partial results of "Operation Freischütz" that fall within this reporting period):

Enemy casualties: 221 bandits killed,
52 bandits captured or deserted,
61 bandit supporters captured,
1 bandit supporter killed.

Captured: 1 heavy M.G.; 3 light M.g.; 1 light mortar; 3 S.M.g.; 50 rifles, 5 pistols; 21 hand grenades; 12,8000 rounds of small arms ammunition; 850 rounds of S.M.G. ammunition; 20 blasting caps; 6 mines; 30 explosive charges; 7 rounds of 52-mm mortar ammunition; 2 binoculars; 2 compasses;

Demolitions and mine accidents: 14
Mines cleared: 8

Own casualties: 1 German soldier wounded, 10 volunteers killed, 16 volunteers wounded, 1 member of the People's Defense killed, 4 wounded.

Document 46

Letter from Headquarters, 2nd Panzer Army to Commander Rear Area 532
25 June 1943

In the appendix you will find a letter from Special Staff Tiger concerning the XV People's Defense Battalion of the Kaminski People's Defense Brigade. The men of the XV Battalion, People's Defense are to be issued both passes and recognition badges to avoid possible incidents. The battalion is not to be moved from Butrye.

Contact with Special Staff Tiger is to be established with respect to this order.

Document 47

Report by Headquarters, XXXXVII Panzer Corps Concerning
"Operation Gypsy Baron"
2 July 1943

During the period from 16/5 to 6/6/43, Headquarters, XXXXVII Panzer Corps carried out "Operation Gypsy Baron" in the wooded area south of Briansk with the 4th and 18th Panzer Divisions, 10th Panzer Grenadier Division, 7th and 292nd Jäger Divisions, the Royal Hungarian 102nd Light Division, security units of Rear Area Commander 532, and the Kaminski People's Defense Brigade.

The mission of Headquarters, XXXXVII Panzer Corps was to destroy the partisan groups, numbering about 6,000 men, in the wooded area Briansk – Desna – Vitemlya – Seredina Buda – Lokot – Lokot to Briansk railway.

The operation was carried out in an area of dense old-growth forest, which in places was very swampy and heavily mined, against a determined, cunning enemy with excellent knowledge of the terrain and equipped with numerous automatic weapons. The following lessons were learned in the course of the operation. Attached are:

a) Report by the 7th Jäger Division (Appendix 1)
b) Report by the 292nd Jäger Division regarding the Eastern Troops (Appendix 2)
c) Report regarding the Lokot People's Defense (Appendix 3)
Appendices 1 and 2 are attached to the original only

1. Preparations for the Anti-Partisan Operation

Operations against partisan bands require thorough preparation by both command and the units. The corps headquarters had to make preparations for "Operation Gypsy Baron" in three days, consequently these were rushed and lacked adequate supporting documentation. Not enough was known about the partisan situation because of the generally passive behavior of the security forces. Consequently planning for the 10th Panzer Grenadier Division advancing out of the area southeast of Briansk was made based on the assumption that there was no concentration of enemy forces east of the Briansk – Navlya railway line. As a result the "Duka" Band, which was located in that area, was able to remain undiscovered in the first days of the operation.

Furthermore, we had no accurate information as to the activities of our security forces on the Desna, and the presence of the Schaum Staff with two battalions was not discovered until encountered on the spot when the operation began. Preparations for "Operation Gypsy Baron" were essentially based on the general knowledge of the enemy and the terrain gained during the winter battles of 1942-43.

Preparations for such an operation must extend:
a) In the Operations Officer's area to:
Thorough briefing of command on the behavior and fighting style of the enemy and the terrain. Use should be made of lessons learned in previous partisan operations. Aerial photos of the affected area to be issued to the units in large numbers.

The troops must be thoroughly trained in anti-partisan warfare and be briefed on the intended conduct of operations.

b) In the Intelligence Officer's area:
Full grasp of information about the enemy.

To this end contact is to be made with agencies which were previously responsible for security in the affected area.

Assignment of as many locals with knowledge of the terrain and agents as possible. Use of prisoners in mine-detecting squads. Increased number of interpreters. At least 15 interpreters are needed for one division.

c) In the Supply Officer's area:
Stockpiling of required supplies behind the attacking units.

Casualty evacuation, securing of booty, establishment of reception camps for the evacuated population and their removal, setting up of prisoner collection points.

2.) Secrecy

The purpose of the buildup to an anti-partisan operation must be kept strictly secret. Prior to "Operation Gypsy Baron" word was spread that the participating divisions were being moved into the areas surrounding the forest south of Briansk to rest and refit.

The buildup must thus be carried out far enough away from the actual bandit area so that the bandits and the population believe the cover story. Furthermore, it has proved useful to give the divisions and units new division numbers when they begin their departure, identifying them as panzer or infantry divisions. It is important that they use their cover designations when they begin their departure movements.

These measures were successful in "Operation Gypsy Baron", first in gaining the element of surprise, and then in achieving encirclement of the partisan area during the concentration phase.

3.) Sealing Off

The entire bandit-infested area is to be sealed off quickly, suddenly and simultaneously at the start of the operation with inclusion of the adjoining march-through areas. The civilian population is to be ordered to remain in its villages. This order must also be issued suddenly, without warning, as soon as the units begin the encirclement, and must be extended to cover an area up to 1 1/2 days march away from the blocking line, making it impossible for the bandits to pass through the area in a single night. All transit and civil passes issued to the civilian population, except for the village elders are to be declared invalid, as it has been found that the civilians are in possession of transit papers of all kinds, issued by various agencies.

The villages in the border areas are to be kept under observation for strangers.

4.) Combing

Commitment of the divisions en masse has proved effective. Elements of the available forces were placed in easily-defensible lines to seal off the area on the Desna, while the bulk of the forces were used from the east and west as "beaters".

The best time of year for anti-partisan operations is the last weeks of April – first weeks of May, because the limited amount of foliage in the wooded area greatly simplifies the search process.

Operations in winter have the advantage that the snow makes it easier to discover bandit tracks than at other times of year.

"Operation Gypsy Baron" showed that the forces were insufficient to thoroughly comb the entire wooded area. The divisions had to fill widths of up to 30 km with seven battalions. It was found that in dense forest one battalion could thoroughly and effectively search an area of 2 km at most. That means that, for a successful operation, a division of seven battalions must be assigned a lane no more than 14 km wide.

5.) Duration of the Operation

Anti-partisan operations that are initiated under considerable time pressure from the beginning inevitably lead to mistakes and failures. Rushing the troops through the bandit area is wron; instead they must be led on a short rein from line to line and forced to repeatedly and carefully search the ground between the lines. In calculating the time required, as a rule it can be estimated that a unit can search a depth of 4 km daily, however, terrain difficulties and actions by the partisans can significantly affect the amount of time required.

6.) Organization of Forces

Organization of the divisions:

Infantry and panzer grenadiers, pioneers and signals battalion fully committed, 1 light artillery battalion reinforced by 1 heavy battery, 1 anti-tank company proved very effective during the operation. Reinforcement by army pioneers for clearing of mines and construction of bridges and roads is desirable.

In the blocking line it can become necessary to bolster the artillery with respect to the large distances covered by the blocking divisions.

Motorized units are, as a rule, less suitable for partisan operations than infantry divisions, which have a greater number of horses and light vehicles.

II. The Enemy

1.) The enemy consisted of several well-organized bands under a unified military command. The makeup of the bands included officers, commissars and NCOs of the Red Army and some "career" bandits, however, the bulk was made up of men from villages in the bandit-controlled area who were more or less forced to serve in the bandit groups. There was also a surprisingly large number of women and children with the enemy.

2.) Fighting Style

The fighting style of the bandits largely corresponded to the information contained in the manuals and leaflets. The enemy only accepts battle when he believes he can destroy smaller elements, has been surprised, has been driven into a pocket, or tries to defend his bases.

From this we have learned that our own forces can only move about in the bandit area in platoon strength or greater and, second, that everything depends on locating the bandit bases through good scouting activities, in order to engage them without warning and destroy them. In every case the resistance of the bands was broken relatively quickly through the local concentration of forces and fire from the heavy weapons.

As soon as the bandits realized that resistance against the relatively stronger "beaters" was hopeless, they either tried to slip away into the forest in groups of 2 to 5 men or concentrated their forces and tried to make a surprise breakthrough at an unobserved place in the blocking line. In the latter case they sent women and children over to us in advance.

No effective counter could be found against the efforts by the bandits to slip away into the forest and hide singly in undergrowth or swamp, under moss and brushwood, or in trees. Only lively patrol activity and thorough laborious searching can lead to the objective here. In some cases the bandits sat up to their necks in the swamp, and when patrols approached they submerged completely and breathed through reeds. When the bandits recognized that the situation was almost hopeless, many tried to make their way to the civilians in hopes of being evacuated with them.

3.) Mines

Detailed information on discovered mines is contained in Appendix 4. Most frequently mined were crossroads, forest lanes, footpaths, tree barricades and approaches to the camps. For marking of enemy minefields also see Appendix 4. Wooden rollers with spikes, pulled by horses on long ropes in front of the vehicles, proved an effective means of locating mines. Appendix 4 only accompanies the original.

4.) Enemy Equipment

In addition to civilian clothing, the bandits wore pieces of German, Hungarian and Russian uniforms. Armament consisted of large numbers of automatic weapons, submachine-guns and machine-guns. Heavy weapons were encountered less frequently, however, one can assume that, given the hopelessness of his situation, the enemy buried heavy mortars, machine-guns and even artillery pieces and will employ them again later. In many cases the enemy employed explosive ammunition and effective silencers.

The enemy was supplied from extensive supply dumps. After these could no longer be reached, during the operation the enemy was supplied from the air with ammunition and American rations. In several cases signal fires (which our aircraft observed the bandits employing at night) tricked the Russian aircraft into dropping their supplies to German troops.

5.) Enemy Camp
Capacity 200 to 1,000 men. Layout and method of construction.

The fighting installations were built in a star shape for all-round defense. Rifle niches and covered two-man shelters branched off from a continuous trench. Larger covered fighting posts with embrasures and dimensions of 2 x 3 m were located at tactically favorable points. In the center of the camp were underground living shelters for 20 – 30 men, kitchen, cobbler, tailor and washing dugouts, also a few saunas.

All installations were well-camouflaged. Well-camouflaged supply holes were located in and outside the camp.

III. Own Fighting Style

1.) General

An effort is to be made to commit the divisions so that the bands are first forced out of the dense and swampy wooded areas into less dense and drier areas, in order to be able to engage and destroy them there.

It is important to hammer into the troops that on finding the enemy they should attack immediately without major preparations. During "Gypsy Baron" waiting until the next day always resulted in the enemy escaping undetected during the night.

2.) Infantry

A complete success can only be achieved if the advance is made in a continuous line of maximum density, sector by sector. Close communication with neighboring units and security at boundaries are of vital importance. Means of communication are light signals, signal whistles, horns, shouts and the like.

Whenever possible, the troops should advance in the direction of forest lanes. This greatly simplifies orientation, contact and follow-up by the vehicles. Every platoon should check its direction frequently with the compass. In easy terrain advancing elements must not press forward too quickly. Care must always be taken, however, to avoid bunching up on the forest lanes. Instead the troops should carefully scan the intervening terrain. The daily objectives should be split up into several intermediate objectives, defined by easily-identifiable terrain features (streams, forest lanes, clearings, etc.). Hourly halts of 15 minutes are necessary to organize the units.

Advancing in wedge formation protects against being outflanked or threatened from the rear. Pre-conditions for this are narrow sectors (max. of 2 km per battalion, 500 – 700 m per company). In the evening forward movement is to be halted in time to permit the establishment of a continuous line of security before nightfall. Movement in the forest during the night is forbidden. The troops must exercise increased vigilance at dawn and dusk. Early in the morning patrols of at least platoon-strength should be sent ahead to the next daily objective. The patrols may only advance away from lanes and roads. In the event of unexpected enemy contact in complex terrain, it is advisable to spray thickets and clumps of bushes with machine-gun and submachine-gun fire. This apparent waste of ammunition saves the units many casualties. Heavy weapons are to be kept close. The light anti-tank gun firing high-explosive ammunition is an effective weapon against partisan bands. If the units encounter stronger enemy concentrations they are to be halted, as many heavy weapons as possible are to be brought into position and artillery support secured. During the attack the enemy is to be engaged frontally by fire only, while his destruction is to be attempted by flanking attack. At the same time, efforts must be made early on to cut off his avenue of retreat.

Reserves are of crucial importance in partisan operations. Breakthroughs of the thin front line by smaller or larger enemy groupings are always to be expected. Their destruction is only possible if reserves are available everywhere. Every company and every battalion must have reserves available close at hand. The regiments and divisions must maintain stronger reserves. In order to be able to destroy larger enemy groupings that have broken through, it is desirable that the divisions have good mobile formations (e.g. the reconnaissance battalion of a panzer division or a bicycle battalion).

3.) Artillery

Artillery fire always has a considerable effect on the partisan bands. Despite all the terrain difficulties, an effort must be made to bring along at least light artillery. Siting positions can be found anywhere, even in dense forest.

Proven orientation methods are:

Needle Method: measurement of needle deviation on any starlit night with the aid of the North Star. The magnet needle showed that, although the maps showed the area to be a magnetic deviation zone, only in isolated instances were there deviations.

Map aiming point method with vertical firing of flares.
Same direction method using straight-line railway lines, forest lanes or roads.
Adjustment fire was usually carried out with combination fuses with detonation points.

Massing of all artillery assets of a division (a reinforced battalion) proved effective in actions against fortified camps or villages in difficult wooded terrain. Massed action is rarely possible in swampy forest. In such cases the use of single guns has proved effective. Their orientation is simplified if they are positioned on straight-line lanes, roads, etc. The use of light field howitzers to lay down direct fire on bunkers and other targets in the forest was not possible on account of swamps and dense undergrowth. The use of numerous forward observers is indispensable in order to maintain flexibility of artillery fire in the forest. Every observer must be prepared to immediately shoot with the entire artillery battalion.

4.) Tanks and Air Force

Tanks are particularly effective in attacks on fortified positions or villages, as is the air force in complex terrain. Air attacks must be planned in advance, however, they should be avoided before the ground attack in order to maintain the element of surprise.

Aerial reconnaissance was relatively ineffective in the dense forest. The detection of campfires did, however, indicate the presence of bandit groups. Night patrols by the air force over the bandit area are necessary, in order to locate signal fires for enemy supply aircraft.

5.) Pioneers

The most important tasks of the pioneers are:

Removal of mines from tracks, roads and important segments of terrain, construction and repair of bridges, support for the infantry in crossing swampy areas and waterways using inflatable boats, destruction of captured camps and defense installations.

The extent of these tasks requires the commitment of strong pioneer forces. A pioneer company should be attached to each regiment. As well, each division should have a pioneer reserve of one or two companies in order to create the necessary cross-links, repair the main supply roads and provide additional mine-clearing teams where heavy mining is found.

A great deal of ammunition and time is required for the thorough destruction of most large bandit camps. Whenever possible the dugouts are burned.

6.) Communications

Firm command is only possible if there are always telephone communications down to battalion level. Only then can command react immediately and correctly to surprises. Maintaining communication is simplified if the regimental command posts are not moved during the day and only repositioned to just behind the front line in the evening. Teams to repair the lines and prevent bandits from tapping in must be sufficiently strong. Overlapping of telephone communications by radio is necessary, and radio has proved effective in maintaining communication between battalions and companies. After 18:00 hours there is heavy interference in radio traffic, making radio communications almost useless in the evening hours.

The entire communications system, including radio stations, must be made sufficiently mobile to follow the infantry anywhere (panye wagons and pack animals).

IV. Supply

In general, supplying the units engaged in large anti-partisan operations presents no difficulties. A prepared system of supply bases in the units' assembly areas is desirable. As the attack proceeds, the divisions set up auxiliary supply bases with mixed supply goods. This eliminates the need for the fighting units to provide security forces and shortens supply lines. Attaching a supply transport unit to each attacking regiment has proved effective.

a.) Replenishment with ammunition up to one initial issue with continuous supplementation was sufficient. Predominantly light artillery ammunition was expended with low total consumption.

b.) Special preparatory measures are not required in the area of rations. In unfavorable terrain and road conditions the establishment of auxiliary issuing stations behind the attacking troops seems appropriate. Carriage of field kitchens is not always possible in swampy wooded areas. Anticipatory issuing of special rations to the men (carriage of gas mask container) seems more practical. Foraging from the land to ease the burden on supply cannot be anticipated in most bandit areas. During the battles only small dumps with potatoes and breadstuff were found. In keeping with the time of year, the necessary special clothing must be delivered in time in order to ease the troops' battle. Mosquito tents and mosquito nets are indispensable during the warm seasons. Rubber boots often represent an additional burden for the men, as they cannot do without their regular boots. Wear on clothing caused by fighting in forests and swamps is severe.

c.) For medical supply, one medical company and one ambulance platoon is sufficient for a division. In the absence of suitable buildings, the special provision of wounded and dressing tents is necessary. To avoid bandit ambushes, main dressing stations should be collocated with units (command posts). In swampy terrain panye wagons are almost always the only means of evacuation. Vehicles transporting the wounded should travel to the rear in groups with escort. The constant availability of a medical evacuation Storch is desirable.

d.) The inoculation of horses against piroplasmosis prevents heavy casualties during the warm seasons.

V. Recovery of Booty

Sufficient preparations must be made for the recovery of booty, in order to avoid the loss of valuable goods. The units generally display little understanding for the necessity of recovery and do not possess sufficient forces to guard it.

a) The use of vehicle services to recover captured weapons and equipment has proved effective. The recovery teams should be attached to the divisions in sufficient strength during the assembly stage and, in cooperation with the units, are to make preparations to secure and recover [captured equipment]. *Towing equipment must be made available by the units.*

b) The allocation of special detachments to collect captured cattle and farming equipment, as well as clothing and equipment is advisable. The captured stocks are generally minimal, usually consisting of small dumps containing potatoes and breadstuff. It has been found that when bandit camps are destroyed, some of the stockpiled supplies are also destroyed or probably were never found at all. The forces must be halted to provide transport space for the removal of captured goods.

VI. Removal of the Evacuated Population and Prisoners

The removal of the population to be evacuated during bandit operations requires thorough preparations. The number of evacuees must not be underestimated.

a) It is advisable that the forces prepare special forces to handle transport to the reception camps. During the operation prisoners and evacuees were sent to the rear by the fighting forces. Heavy protection and long distances deprived them of forces equivalent in strength to a battalion. It seems more practical to form escort detachments from non-combat personnel of the divisions.

b) The number of reception camps to be set up is based on the anticipated numbers of civilians to be evacuated. The camps are to be sited so that the forces do not have to send evacuees long distances, even as the attack progresses. They are to be sited around the bandit area, as the outflow cannot be directed to just one side of the pocket. In setting up the camps, the strict separation of civilians who have been disinfected from those who have not yet been disinfected is to be anticipated.

This results in the following organization:
a) camps for non-disinfected civilians
b) camps for disinfected civilians
c) delousing facility

The following personnel are required for a reception camp:

Camp commander

Medical officer with aides

Rations officer

Military police as security agency

The stockpiling of food is based on the anticipated number of evacuees and the probable timing of their departure. It should not be assumed that the population in the bandit area will possess sufficient foodstuffs.

With the help of delousing platoons and delousing barracks, the large-scale delousing of civilians ran smoothly. Provision must be made in the reception camps for fulltime medical and hygienic monitoring of the evacuees.

c) Sufficient transport space must be made available on a timely basis for the fast transport out of the evacuees, in order to avoid lengthy stays by civilians in the camps. Special guards are to be assigned to the transports. Thought is to be given to providing sufficient food and medical attention.

The most advantageous location for prisoner of war collection camps for partisan band members, deserters and evacuees of military service age is near the reception camps.

VII. Results of "Operation Gypsy Baron"

1,568 prisoners
869 deserters
1,584 enemy killed. The number of dead is in reality significantly higher, as it has been found that the bandits bury their dead immediately after the fighting.
15,812 evacuated civilians
207 destroyed camps
2,930 destroyed bunkers and dugouts
11 pistols
1 revolver
1 flare pistol
1,117 rifles, 181 of them automatic, 26 rifle barrels
88 submachine-guns
124 machine-guns, also numerous machine-gun carriages and drums
2 rifle grenade launchers
55 mortars
14 anti-tank guns, 2 anti-tank gun barrels
1 20-mm tank cannon
2 light hunting rifles
28 anti-tank rifles
9 light artillery pieces
12 heavy artillery pieces
3 tanks, including 1 T-34
2 armored cars
2 aircraft, including 1 with radio equipment
1 radio station with 2 radio sets, also 8 radio sets (2 of them Hungarian)
1 radio dynamo
1 binoculars
7 field telescopes
1 gas mask

92 boats captured or destroyed, numerous mines disarmed or detonated
165,720 rounds of rifle ammunition
Approx. 30,000 rounds of submachine-gun ammunition, approx. 11,000 rounds of machine-gun ammunition
More than 1,000 rounds of artillery ammunition
Approx. 1,900 rounds of mortar ammunition
562 rounds of anti-tank rifle ammunition
300 kg of explosives, numerous explosive charges
1 headquarters camp with printing press
2 tire dumps with about 120 tires
1 skins dump
1 vehicle motor with tires for 1 vehicle
2 trucks
5 field kitchens, 1 kitchen installation
1 bakery
1 field forge
1 shoemaker's workshop
1 ordnance shop
1 lokomobile (portable engine)
2 tractors
30 sets of harness, 3 saddles
4 limbers
110 pairs of skis
183 sleighs
316 horses
380 cows
717 panye wagons
Clothing and equipment for about 500 men
25 parachutes and supply containers (ammunition, American rations and flour).

VIII. Preserving the Success of a Completed Anti-Partisan Operation

To preserve the success achieved in an anti-partisan operation it is necessary to occupy the entire cleared area with security forces. These elements must establish strongpoints in the forest, from where they can continuously patrol the entire area in strength and prevent the bands from reestablishing themselves.

The struggle against the bandits must also be prosecuted actively. If the security forces remain passive and limit their activities to guarding lines of communication, within a very short time the success of an anti-partisan operation will have been for nothing. It is important that

a) command of the security forces in a bandit area be in the hands of one man, so that forces can be concentrated in one spot if required,

b) that the troops tasked with combating the partisan carry out this mission for some time, so that they become familiar with the special nature of anti-partisan warfare and the terrain,

c) Eastern and People's Defense units be brought in, for, because of their make-up and life in the forest, they are by nature better suited for the struggle against the bandits than the German soldier.

IX. Lessons in the Intelligence Field

1.) Enemy Intelligence

The lengthy preparatory work, conducted mainly by organs of the Abwehr in the form of prisoner interrogations and through the employment of agents, produced material about the position of camps, strengths of the various bands, names of officers, mining of roads, etc. Concerning the grouping of the bands, while we knew where the base camps were, prior to the operation there was uncertainty as to [partisan] movements. As a result, we were not fully aware of the movement of the Duka Brigade into the area surrounding Verkhepolye. Nevertheless, the available intelligence information was of great help and created trust among the command and forces after their reliability was demonstrated by the facts.

Likewise, the traffic directors prepared in advance did good work. Undercover agents who accompanied the forces were able to spot important persons among the prisoners and dead.

During the operation the intelligence focus was on the interrogation of deserters and prisoners, which made it possible to locate fortified camps and occupied settlements not marked on the maps on a timely basis, as well as enemy movements. It proved to be of decisive importance that such interrogations were carried out and evaluated as quickly as possible. For the forces, this was only possible if they had been provided with interpreters (meaning ones trained in interrogation techniques) in sufficient numbers. The required knowledge of the enemy was gained thanks to the interrogation assets provided by the army, which were employed selectively, and the assignment of Abwehr I and III [secret intelligence and security/counter-espionage, respectively]. Captured papers (diaries of several bandit groups, lists of the agent network and other information about the organization) showed that the bandit organization around Briansk already had its beginnings in July-August 1941.

Aerial reconnaissance added to our picture of the enemy (visual observation of campfires and herds of cattle), as it made it easier to follow the movements of the fleeing bands. Clues were also provided by reports on bridge-building, roads in use, presence in villages, anti-aircraft fire and parachutes hanging in trees.

Signals intelligence proved of little use during "Operation Gypsy Baron"; the reason for this failure must be sought in its rushed use in unfavorable terrain influences.

It is important that intelligence officers compile all intelligence in maps or file cards, so that a relatively accurate assessment can be made from the mass of conflicting intelligence. For this purpose a file card should be made for every village, for every camp and for every bandit group; the campfires and herds of cattle must be entered on the file cards each day in different colors, in order to identify enemy movements. Food storage facilities, ammunition dumps, lighting of enemy airfields and drop points, in particular, must be discovered so that the enemy's supply efforts can be disrupted.

2.) Military Intelligence

a) Scrutiny of civilians living near the front:

In order to prevent unreliable elements from moving in and to detect on a timely basis the presence of small groups of partisan infiltrators, the populations of the most important villages were checked each dawn. No significant in-migration was discovered. A few members of bandit families were picked up. A number of administrative shortcomings came to light, however, which hampered the scrutinizing process. In many villages in the self-governed district of Lokot, for example, many lists of residents were not up to date, and west of the Desna the shortcomings described in the corps headquarters report of 12/4 (to Field Commander Briansk) were again observed (expired passes, issuing of passes by sub-agencies of the local military posts). Other measures were carried out, including sharp restrictions on travel and a complete ban west of the Desna.

b) The most important tasks of the military police and security service were scrutinizing the populations of areas evacuated by the partisans. A large number of band members (men and women) and local self-defense forces were found among them. Given the large numbers of evacuees (16,000) and the limited number of military intelligence assets available, checks could only be made randomly. Numerous civilians had to be moved out without adequate scrutiny, consequently it must be feared that there were further suspicious characters among the evacuees. Again, notice should be taken of the dangers that can arise from overly-hasty resettlement, deportation to the Reich to work, or even recruitment for Eastern units.

With the assistance of genuine defectors and reliable mayors from the surrounding area, a number of criminals were arrested.

3.) Active Propaganda

To degrade the partisan bands and fragment their resistance, the intelligence section dropped a total of 840,000 leaflets during the operation. The effect can be characterized as good; many deserters came in, some even with their weapons.

Desertions were encouraged by the rapid dissemination of the information that we do not indiscriminately shoot every person from the bandit-infested area.

The deserter liaison and care sections formed quickly by the divisions were committed in the collection camps but achieved nothing significant; their action should be seen as a practice run and training.

Loudspeaker trucks, which could have done good service encouraging and educating the population near the front, were not available.

4.) Spiritual Care

There was scarcely any opportunity to provide spiritual care to our own forces during the forest fighting; to counter the dulling effect of the difficult action, value was placed on making sure that the daily news (OKW reports, "Das Neueste" and when possible the "Army Newspaper") reached the troops.

Document 48

Report by High Command, 2nd Army to Headquarters, XX Army Corps
The Behavior of German Soldiers in the Self-governed District
Is Negatively Affecting Relations with the Kaminski Brigade
13 August 1943

The following report by the liaison officer to Kaminski is being sent for your information.

Numerous excesses by the forces within the self-governed district, especially seizing the cattle of People's Defense men, is having an extremely negative effect on the morale of the population and the People's Defense and is destroying trust in the Wehrmacht. 106 People's Defense men have already deserted; probably gone over to the partisans. Kaminski has stated that he is unable to accept responsibility for threats to the reliability of the People's Defense and is considering asking that he be relieved if the previous behavior of our forces continues. He is also urgently requesting that steps be taken immediately.

To the south, the self-governed district extends a considerable distance into the current battle zone of Headquarters, XX Army Corps. Appropriate measures must be taken to ensure that the mentioned excesses by the forces cease.

Document 49

Report by Quartermaster, 2nd Army Regarding the Kaminski Movement
16 August 1943

The Kaminski Movement is being trekked out of the Lokot area via Seredina Buda, initially into the Gremyach – Pogar area west of the Desna.

As per special orders from Army Group Center dated 11/8/43, the Rear Area Commander 532 will carry out the resettlement from the Lokot area into the area of Field Commander 181 Lepel in consultation with Bef. H. Geb. According to available information, initially

1,500 – 2,000 People's Defense people are to be moved by rail from Seredina Buda to Vitebsk, while beginning 20/8/43 four trains are to be dispatched daily with civilians, cattle and movable possessions.

For part of the population, a foot march via Seredina Buda into the area surrounding Pogar (from there rail transport) is envisaged.

As advised by Hauptmann Peschorner, Rear Area Commander 532's liaison officer, it is planned to route the Kaminski movement via Seredina Buda – Lukashenkov – Prokopvka – Novgorod Seversk – Pushkari – Gremyach – Pogar. Nothing further is known yet. Rear Area Commander 532 was directed to, in closest consultation with Rear Area Commander 580:

1.) Provide monitoring and traffic control for this movement through the use of military police at the most important junctions and bridges plus the use of mobile patrols,

2.) determine how and where this movement can be fed,

3.) determine who will be responsible for detraining in Pogar,

4.) when and in what strength this movement should be anticipated,

5.) to determine if bridge conditions allow a shorter route to be taken through the army area to Pogar.

Major Blume was ordered by me to remain in the closest contact with Hauptmann Peschorner and keep me informed.

Document 50

Letter from the Head of *Einsatzgruppe B* of the Security Police and of the Security Service to the Commander of Counter-Partisan Units *SS-Obergruppenführer und General der Polizei* von dem Bach Regarding Kaminski and the Self-governed District of Lokot
28 September 1943

With the dissolution of the army area and the withdrawal of the Headquarters, 3rd Panzer Army boundary to the south (the exact border runs along the southern border of the rayon of Lepel – Chashniki – Senno – Begushevskoye), the entire of the self-governed district of Lepel is now completely under the jurisdiction of Headquarters, 3rd Panzer Army.

Regarding the Kaminski matter, Headquarters, 3rd Panzer Army has made the following ruling:

Territorially, Kaminski's jurisdiction is limited to the rayons of Lepel, Chashniki and Ushachi, of which the latter is completely controlled by the partisans. Within this area Kaminski retains all of his previous authority. Effective immediately, Hauptmann Könnecke's liaison staff is attached to Headquarters, 3rd Panzer Army. The German military administration and post commanders are being withdrawn from the Kaminski area. The liaison staff will, however, retain a number of field offices, enhancing German monitoring abilities.

Following the Kaminski People's Defense Brigade's move into the Lepel district, at the instigation of the 286th Security Division, which was responsible for the area at the time, an apportionment of the armed forces within the area was undertaken. This parceling-out was not entirely in keeping with Kaminski's wishes, whose original intention was to concentrate as many of his forces as possible in Lepel, from where he could keep a better eye on his soldiers, who had been more or less uprooted by the resettlement, and thus reduce their susceptibility to enemy propaganda. From Lepel various forays were to be made to pacify an increasingly large portion of the surrounding area. At present the Kaminski Brigade is based at the following locations:

1. Rifle Regiment – Lt.Col. Galkin – in strongpoints guarding the roads east of Lepel to Botsheykovo.

2. Rifle Regiment – Lt. Golyakov, previously Major Tarasov – Senno

3. Rifle Regiment – Major Turlakov – Beshenkovichi and strongpoints along the road from Beshenkovichi in the direction of Vitebak, plus outposts along the Ulla.

4. Rifle Regiment – Major Proshin – Lepel with outposts west and north- and southwest of Lepel.

Guard Battalion (Special Purpose Motorized Battalion) – Lepel

Armored Battalion – Hptm. Samsonov – Lepel. Only 1 T 34 tank and 1 KV I are functional because of a lack of fuel.

The units' armament can be seen as satisfactory. The only complaint is the shortage of ammunition, but there, too, help is expected. There has been a slight improvement in uniforms and equipment compared to what they had in Lokot, but it is still unsatisfactory. There is a shortage of coats and boots, in particular. Given the present unfavorable, wet weather and later the arrival of cold weather, these factors can reduce the operational capabilities of the troops to the point that combat operations outside their bases becomes impossible.

The food situation of the self-governed district is worse than in Lokot, because the troops are forces to rely almost exclusively on Wehrmacht rations and cannot obtain additional food from local farms as before. With the Russian soldier's great dependence on a generous bread supply, this will result in a drop in operational readiness and willingness to fight.

At present the morale of the force is extremely low. Signs on unreliability are growing, susceptibility to enemy propaganda is rising. According to the latest information, approximately 300 men deserted from the unit based in Senno. The situation was only restored through the determined intervention of Kaminski's deputy. Kaminski recognizes the serious threat that the enemy's effectively-conceived propaganda poses for his men, *and he complains about the slowness and inability of the Lepel Propaganda Section, which makes a planned and convincing counterpropaganda program impossible.*

Regarding the overall situation, it is also of importance that because of the dispersal of his units ordered by the 286th Security Division, Kaminski will no longer be able to carry out the large-scale attack against the bandits in his area as originally planned. Instead of regiments he can now only commit battalions. Therefore the planned encirclement of the partisan bands, which should have led to the liberation of 50% of the self-governed district, is also no longer possible.

Kaminski repeatedly stresses that he has trust in his officers and men. The general view held by the Germans, however, is quite the opposite. There has been a visible drop in the morale of the local Russian population since the arrival of the People's Defense Brigade.

This development is the result of friction with the refugees from Lokot and the inadequacy of the measures carried out by Kaminski. After the withdrawal of German troops from the strongpoints the pro-German people fear for their safety, as they have no trust whatever in the Kaminski People's Defense Brigade. Representative of the antagonism between Kaminski and the local Russian population is a speech by Kaminski's propaganda agent at an information meeting in the movie theater in Lepel on 23/9/43, in which the entire blame for the miserable conditions in Lepel and the partisan movement was laid entirely on the population of the area. Some idea of how badly the people want German military units to stay in Lepel may be gained from the rapid spreading and exaggeration of rumors, according to which new German units are already on the way. In actual fact two bicycle battalions are being stationed in Lepel.

Document 51

Situation Report Sent by Headquarters, 2nd Panzer Army to the
High Command of Army Group Center
28/9/1943

1. Bandit Situation in the Panzer Army Rear Area (1 map)
With the new drawing of borders and the expansion of the army area to the southwest, there are now several sources of danger in the 3rd Panzer Army's rear area which give cause for serious concern:
These are:
a) the bands in the Rosono area
b) the bands in the Vitebsk – Polotsk – Lepel – Senno area (area of Administrative Headquarters 181) and the neighboring area to the west.

c) The Kaminski Brigade and the accompanying population from the Lokot area in the area around Lepel.

In detail:

1.) While the transfer of the army's northern border to the Dryssa has resulted in the Rosono area leaving the army area on the maps, the bandit situation in the area surrounding Polotsk has not changed. All of the bands in the area south of the Kalinin region border (general line Osveya – Yeserishche) are oriented towards Polotsk and the Nevel – Polotsk and Vitebsk – Polotsk – Dvinsk rail lines. According to captured papers, the strength of the White Russian brigades deployed in this (southern) part of the Rosono region has grown even further. At present they number more than 11,000 men.

As the brigades have grown, they have also shifted to the west. The area north of the Polotsk – Dvinsk rail line is now occupied by bandits as far as the old Latvian border. There are two newly-formed brigades there with a total strength of 1,500 men. Bands from the west and south have also turned up east and southeast of Dzisna. Bands have moved into the area north of Obol for attacks against the Vitebsk – Polotsk line; moreover several demolition squads have been committed from the south.

To date, efforts to counter the attacks by these bands against the Nevel – Polotsk and Vitebsk – Polotsk – Dvinsk lines by drawing on all available forces have only been partially successful. An intensified effort against the bands on the approaches to the railways is no longer possible. The result of this has been further encroachment by the bands into the area near the lines and mining of the roads there.

2.) While there are still scattered German strongpoints in the Vitebsk – Polotsk – Lepel – Senno area, the area is controlled by the bands in a way that is making it increasingly difficult to continue to maintain these strongpoints.

The bandits have now achieved a strength of about 15,000 men in the entire region. Through forced recruiting and the intake of native units (in particular the Drushina units under the command of Colonel Radionov in the area west of Lepel with a strength of about 2,000 men), the brigades have so grown that they are capable of forming new ones through division. Their weaponry, especially in automatic weapons, has improved significantly. Several tanks were even observed in the area northwest of Senno.

To a growing degree our own strongpoints are being cut off from the outside world. Traffic can only be maintained on the Vitebsk – Lepel road through the use of powerful convoys. There are no telephone communications because kilometers of line have been destroyed and the telephone poles cut down. Log barricades have been set up on the road to Lepel and future use of the "military road" from Lepel to Minsk has been rendered impossible, for according to residents, southwest of Lepel the pavement has been torn up for a distance of 15 km.

Attacks on our strongpoints have increased recently, and a large-scale attack on Senno is said to be imminent.

3.) The Kaminski Brigade (about 6,000 members of the People's Defense) and the population from the Lokot area accompanying it (previously about 25,000 persons) moved into the Lepel area by the beginning of September 1943.

Although Administrative Headquarters 181 Lepel made preparations for a smooth resettlement and detailed plans concerning allocation sites and numbers were drawn up, faulty work by Kaminski's people resulted in the quartering of the refugees not taking place as planned. Lepel and the surrounding area were overpopulated, resulting in ill-feeling among the previously pro-German native population.

Kaminski's People's Defense units only were quartered in the rayon of Lepel as follows:

1. Rifle Regiment – Lt.Col. Galkin – in strongpoints guarding the roads east of Lepel to Botsheykovo.

2. Rifle Regiment Senno

3. Rifle Regiment Beshenkovichi and strongpoints along the road from Beshenkovichi in the direction of Vitebak plus outposts along the Ulla.

4. Rifle Regiment Lepel

Guard Battalion Lepel

While, with the growing unreliability of all eastern forces, the "People's Defense" could no longer be viewed as absolutely reliable; a number of incidents, especially the desertion of elements of the VIII People's Defense Battalion in Senno on 23/9/43, have given cause for serious doubts. The investigation into this incident revealed a regular conspiracy, whose goal was to eliminate Kaminski and his closest advisors, hand the People's Defense over to the partisans and thus place the entire district of Lepel in their hands. Even though the decisive intervention of Kaminski and Administrative Headquarters 181 Lepel, especially the arresting of a number of officers, initially prevented the revolt from spreading, further appearances of breakdown should definitely be expected because of the present conditions. First and foremost, activity and pressure from the bands is now constantly increasing—following the withdrawal of the 2nd Battalion of Security Regiment 931, previously deployed in the Lepel, by order of the army group. The enemy's propaganda has had considerable success recently—mainly through the spreading of rumors—resulting in the desertion of many OD people and foreign auxiliaries to the bands.

The mood of the People's Defense is characterized as depressed. While Kaminski himself believes that his officers and men are loyal—while he is presently master of the situation, in case of emergency he will be unable to prevent further irregularities with his own forces.

If the present situation in the Lepel area does not undergo a quick and radical change through occupation by German troops, there is the danger that enemy propaganda will gain further influence on the People's Defense, already especially susceptible to it, and thus initiate a development that could lead to a very critical situation in a short time.

II. Situation of the Security Forces in the Panzer Army Area

a) At present the panzer army has security forces totaling 9 security battalions

b) Also attached to the army, but presently deployed in the area of Headquarters, 16th Army:

Grenadier Regiment 406 with 3 battalions,
Security Regiment 601 with 2 battalions.

c) Needed to guard rail lines and roads:

Krynki Station – Vitebsk – Polotsk – Dryssa 5 battalions and alert units,
Polotsk – Vetrino 1 battalion,
Polotsk – Nevel within the panzer army area 3 battalions,
Vitebsk – Nevel within the panzer army area 1 battalion and alert units,
Vitebsk – Orsha within the panzer army area 1 battalion and alert units,
Total 11 battalions.

The missing 2 battalions and the 3 security battalions presently deployed in the "Panther Position" are replaced by 4 battalions of the 391st (Field Training) Division and 1 battalion of the 390th (Field Training) Division (this is only available temporarily).

As soon as the field training division has to release the trained recruits, the battalions will no longer be available for security duty.

d) In the self-governed district of Lepel the panzer army is forced to protect the roads militarily in order to keep open traffic and supply. Lepel is not in a position to do this.

Required for this are:

Vitebsk – Lepel road 1 security battalion
Bogushevskaya – Lepel road 1 security battalion
Ulla – Lepel road and Polotsk – Lepel road 1 security battalion

Five more security battalions are required if the panzer army does not want to be driven into a hopeless situation in its rear. New units must be sent in, or Headquarters, 16th Army must return Gren.Rgt. 406 and Security.Rgt. 601 to Headquarters, 3rd Panzer Army.

With respect to this, it is noted that these forces will suffice to guard the panzer army's lifelines and give the commander of the self-governed district of Lokot the backing needed to prevail against the bands and his subordinates. As before, however, cleaning up the rear area remains out of the question.

Document 52

Report by the Liaison Staff to the Self-Governed District of Lepel
regarding "Operation Hubertus"
31 October 1943

Purpose of the operation was:
1.) Open the Senno – Chashniki road, in order to move the approximately 3,000 evacuees from Lokot in Senno to Chashniki.
2.) To pacify to the maximum extent possible the area Beshenkovichi – Senno – Uzvayka River - Chashniki
Approximately 2,000 members of the People's Defense took part in the operation and were divided into five battle groups, together with the Lepel OD.
The plan of operations was laid down in People's Defense Brigade Headquarters Battle Order No. 3 of 2 October 1943. The army provided two radio stations, one of which stayed in Lepel, while the other was assigned to the operations staff. The operations staff consisted of:
  Brigade Commander Kaminski
  Lieutenant-Colonel Shavykin, chief-of-staff
  Major Frolov, operations officer
  Captain Kapkayev, intelligence officer
  Captain Bakshanski, special appointee for propaganda
Also attached to the operations staff:
  Hauptmann Köneke, liaison officer, with
  Sdf. (Z) Pommer as interpreter
  SS-Obersturmführer Loleit, Reichsführer-SS liaison officer
  SS-Untersturmführer Johannson, SD-EK 9
The operation began according to plan on 16 October after the battle groups designated in the order had moved into their start positions on 15 October. The first part of the operation proceeded according to plan. The designated objectives of the day were reached, although significant difficulties arising from the complete destruction of all crossings and roads had to be overcome. The bands defended the villages they occupied with varying degrees of determination. In some places there was tough fighting, especially in the villages of Shalami, Ossovets, Vodooyevo and Lasuki.
The bands had generous supplies of ammunition and many automatic weapons. On the other hand, they lacked heavy weapons and, when they had them, ammunition. Nowhere did they stand up to tanks. On the other hand, they stood up quite well under artillery fire—for example at Lasuki. During the burning of the villages of Shalami and Ossovets it could be seen that there were ammunition dumps in several of the houses.

The local population stated, and this was confirmed by prisoner statements, that partisan brigade commander Alexeyev had given the order to stand up to the attack at all costs. He had formed rear battalions that were supposed to prevent his forces from withdrawing by force of arms. Near Vodopoyevo, in addition to 5 otriyade of the Alexeyev Brigade, an otriyad of the "Smolensk Regiment" was detected, which according to prisoner statements had come to the former's aid from Saprudye 68/84 the day before.

The bands initially withdrew to the south. According to residents, some of the bandits declared that resistance against the RONA with its tanks and heavy weapons was pointless and that they were withdrawing to Chereya. In other places it was discovered that the bandits had spread the rumor that attackers were not the RONA, but German-backed Vlasov troops.

The attempt to encircle the retreating bands in the bend of the Yzveyka River failed, as the communications assets were lacking to commit all of the battle groups according to a plan and at the right time. The bands were able to flee to the southwest.

The bandit attack on Chashniki on 19 October made a change of plan necessary. A battle group had to be diverted to relieve the village, and early on the 21st it liberated the place, most of which had been occupied by the bandits. The remaining groups could not continue the operation for three days because of extraordinary difficulties in bringing up the necessary quantities of ammunition and fuel from Senno.

Meanwhile the situation in Chashniki had worsened again. Under continuous bandit attack, the troops in the village were in danger of having to cease fighting because of lack of ammunition. For this reason, all other battle groups were sent to Chashniki on the 24th. Subsequently there were no further serious combat operations. The bandits limited themselves to attacking several smaller villages in the surrounding area but were repulsed everywhere. Leaving the 3rd People's Defense Regiment to guard Chashniki seemed sufficient, allowing the attack on the main bandit nest of Volosovichi to begin on 25 October.

The attack force was organized into three battle groups, in order to sweep the widest possible area. Reached on 25 October were:

By the northern group (5th Rifle Regiment) Zhurovka 28/76

By the central group (2nd Rifle Regiment and Operations Staff) Lyakovichi 28/72

By the southern group (XIII/5th Regiment and Guards Battalion) Lyakovichi 32/72

The concentric attack on Volosovichi was continued on 26 October 1943 and the town was taken against minimal resistance at 10:00.

Bandit telephone lines were discovered and destroyed in Lyakovichi and Volosovichi. The villages—especially Volosovichi—were fortified with carefully-built bunkers and defense positions (in some cases communications trenches more than 100 meters long).

The defense positions were essentially laid out for a defense facing northwest (from the direction of Lepel!), consequently they were of no use against the attack from the southeast. The effects of the German air attack on Volosovichi were clearly visible, however only houses, dugouts and commercial buildings were hit, not the well-camouflaged bunkers. According to prisoners, the bands withdrew towards the large wooded massif southwest of Volosovichi . Combing the extensive area of forests and swamps with the available forces appeared hopeless. On the 25th and 26th of October, therefore, the area Volosovichi – Svyada 08/72 – Great Polus'tseviche 12/82 – Cherny 20/81 was carefully combed. There were no further serious contacts with the enemy.

At 14:00 on 27 October all battle groups arrived together in Lepel.

According to a report by the brigade staff, the enemy suffered the following casualties during the fighting, including the battles for Chashniki and Lepel:

    562 dead
    35 captured

The number of wounded could not be determined. It must be high, however, for according to statements by local residents about 200 wounded were evacuated in panye wagons from Lyakovichi alone.

    Own casualties:
    34 killed
    61 wounded
    38 missing

Also lost were:

2 light M.G.	6 heavy M.G.	1 S.M.G.	1 artillery piece
4 mortars	60 rifles	1 BT 7 tank	
1 T 34 tank			

Captured were:

2 heavy M.G.	13 light M.G.	13 S.M.G.	139 rifles
5 anti-tank rifles	1 mortar	3 revolvers	
4 semiautomatic rifles			

Destroyed in battle: 1 T 26 tank, 1 BT 7 tank

Observations and Lessons

The People's Defense performed well offensively. Some attacks were carried out with courage. The units were not of equal worth; the personality of the unit leader was always the determining factor.

The main fighting power of the People's Defense lies in its tanks and heavy weapons, for the partisan bands have nothing equivalent with which to counter them.

Defensively, the People's Defense is less effective. It lacks the necessary persistency. Faith in its own strength falls rapidly when ammunition runs low.

Firm command was lacking throughout the entire operation. The main reason for this is the absence of the necessary communications between the operations staff and the various battle groups. Providing the People's Defense with radio equipment and telephone links is absolutely essential in future operations.

Supply proved to be extremely difficult. The necessary means of transport were lacking, and the supply dumps were too far away. In future it will be necessary to set up supply dumps near the area of operations.

Advancing over the badly-damaged roads required a great deal of pioneer work. The fighting troops carried this out relatively well and quickly, although the available means were extremely limited. The establishment of pioneer platoons with the necessary equipment is desirable.

Mounted battalions are needed for reconnaissance in the swampy, trackless terrain and for rapid pursuit of the fleeing enemy. The brigade has already recommended the formation of a cavalry platoon for each regiment. The necessary horses are present, however saddlery is required.

Subsequently, it can be said that the objective of the operation was partially achieved. During the fighting approximately 2,000 civilians were transported from Senno to Chashniki. The remaining approximately 650 people could not be dispatched because of a shortage of transport capacity. The destruction of partisan bands in the area of operations could not be achieved as the forces committed were inadequate. Nevertheless, the bands were driven from their previous locations and seriously harassed. If this harassment is continued, the regular supplying of the bandits will be seriously disrupted and the bands' influence on the civilian population will diminish significantly.

Document 53

Special Order by the Commander of the Security Police and the SD in White Russia and Ruthenia Regarding the Participation of the Security Police and the SD in "Operation Spring Festival"

10 April 1944

1) Each battalion of Battle Group von Gottberg (and, with the agreement of Headquarters, 3rd Panzer Army, the attached Wehrmacht elements) is being assigned a motorized squad of the Security Police and the SD of 1 officer and 2 men (including interpreter). The squads' mission:

a) Interrogation of prisoners and deserters,
b) Collection and evaluation of captured papers,
c) Other enemy intelligence
d) Intelligence information from the battalion commander.

2) Each of the four Einsatzgruppen will be assigned an SS officer of the Security Police and of the SD (with interpreter and vehicle). Mission of the SD officers:

a) Command of the Security Police and SD personnel attached to the Einsatzgruppe.

b) Visual inspection of the material captured by the squad
c) Intelligence information from the Einsatzgruppe leader.
3) The Security Police/SD squads will convey captured material daily to the SD officer attached to the Einsatzgruppe. The SD officer attached to the Einsatzgruppe will report daily to the intelligence officer attached to battle group headquarters and regularly direct all material to him. Persons who can provide particularly important information, especially all brigade and battalion commanders and commissars, plus members of senior staffs, etc. and all radio operators, are to be immediately conveyed to the intelligence officer attached to the battle group headquarters.
4) The following assignments will be made in carrying out Articles 1) and 2):
a) to Einsatzgruppe Rehdanz (command post Krulevshchizna):
SS-Hauptsturmführer Benitzki with vehicle, driver and interpreter from Adst. Glebokie and 6 squads (2 squads from Adst. Vileyka, 2 squads from Adst. Glebokie, 1 squad from Adst. Baranovichi, 1 squad from Adst. Lida).
b) too Einsatzgruppe Anhalt (command post Dokshytsy):
SS-Hauptsturmführer Dr. Steinhäuser with vehicle, driver and interpreter from the BdS (Commander of Security Police) office in Minsk plus 7 squads (all from the BdS office in Minsk). The Security Police/SD squad attached to the Dirlewanger Battalion under the command of SS-Untersturmführer Amann is also attached to SS-Hauptsturmführer Dr. Steinhäuser for the duration of the operation. There is no need to provide another squad to the Dirlewanger Battalion.
c) to Einsatzgruppe Kaminski (command post Beresino):
SS-Obersturmführer Loleit with vehicle and driver from EK 9 and 6 squads (all from EK 9).
d) to Einsatzgruppe Krehan (command post Pyshno):
SS-Untersturmführer Menge with vehicle, driver and interpreter from EK 9 and 5 squads (3 squads from SK 7a, 2 squads from Adst. Baranovichi)
I entrust SS-Hauptsturmführer Dr. Seckel, intelligence officer (Ic) attached to battle group headquarters, with the overall command of the forces of the Security Police and SD (less reinforced Police Battalion 23) taking part in "Operation Spring Festival".
5) In agreement with the Einsatzgruppen commanders, the forces are to be thoroughly instructed,
a) that, given the nature and closeness of the Ushachi area, a great intake of captured papers is to be expected with certainty, from which important information, not only for the conduct of the operation itself, but also concerning the structure and organization of the entire bandit movement and probably the illegal communist party may be obtained.
b) that, in general, special attention be paid to the locating of captured papers.
c) that all papers—with the exception of personal documents—be taken from all prisoners.
d) that attention be paid to the presence of such papers (orders, passes, certificates, letters, leaflets, etc.) during searches of shot persons, of houses, bunkers, items of baggage, equipment, etc.

e) that all prisoners and deserters are delivered immediately to the nearest Security Police/SD squad and all captured papers are conveyed there immediately.

The SD officer attached to the Einsatzgruppe commander is responsible for providing the necessary instruction.

Document 54

Extract from the Assessment of the Enemy Situation in the Lepel – Ulla – Polotsk – Dokshytsy Area by the Senior SS and Police Commander
Central Russia and White Ruthenia
11 April 1944

Map Material 1:100,000   N 35 III East and West
   N 35 VI East and West
   N 35 V East.

1. General Overview

The area Lepel – Ulla – Polotsk – Dokshytsy, also known as the greater Ushachi area, is bordered in the south and southeast by the Dokshytsy – Lepel – Kamen – Ulla road, the Dvina River in the northeast and the Polotsk – Molodechno rail line in the northwest and west. The center of the area is the rayon of Ushachi (Vitebsk region). From the north through west to the south it is bordered by parts of the following rayons: Vyetrina (Vitebsk region), Plissa (Vileyka region), Dokshytsy (Vileyka region) and Lepel (Vitebski region). The southwestern part of the area is a difficult-to-access area of forests and swamps, which via a land bridge to the northeast becomes an extensive area of lakes. Encouraged by these conditions, small plundering bands initially formed in this area. Through skillful leadership, lively propaganda among the civilian population and planned supply from the air from Moscow, by the late summer of 1942 these already posed a considerable danger to lines of communication and a threat to our strongpoints, causing them to be abandoned one after another. In the course of further development a closed partisan band area was created, which was protected against surprises from the outside by lines of sentries, civilian checkpoints and a systematic arrangement of field positions, bunkers, roadblocks and mines. The roads within the area are believed to have been rendered impassable by the destruction of bridges, erecting of barriers and in some places even by tearing them up. The civilian population from the border regions was forcibly evacuated to the center of the area and combat brigades were moved up to the borders to screen the area.

According to our information, the leader of the partisan brigades in the rayon of Ushachi is "Lobanok". It should be assumed that the brigades in the rest of the rayon are subordinate to him for tactical reasons. Lobanok is probably identical to the former commander of the "Dubrovski Brigade" (F 114) Lobanok, Vladimir, age about 30, average height, lean, dark blonde, as the "Labonok Brigade" (F 126) was formed from the "Dubrovski Brigade" in the summer of 1943. Further light is shone on Lobanok as the probable leader by the fact that he commanded all of the brigades in the area during "Operation Cottbus" (early 1943). Recently an order was supposedly issued to the brigades under Lobanok to hold the area at all costs until the Red Army arrives. Air support was promised against larger German attacks.

The total strength of the bands is estimated at about 14,000. Its armament and supplies can be characterized as adequate, however, it appears that relatively few heavy infantry weapons are present. This may have changed considerably, however, due to the exceptionally high level of supplies dropped from the air recently. While about 50 supply flights were reported during the period from 15 December 1943 to 14 January 1944, and 80 from 15 January to 14 February 1944, according to preliminary reports more than 180 aircraft entered the area between 1 and 31 March 1944.

Most of the brigades have a strong Red Army soldier presence and are led by officers of the Red Army. Discipline and fighting morale are therefore considered good. The majority of the bandits have never been in combat against German units, however. In keeping with the previous unhampered development in the Ushachi area, morale among the population and the bandits is good. "Operations Cottbus" and "Street Cleaner" carried out in the spring and winter of 1943, respectively, only involved the bands in the southwestern part of the area. The attacks carried out by the Luftwaffe and the bombardments of camps and partisan-occupied villages in autumn 1943 only caused a temporary disruption and movement of a few band units. The activities of the bands in the greater area consist mainly of:

a) Harassing German supply traffic through Lepel to the front;

b) Harassing and interrupting railway traffic on the Molodechno – Polotsk line, where series of demolitions have again taken place since the beginning of the year;

c) Destruction of German strongpoints on the supply roads and in the area near the front.

In addition to the partisan brigades, there are also Red Army units (reconnaissance teams and pioneers) which carry out acts of sabotage, keep watch on all of our movements, continuously supply the Red Army with intelligence and are active as far as the Polotsk – Glebokie – Molodechno area. Massed attacks against roads, strongpoints and rail lines (also see "Rail War" in August 1943) in cooperation with new advances by the Red Army are to be expected at any time. A penetration by the Red Army into the Ushachi area would pose an extraordinary threat to White Ruthenia. Furthermore, the situation in the area, combined with the serious situation at the front, poses a constant serious threat to her—especially as almost nothing is known about the intentions of the bands in the area.

II. Band Situation:

For a better overview the area is divided into four sectors:
1) Northern Sector (area S of Polotsk to abeam Voron'ech' 02/34),
2) Eastern Sector (area SW of Dvinsk to chain of lakes)
3) Southern Sector (area N of the Pyshno – Lepel – Kamen – direction Ulla road)
4) Western Sector (area Polotsk – Molodechno rail line and Dokshytsy – Lepel road)
5) Core Area Ushachi

As to 1) Northern Sector:

The entire sector is under the control of the extremely powerful "Melnikov Brigade" (Chapayev F 7), which was transferred from Ushachi to Tutovlya 22/38 with the mission of protecting the Ushachi area to the north. The construction of fortifications was pursued on a considerable scale. A defense line 5 to 10 km deep was created from Lyakhovtsy 88/32 through Navlitsy Lake 94/36 to the east to Turovlya 22/38, which is further guarded by forward field fortifications and patrols, including sentries in a patch of small trees east of the bridge 500 meters S of Boyuchevo 88/36. There is also a partisan radio station about 7 km S of Polotsk 12/44.

The fortifications in the area Navlitsy Lake 94/36 – Sakorki 04/40 – Saosorje 16/40 and Turovlya 22/38 must be characterized as extremely strong. The fortifications, concrete bunkers etc. set up near Gomel 12/32 reveal that the bands see this place on the one hand as the key northern position to the chain of lakes, and on the other as a possible rally point. As well, the place is significant because the presence of a band headquarters is to be expected (several telephone lines come together in the town) and there is a radio station there. The roads from Polotsk into the northern sector have been rendered impassable through the destruction of bridges and installation of log barriers and are guarded by sentries and bunkers.

"Melnikov Brigade", now "Chapayev" (F7)

Commander: Melnikov – chief-of-staff and commissar Koronovski – strength 2,500 men in 11 battalions. Headquarters: in Turovlya 22/38, the rear the "Koniev Battalion" with 450 men. Radio station: at headquarters, also radio stations at each battalion headquarters. Armament: 3 – 4 122-mm artillery pieces, 4 76-mm guns, 4 45-mm anti-tank guns, machine-guns and submachine-guns. Occupied villages: 3 battalions between Shelkovo 18/46 and Turovlya 22/38. Main body in Saskorki 04/40 area. Each battalion has a patrol of 35 men equipped with 3 automatic rifles with silencers plus rifles and submachine-guns.

Eastern Sector:

Deployed to protect the eastern sector, the "Tyabut" (F 16), "Lenin" (F 14), "Bareyka" (?) and "Kozmin" (?) Brigades have occupied the hills SW of the Dvina and have established defense positions, building field fortifications and bunkers. Particularly well-built field positions are located on the SW bank of the Dvina from Novo – Dvor 26/40 to Yanpolye 28/34 and from Usvitsa II 30/30 to Adelino 32/26. Total strength of the forces stationed there about 3,000 men. Focal point 0 Gomel 12/32 to the Dvina, protected by dense forest and swampy terrain. Bridgehead on the east bank of the Dvina near Nemersl 26/36 and Litvinovo 28/42; from there frequent band rotations across the Obol River near Tolkachovo 34/40 through the main line of resistance to the Red Army. Observation platforms provide an improved view of the approaches. Most of the roads have been mined and are of limited use in bad weather. Near Mal. Bortniki 40/16 intelligence radio station Oleny.

"Tyabut Brigade" (F 16). Commander: Tyabut – strength: 1,000 men in 7 battalions – Headquarters: N of Belashi 26/32. Armament: 2 guns, mortars, machine-guns, anti-tank rifles, rifles with silencers. At brigade headquarters observation posts from which the bank of the Dvina can be watched. One battalion in Ostrovlyane 28/32, raised observation platforms there too. According to unconfirmed report transferred to Bobynichi 90/28.

"Bareyka Brigade" (no number). Based near the village of Kisseli 24/34. Camp in grid squares 22/34 and 24/34. Otherwise nothing known.

"Lenin Brigade" (F 14). Commander: Sakmarin – chief-of-staff: Isofakov – commander: Sipkov/ Strength: 1,000 men in 7 battalions – Headquarters: in Bystriki 26/26. Armament: machine-guns, automatic and other rifles.

"Kozmin Brigade" (no number) based at Podgay 26/26. Nothing more known. At present the ice of Tottsha Lake 18/24 is being used as an airfield, with single- and twin-engined aircraft landing there during the day.

Southern Sector:

The enemy's in-depth blocking line runs N of the Ulla – Kamen road, bolstered in places by concrete bunkers, and is continually being augmented by the construction of new field fortifications. The total strength of the "Romanov" (F 13), "Utkin" (F 125), "Lobarov" (F 126), "Alexeyev" (E 1) Brigades and the "Smolensk Brigade" (E 15) brought in from the northern sector as reinforcement can assumed to be 9,000 men. The massing of such strong partisan forces gives the sector increased importance. Elements of the "Lobanok Brigade" (F 126) have occupied the villages east of Pyshno 94/92. Strong forward field positions E of Voron' Lake 04/98 to Saborovye 10/98. Between Kiselevo 16/06 and Zayesvino 30/08 strong defensive installations are blocking the southern approaches to the chain of lakes. Further field fortifications to 1 km N of Karbani 02/06. East of Karbani 02/04, 1.5 km NE of Shary 08/06, 1 km NE of Raguzkije 00/04, S of Vel. Dolzy 92/04, W of Voron' 04/98 with machine-gun positions, machine-gun position in forest W of Asarenki 04/00. Field

positions W of Samoshye Lake 92/02 and between Sunitsa 94/00, also Porovno 96/02. On hill SW of Uroda 22/06, in Rakovtsy 18/06 and on high ground to the west there are bandit sentries that immediately raise the alarm at the approach of German units. The roads in the bandit area are passable by medium vehicles in dry weather, provided they have not been torn up or rendered impassable by trenches or log barricades. The Lepel – Kamen road is always mined. Log barricades have been detected on the Voron' 04/98 – Ushachi 04/00 road W of Asarenki and the Noviny 06/04 – Shary 06/06 road. Bridge at the crossroad 04/98 on the Voron' – Ushachi road, another 700 m E of the crossroad 06/00 on the Voron – Vatslavovo road. All bridges on the main and secondary road in Voron 04/98 destroyed and log barricades 500 meters from crossroad 04/98. In Tserkovishche 90/00 bridges destroyed and log barricades. The Voron 04/98 – Ushvitsa 32/28 road has been rendered impassable through the destruction of all bridges and the laying of log barricades and ditches and is guarded by field emplacements. Bandit radio installations identified near Saborovye 12/98.
[…]

Document 55

Operational Order by Battle Group von Gottberg for "Operation Spring Festival"
11 April 1944

I. Enemy Situation
The greater Ushachi area forms a closed bandit area. The bands are composed of powerful units made up of left behind, dropped off or infiltrated Red Army personnel. The civilian population in this area fully supports the bandits. Heavy mining, with well-constructed, camouflaged positions and powerful resistance, is to be expected. In the event of an attack in this area the bandits can call upon air support from the Red Army.

II. Mission
In consultation with Headquarters, 3rd Panzer Army, Battle Group von Gottberg will conduct operations to clear the partisan-held Ushachi area. The operation is code-named Spring Festival.

    3.) *Own Forces:*   *SS Police Regiments 2, 24, 26*
    SS Special Battalion Dirlewanger
    Police Battalions 57, 62
    Reinforced SD Battalion 23
    III Battalion, Police Rifle Regiment 31
    II Battalion, Police Rifle Regiment 36
    1 company of the Military Police Special Operations Command
    12th Police Panzer Company
    Flak Battalion I, Detachment H.Q. Reichsführer-SS

Group Kaminski: 1st Regiment
5th Regiment
Guards Battalion
Canine Battalion
17th and 18th Motorized Military Police Platoons
TN Company

Detached by Headquarters, 3rd Panzer Army:
Security Regiment 64 (Security Battalions 722, 839, Regional Defense Battalion 330)
Pioneer Battalion 743 horse-drawn (less one company)
3rd (Flak) Platoon, Anti-Tank Battalion 256
1 company from Army Heavy Anti-Tank Battalion 519
(S.P. 88-mm anti-tank guns)
1 battery from Assault Gun Brigade 245
Road Defense Platoons Werner and Blücher
Armored Train 61

Detached by the Commanding General of Security Forces and Commander of White Ruthenia:
Panzer Company Center
1 medium battery

Detached by the Senior Pioneer Command 2:
1 company of Pioneer Construction Battalion 784
1 company of Pioneer Construction Battalion 730

General blocking line, Krolevshisna road – Ushachi intersection with rail line near Leninsk Luch (11 km SW of Polotsk)

From Senior Pioneer Command 2:   Pioneer Construction Battalion 730 (less 1 company)

Pioneer Construction Battalion 731 (less 1 company)

From Senior SS and Police Commander Ostland:
10 battalions and elements of Army Group North

The Commander of Security Police and SD White Ruthenia will provide Security Police and SD liaison officers to the various groups. SD detachments up to battalion command posts. Mission and duties of the SD detachments as per special order (included as Appendix 1).

Air Commander 1 to provide air support.

Seizure of workers, cattle and agricultural products as per "Special Directives for Seizure" (included as Appendices 2 and 2a).

Supply of forces as per "Special Directives for Supply" (to be issued to the units).

Own intentions:

Encirclement and destruction of the enemy in the area surrounding Ushachi. […]

Appendix 2 to the Operations Order for "Operation Spring Festival"
  Special Directions –
for the seizure of workers and agricultural products.
I.) The commanders of the 4 operations groups
   1. Oberst Krehan
   2. Brigade Commander Kaminski
   3. SS-Obersturmbannführer Anhalt
   4. Major der Schutzpolizei Rehdans
are being provided collection and escort detachments to provide support and transport away prisoners, workers and agricultural products to the reception camps in
   1. *Sloboda, about 10 km NW of Lepel*
   2. *Drekhovo, about 22 km W of Lepel*
   3. *Torguny, about 5 km NW of Dokshytsy*
   4. *Babiche near Krulevshchizna*
These detachments are to be differentiated as follows:
a) Pure guard detachments at the preceding reception camps.
b) Escort and security detachments from the operational areas to the reception camp and further to the prisoner collection points and collection sites for workers and agricultural products.
   c) Seizure detachments for agricultural products and workers [...]
   II.) Each of the operations groups will be provided an officer to oversee the collection of agricultural products and workers. For collection of agricultural products and workers by the battalions, the individual operations groups will be assigned agricultural-officers and work action men as follows:

	Agr.-Officers	Work Action men
1. Operations Group Krehan	7	7
2. Operations Group Kaminski	7	7
3. Operations Group Anhalt	9	9
4. Operations Group Rehdans	11	11
III.) The Reception Camps in	1. Sloboda	
	2. Drekhovo	
	3. Torguny	
	4. Babiche	

will each be assigned 2 agricultural and work action men, who are to:

a) separate animals for slaughter and productive livestock,

b) send those incapable of work back to as yet undetermined exclusion areas. Each operations group is being assigned 1 officer and 40 men to guard and transport out prisoners, workers and agricultural products from the operations area.

IV.) Departure and Economic Supply

The seizure, guard and security forces will be dispatched to the operations group command posts on a timely basis. Economic supply in the area of operations is the responsibility of the units to which these forces are assigned. The same applies to the forces of the SD and for vehicle drivers.

V.) Feeding of Prisoners, Deserters and Workers

Food is to be taken from the agricultural products delivered to the reception camps, which are to be distributed by the agricultural officers in these camps. Workers and deserters are to be given preference in the distribution of food.

VI.) Transfer of Prisoners, Deserters and Workers

The officers of the guard detachments in the reception camps will transfer these as follows:

1. Reception camp under Operations Group Krehan in Sloboda to Borovka approx. 10 km northeast of Lepel (capable of holding 600 prisoners) and Borovno approx. 7 km east of Lepel (capable of holding 500 men, workers only).

2. Drekhovo Reception Camp under Operations Group Kaminski to Parafinov (for 1,200 men), prisoners to be separated from workers.

3. Torguny Reception Camp under Operations Group von Anhalt likewise to Parafinov.

4. Babiche Reception Camp under Operations Group Rehdan to Gleboki (Army Collection Center 8 ready to accommodate 400 prisoners and workers […]

XII.) Establishment of Restricted Municipalities

The operations groups will designate restricted communities in their sectors which will accommodate elements of the population incapable of work (cripples, the sick, old people and mothers with children, of which more than half are under ten). These restricted municipalities are villages far away from the main roads.

The operations groups will report the selected villages to the battle group supply officer by 18 April 1944, thereupon every third day if more are established. All houses in these restricted municipalities are to be spared, as they are also earmarked for the non-working population from the areas of the divisions of 3rd Panzer Army. The Beresino – Parafianov field railway is also available for the transport of prisoners and workers.

Appendix 2a to the Operations Order for "Operation Spring Festival"

BULLETIN
For Seizure of Local Residents and Economic Goods during
Rain Shower and Spring Festival

In most cases those guilty of the atrocities committed by the bandits are the bands' officers and fighters. Women and children are often forced into the forests to join the bands. Atrocities are unworthy of German soldiers, avoid them! Be hard when it is necessary, but be fair.

The enemy employs every means, therefore be watchful and do not trust the population in the areas held by the bands!

1.) Bandits

a) Destroy bandits in battle,

b) prisoners, including bandits who have deserted (if the bands display any tendency to desert they are to be given the opportunity to do so – every deserter saves fighting and blood), are to be transported under heavy guard to the designated prisoner collection points, provided they are not taken charge of by the GFP accompanying each battle group and interrogated and sentenced on the spot. In this the rule must be:

No prisoners or bandit deserters are to be shot until a thorough interrogation by the GFP or Abwehr team has taken place. Only in this way can important information about the partisan band command and organization be gained for evaluation for future anti-partisan operations.

2.) Remaining Population

Guideline: send no excess eaters and bothersome cohabitants to the rear! But seize every possible, meaning only healthy and fully capable workers for the homeland and the building of positions!

Businesslike strict handling with no unnecessary cruelty! Mothers are not to be forcibly separated from their small children!

Execution: if representatives of the labor administration have been assigned to the unit, it is their responsibility to sort out the workers based on their qualifications.

Otherwise the unit is to divide the population it encounters into the following groups:

a) men of 15 – 60 years fit for military or labor service – transport to prisoner collection point (see 1.b) as they are definitely suspected bandits. Whenever possible allow them to take along work clothing for summer and winter and food for two days! At the prisoner collection points they will be examined by Abwehr agents for concealed bandits, which after interrogation will be sentenced according to their bandit activities.

b) cripples, sick, old people, plus women and children, of which more than half are under 10 years – transport to specially-designated municipalities for resettlement (restricted municipalities, (see 4.b). Do not prevent them from taking the necessary possessions as hand luggage. Under no circumstances direct them to the collection points in the rear!

c) women of 15 – 60 years capable of work, including mothers with children, if at least half of them are over 10 years – transport under guard to the nearest worker collection point! Whenever possible, have them take along adequate work clothing for winter and summer, likewise food for two days, where appropriate leave 1 or 2 panye wagons for such baggage.

3.) Economic Goods

Guideline: seize everything! Exception for restricted municipalities as per 4.b. Execution: Provided an agricultural officer has been assigned to the unit, he is responsible for the disposition of acquired commodities as per A.Wi.Fü directive with the assistance of the unit commander.

a) Transport cattle and horses, food, equipment and other commodities to the nearest economic collection detachment or describe accurately for pickup (type, quantity and location)!

b) No unauthorized use of found goods, as food for the workers is vital for the supply of the forces!

c) In the restricted municipalities (see 4.b) leave stocks and farming equipment for the scanty existence of the residents!

4.) Villages: apart from direct combat operations, destroy no villages which:

a) are 3 km on either side of the main roads,

b) are required for restricted municipalities. Restricted municipalities are those specially-designated villages which—situated far from the main roads—are earmarked to accommodate elements of the population incapable of working (see 2.b). If possible, spare all the houses there, as several thousand non-work-capable civilians will have to be evacuated from the division areas into the former bandit areas.

5.) Collection Points are being set up:

for prisoners, workers and agricultural products

       I. in Sloboda
       II. in Drehkovo
       III. in Troguny
       IV. in Babiche

Each unit will convey prisoners, workers and commodities brought in by it to the nearest collection point. Each collection point is responsible for conveying these to the next collection point in the direction of the panzer army camp (see 6).

6.) Panzer Army camps are located:

a) for prisoners

      in I. Parafianovo (Dulag 230)
      in II. Glebokie (AGSSt 8) and
      in III. Borovka (strongpoint on the Lepel – Kamen road)

b) for workers

        in I. Parafianovo
        in II. Glebokie
        in III. Borovna, 7 km east of Lepel.

Document 56

Combat Report from "Operation Spring Festival"
by Battle Group von Gottberg
12 May 1944

16/4/1944. After completion of preparations for "Operation Spring Festival" to destroy strong partisan forces in the greater Ushachi area, assembly of the forces of Battle Group von Gottberg brought in by rail and road was completed on 16/4/1944.

To temporarily prevent attempts by the enemy to break out to the W, Operations Group Rehdantz launched an attack with advanced left flank and without encountering significant resistance reached a general line Oiszozolovka – Ivanovschchina – NW Zupolovo.

17/4/1944, After overcoming minor enemy resistance in the area of Operations Group Anhalt, the objective of the day was reached in the general line Beresino – Berespilye – Kovly – Nieszczierowszczyzna – Recznie – Bielski – Zaszczesle – Holubicze – Polesio. The muddy period which began in mid-April is already negatively affecting the advance by the troops. Bringing up supplies, the combat trains, the heavy weapons are all encountering serious difficulties.

On 17/4 Operations Group Anhalt established a bridgehead near Czerniczka-Recznie after gradually overcoming stiffening enemy resistance.

The main body of forces in Battle Group Jeckeln was in the blocking line by 17/4. Battle Group Jeckeln assumed responsibility for sealing off along the rail line together with attached units from Army Group North.

Operations Group Kaminski command post: Lipnyaki.
Operations Group Anhalt: Dokshytsy
Operations Group Rehdantz: Krolevshisna
Battle Group Jeckeln: Vetrino

During the night of 7/4/44 the Read air force bombed the town and area of Lepel heavily. At the very start of the operation heavy enemy air supply activity was detected in the Ushachi area.

18/4/1944. Operations Group Kaminski attacked northwards from its start position with the main body of its forces. Stubborn enemy resistance was encountered in the area of the village of Vetche after stronger enemy forces had been thrown back towards the north in the Anionovo – Khramenki area.

Operations Group Anhalt established a bridgehead 2 km NE of Kovly, and after overcoming extremely stubborn resistance drove off the enemy towards the NE. The bridgehead was expanded during the night. In the Czerniczka area the enemy resisted and then withdrew towards the east.

The advance battalion of Operations Group Rehdantz overcame weak resistance near F.Bor, however, the rest of its forces remained in the line previously reached. After extreme difficulties the objective of the day was again reached on 18/4/1944, in a general line Kulevschchinna – south end – Vetche – Selevki – Berespolye Point 187.7 – Travki – Czerniczka – Pieszczenowka. From there the objective of the day line was as on the day before.

19/4/1944. Operations Group Kaminski took the village of Vetche and the hills to the north. The enemy moved in strong reserves, however, resulting in heavy back and forth fighting, during which the village changed hands several times. Finally, under heavy enemy pressure, Vechi had to be abandoned. While Operations Group Kaminski's right wing held the line Postolka – south edge of Vetche against fierce enemy counterattacks, its left wing remained in the Belki area as the road leading northwest was very heavily mined and blocked by deep log barricades. Several casualties were caused by mines.

After overcoming stiff enemy resistance near Otrubok – Petrovshchina, Operations Group Anhalt succeeded in reaching the general line Staroy. Selo – NE exit from Otrubok – Potaszina – left group boundary. During the night a bridgehead was established across the Tacherniza at Osovek, and after fierce resistance the enemy was driven off to the east.

After overcoming enemy resistance in the Borysowe – Lady area, Operations Group Rehdantz reached the general line Borysowo – Lady – Otliwiki – Dewidki – Kolano – Borove. By this day 21 bunkers and 13 bandit camps had already been destroyed.

20/04/1944. Operations Group Kaminski held the line it had reached against powerful enemy resistance under the most difficult conditions and repulsed numerous enemy counterattacks by powerful units.

The muddy period had a negative impact on the delivery of heavy weapons, whose use was not yet possible.

After overcoming strong enemy resistance, in the morning hours of 20/4/1944 Operations Group Anhalt took the hills near Point 196.7 and forced the enemy to withdraw from Erzhepol'ye – Chernitsa in the direction of Lesiny. Because of heavy air attacks the day before, in the Chernitsa II area the enemy had already withdrawn towards the east with heavy losses. The powerful fortifications discovered by our reconnaissance in the Lesiny area were systematically destroyed by precision air attacks. After 3 1/2 hours of artillery preparation, the creation of a bridgehead was forced over almost impassable swampy terrain near Horonovo-(Svatki).

During the night of 20/4/1944 enemy transport gliders carrying 17 hundredweight of explosives were deceived by a landing beacon and induced to land in the Chernitsa II area. The enemy's supply flights into the Ushachi area reached the number 180 during the night.

The continuous rain gradually made the terrain so impassible that heavy weapons could only be brought forward by hand. There were no more roads usable by motor vehicles, not even tracked vehicles. A few farm tractors were put to use. Some of the men had had only cold rations for three days, some had no food at all.

The 3rd Panzer Army had already made the suggestion to stay in place for several days until the worst of the muddy period was over.

Despite all difficulties, the battle group commander decided to continue to attack so as to give the enemy no time to bolster his fortified positions. Radical measures were introduced, such as bringing in thousands of workers to build roads, taking command of all Todt Organization assets, bringing in food and ammunition by means of pack columns, and in fact they succeeded in getting past the period of difficult terrain conditions. While Operations Group Kaminski held its line despite heavy enemy pressure, Operations Group Anhalt and Operations Group Rehdantz reached the general line Erzhepol'ye – Chernitsa I – Point 184.8 – Point 177.0 – Modelo – Fw.Barbarovka – Lubovo – Przewoz – Borovoe – Uhaly – Uiabki.

21/4/1944. After completing a partial operation to clear the terrain in the south Lepel area, Operations Group Rehan had the necessary freedom in its rear to assemble its forces and protect the attack on the battle group's right wing. Attacking on 21/4/1944, Operations Group Krehan broke through the enemy's forward outposts and reached the general line south edge west Oron – Seo – Osye – Svertsno. After fierce fighting, Operations Group Kaminski took Wetche and fought its way into the enemy's heavily-fortified positions in the general line Logo – Bushenka. Approximately 200 of the enemy were encircled, after which 180 enemy dead were counted.

With support from heavy weapons, Operations Group Anhalt took the fiercely-defended villages of Chernitsa and Svistopolye. The enemy withdrew before the group's right wing back across the Chernitsa. On Operations Group Anhalt's left wing the enemy withdrew just one km to the east and then began fighting again. After a flanking attack the enemy was again put to flight.

According to prisoners, the enemy sent back 60 panye wagons loaded with the dead. In general it was observed that the enemy also took all of the people and cattle with him when he withdrew. Although Lesiny had been bombed by Stukas on 20/4/44 and again on 21/4/44, the village could not be taken, as the enemy in the Lesiny area held on grimly in well-fortified positions with numerous supporting heavy weapons.

After overcoming stubborn resistance, Operations Group Rehdantz, with Fw. Barbarowka and the advance battalion, took Vitovka on the right wing. Czyste, which was heavily fortified and tenaciously defended by the enemy, could not yet be taken. On Operations Group Krehan's left wing, Operations Group Kaminski succeeding in reaching its objective of the day, the line Babashkov – Useche – south edge of Buyenka – Gora – Klovo, while its left wing reached Nov.Selo. After overcoming severe terrain difficulties, Operations Group Anhalt's right wing reached the general line Hornovo – Asony – Hornovo – Wiercinski. Making contact with Operations Group Rehdantz on the right wing was not yet possible. Operations Group Rehdantz held the line Czyste – Lubov, bent its left wing forward through Ostov-Bozki to Madozierze, barricaded the narrows between Szo Lake and Dolho Lake and, following the shore of Dolho Lake, sealed off the area to the left operations group boundary. Road conditions remained catastrophic; the mined and muddy roads did not permit regular supply traffic, and demanded the most strenuous exertions from every single man.

Battle Group Jeckeln pulled Blocking Group Grave from its former blocking position and moved it into the Vetrino area. Battle Group Jeckeln reconnoitered the ground before it and found it heavily mined. It also discovered well-constructed and wired enemy positions to the SE of the rail line. Once again numerous supply flights into the Ushachi bandit area were reported. The enemy's intentions were now clearly recognizable: the Ushachi area was to be held at all costs, with the recapture of the outer defenses in the core area.

22/4/1944. On 22/4/1944 Operations Group Krehan ran into stubborn resistance near Voron.

Launching repeated attacks, Operations Group Kaminski took the heavily fortified villages of Usochi – Novoye – Zhitye – Kurtslevshchina – Sloboda by storm. While the enemy there only withdrew slowly to the north after bitter fighting, in the area of the general line Rudnya – Mal. Dolzy – Logi – Bushenka he held on with all available forces. During the night Operations Group Kaminski had to fight off three heavy enemy attacks.

In the area of Operations Group Anhalt a focal point gradually developed on the right wing. In the early hours of the morning there was a heavy enemy barrage from heavy weapons. […]

After taking Lesiny and Pukhnominki, OGR Anhalt advanced into the Sarubovshchina area as far as Teerofen. This territorial gain came at a heavy cost in casualties. The air force and the heavy weapons, in particular, played a major role in this success. The Anhalt Group advanced its left wing forward in the general line Krovnica – Losina, where contact was made with the right wing of the Rehdantz Group.

Operations Group Rehdantz had meanwhile cleared the wooded area near Losina of bandit elements and forced a crossing of the Szosza near Kobylanka against the fiercest enemy resistance. During the night fierce counterattacks had to be repulsed in this area. Battle Group Jeckeln reconnoitered successfully and a bravely-executed assault operation brought in four prisoners. Opposite Battle Group Jeckeln's sector the enemy's intentions were clear, to bolster his defense positions and mine and wire the foreground in order to meet an attack from the north.

Operations Group Rehdantz moved its command post to Kaleczpolo.

25/4/1944. The enemy's point of main effort gradually developed opposite the Kaminski Group and the right wing of the Anhalt Group. To prevent a loss of contact, the Krehan Group remained in the Vorovka – Ostrovo – Point 167.0 – Suiniza – Polosno line it had won the day before and again thoroughly combed the wooded area in its rear.

While the right wing of the Kaminski Group was holding its line on 22/4, it succeeded in taking Logi, where the chief-of-staff of the Alexeyev Brigade was captured. The enemy lost many killed and booty and important maps fell into our hands.

Throughout the day the Kaminski Group's left wing was involved in fierce offensive fighting in the Bushenka – Sabolotye area. Not until noon could Khramonki be taken and contact established with the Anhalt Group. In the evening the left wing was in front of Voloki. The enemy had meanwhile moved up reserves and during the evening repeatedly renewed his attempts to break through in the Logi – Voloki area. Continued rain left the roads almost impassable.

On 25/4, on the Kaminski Group's left wing, Operations Group Anhalt attacked from the Chernitsa – Sabolotye area and made close contact with the Kaminski Group. The left wing took the villages of Mikuliny – Buski, Krovnica, Dubivce. In difficult fighting, stout bunkers and field fortifications in this wooded area were stormed and destroyed. Enemy cavalry, who retreated headlong through Dubovico to the east, drowned in the swamp east of Dubovico.

During the night of 25/4 powerful enemy forces attacked in the Szonza area and tried to break through. The attack was repulsed with heavy losses. During the course of 25/4, a surprise attack was launched against enemy positions identified in the wooded area 1.5 km east of Kobylanka with support from heavy weapons. The positions were destroyed and numerous prisoners were taken.

Battle Group Jeckeln again conducted successful patrol and assault operations forward of its blocking position.

Following a successful night attack, on 25/4 the general line Borovka – Ostrova – Suiniza – Polosno – Tartak – Mal.Dolzy – Point 188.9 – Saswidok – south edge of Voloki – Teerofen – Hornovo – Wiercinski – Losina – Point 182.0 – Nadozierze – shore of Dolhe

Lake was reached. Strong enemy resistance had to be overcome, especially at Hill 173 in the area SW of Szo Lake. This area of swamp and forest favored the enemy in his well-fortified positions, especially during the muddy period, while our attack forces had to struggle to the point of exhaustion against a determined enemy and difficult terrain.

26/4/1944. After overcoming determined enemy resistance, the right wing of Operations Group Krehan advanced to Dvor Shary, cleared a wooded area in the Barsuki area and, after fierce fighting with air support, took Provno. It also stormed the hill south of Yusofatvo and opened the way for the capture of the town. The right wing advanced to abeam Zamosh'ye and took the eastern part of the village.

The right wing and center of Operations Group Kaminski remained in the line it had reached the day before while, after heavy fighting, the left wing reached the forest clearing 1 km NW of Bushenka. The count of enemy dead reached 89.

Despite several attacks with powerful support from the heavy weapons, it was not until the evening hours of 26/4 that the right wing succeeded in driving the hard-fighting enemy out of Voloki and taking the village. The enemy's plan was obvious: he wanted to prevent a further advance by our forces at all costs and planned to pin down and destroy Kaminski's and Anhalt's attack forces in the maze of forest and swamp. The achieved line was held through the night against numerous enemy attacks. The Anhalt Group's left wing and the Rehdantz Group held the line they had reached the day before. We suffered numerous casualties as a result of the enemy's mining of the road and the wooded area.

27/4/1944. The enemy launched counterattacks in the Yuzefatovo area in the early morning hours of 27/4, however these were repulsed. The Red air force carried out heavy attacks during the night of 27/4 and during the day committed several close-support units against our attack forces. The crisis that had arisen several days earlier in the area of the Kaminski and Anhalt groups, caused by fierce enemy resistance, was not to be underestimated. The battle group commander personally intervened in the command of both operations groups and cleared up many difficult situations, carried out a reordering and regrouping of the units whenever it seemed urgently necessary, and made the decision to hold the line as it was.

This development in our situation was only possible because the units of the 3rd Panzer Army that had attacked from the east on 10/4 had stopped in a natural blocking position following the Gemel – Beloye chain of lakes and had gone over to the defensive there. Recognizing the situation as the operation was proceeding, the enemy pulled strong elements and all his reserves from the northeast and east of the Ushachi area and massed his forces opposite the Kaminski and Anhalt groups, resulting in a determined, and for the enemy successful, defense. While the entire civilian population was building fall-back and defense positions in the rear area, the enemy was even able to launch sustained counterattacks with *powerful forces, which many times placed the Kaminski and Anhalt groups in the most difficult situations. After the battle group commander assessed the situation, the suggestion was made to 3rd Panzer Army that it leave the blocking position it had been in since 17/4 and attack towards the west in order to force the enemy to loosen his main effort against Battle Group von Gottberg. Simultaneously the battle group commander committed the air force units, which launched precision strikes against identified defense positions and troop concentrations from the early morning until the late hours of the evening. Furthermore, orders were issued for the establishment of bridgeheads near Samosöjo and Tartak, in order to pin down the enemy forces frontally and then strike from the flank with powerful spearheads.*

With support from the air force, the Kaminski group succeeded in establishing the bridgehead near Tartak. Strong enemy resistance prevented the bridgehead from being expanded during the day. The Kaminski group had to go over to the defensive on the entire line and repel two serious breakthrough attempts by the enemy in the Svidok area.

After overcoming stubborn resistance in fierce forest fighting, Operations Group Anhalt stormed and took the hill in the clearing due NE of Voloki. While the enemy was forced to abandon this hill, he attacked our positions from the Krasny – Ostrov – Filippovka area with powerful forces. He succeeded in penetrating as far as the regimental command post in Zarubovshchina, but then was driven back again with heavy losses. The fanatically-fighting enemy left behind neither weapons nor the fallen, instead taking everything with him to prevent us from gaining an insight into his losses. During the morning fighter units of the Red air force were again over our positions.

With support from heavy weapons, Operations Group Rehdantz broke through the enemy's system of defenses in the Szo Lake area. Attacking northward from the area of Point 182 – 183.7, it reached the village of Szo in heavy fighting with air support. The village fell into our hands after bitter house-to-house fighting. The Rehdantz group's left wing also attacked and broke through enemy bunkers and field emplacements in the narrows between Szo Lake and Dolhe Lake and carried the attack forward into the area east of Pinski. The enemy repeatedly regrouped and offered stubborn resistance.

Opposite Battle Group Jeckeln's sector the enemy was generally observed to be digging in and appeared to be feverishly and with all means bolstering his main line of resistance. On this day Battle Group Jeckeln reached the general line Dvor – Shary – south tip of Ugly – Barawzy – Yusofatova – Forovno – Zamosh'ye in the area of Operations Group

Krehan. The Kaminski group held its achieved line. On the Kaminski group's left wing, the Anhalt group reached the north edge of the hill near letter "V" in Voloki. From there the line followed a generally northwest direction through the letter "V" in Zarubovshchina – dotted road veering northwest 1.5 km SW of Filippovka, and from there as per the previous day.

Operations Group Rehdantz reached the general line Losina – No. 264 – No. 261 – Point 183.7 – Dabrova collective farm – Fw.Prueniki – north tip of Szo Lake – north edge of Piski – Kaminnka.

Battle Group Jeckeln remained in its blocking position. The weather cleared temporarily and made the various supply roads relatively passable for horse-drawn and tracked vehicles.

28/4/1944. There were numerous supply flights into the greater Ushachi area during the night of 28/4, and simultaneously the Red air force heavily bombed the Anhalt group's positions and the villages of Tartak, Rudnya and Logi. In the early morning hours, after overcoming stubborn resistance, the Krehan group forced a crossing near Zamosh'ye, took the west part of the village and there established a bridgehead, which was expanded later in the day. In a subsequent advance to the west the village of Tserkovshche and Hill 183.4 to its southwest were taken. The enemy resisted our attack fiercely and withdrew slowly toward his prepared positions, contesting every meter of ground. After heavy fighting, the Kaminski group succeeded in breaking through the enemy's southern defense line and taking the enemy positions by storm. The enemy brought in fresh reserves, however, and our forces were forced to pull back to their start positions. Prisoners stated that the Kaminski group and the right wing of the Anhalt group were facing at least 2,000 men of the "Rodyanov" and "Alexeyev" Brigades.

In the early morning hours the right wing of the Anhalt group went to the attack towards the northeast from the line it had reached earlier. The enemy resisted fiercely, halted our attack, and then launched a powerful counterattack. With support from all heavy weapons the enemy was beaten back, in part in hand-to-hand fighting, with heavy losses.

During the morning nine Russian close-support aircraft approached the Rehdantz group's line, but they were driven off by anti-aircraft fire. By the evening of 28/4 Battle Group von Gottberg had reached the general line road fork near Karbani – southern edge of Ugly – Baeawzy – Yusufatovo   Point 175.8 – Tartak bridgehead – northern edge of Rudnya – Hill 188.9 – southern edge of Sawidok – crossroad 1.5 km east of Voloki – letter

"N" in Teerofen – bend in road 500 m NE of the number 6.0 – western edge of forest clearing due west of Ostrov – letter "F" in Filippovka – No. 271 – No. 264 – No. 261 and northern edge of swamp island to its west following the road in the direction of Koshany to No. 256 – southern tip of Biale Lake – western edge of the chain of lakes to Fw. Szo – letter "l" in Yanopol – Horanie – Kamonka. The enemy had recognized the danger facing him from the area of the Zamosh'ye bridgehead and exerted heavy pressure on our forces from the area of Wel. Dolzy. By maintaining a strong screening force to the north, however, it was possible to achieve the conditions necessary for a further advance to the west. So as not to hamper the flanking thrust by the Krehan group, the commander of Battle Group von Gottberg had a Stuka unit drop supplies to the assault force on the evening of 28/4. This was to avoid threatening the success that was to make an impact in the coming days.

29/4/1944. While, during the course of 29/4, the IX Corps advanced against at times stubborn resistance to our line northwestern tip of Cherstvyatskeye Lake – Bolotniki – Vashkovo, Battle Group von Gottberg also succeeded in pushing its right wing forward to the general line Vashkov – Svon – Zamosh'ye; and there the enemy was driven across the Oshatsha to the northwest.

With air support, the Kaminski group was able to expand the Tartak bridgehead and attack and seize the villages of Pushishche and Saoserye. The ceaseless air attacks, which had begun in the early morning hours and were concentrated in front of the Kaminski and Anhalt groups, the flanking attack by the Krehan group and the right wing of the Kaminski group, the joint attack by the Kaminski and Anhalt groups with support from all heavy weapons, had finally broken the ability to resist of the powerful enemy in this area. In fierce fighting, the left wing of the Kaminski group broke through three fortified defense lines, inflicting heavy losses on the enemy, and behind the third discovered two mass graves containing the bodies of 110 enemy fighters. After overcoming stubborn resistance, the Anhalt group stormed and took the villages of Krasny, Ostrov and Ulyanov. The same day the Kaminski group took the village of Kortschi. The Rehdantz group experienced heavy air raids on the villages of Sloboda and Kaletspole; however, because of the many duds little damage was caused. An attempt by the enemy to break through in the Losina area was repulsed with losses to the enemy. The Red air force also made attacks on Battle Group Jeckeln's sector.

On this day the battle group reached the general line Vashkov – Svon – Samachje – Tartak – Point 192.5 – Korshi – Point 194.7 – Ulyanovka – northern edge of Ostrov – western edge of Filippovka – Samchowo – No. 269 – Losina, while the Rehdantz group remained in the line it had reached the day before.

While the 3rd Panzer Army temporarily attached the Krehan group to IX Corps again and sent it additional forces from the 95th Infantry Division, the battle group moved Blocking Group Grave to the left wing of the blocking position to relieve elements of the

Rehdantz group and formed the bulk of the Rehdantz group for an attack. This was done to carry out a plan by 3rd Panzer Army on 30/4, namely to alleviate the difficult situation facing Battle Group von Gottberg by means of a partial encirclement from the southwest through Wel. Dolzy and northwest through Klapzy. Orders were issued for this offensive operation to go ahead on 30/4.

During the afternoon and towards the evening of 29/4, our ground and aerial reconnaissance and intelligence discovered that the enemy had withdrawn the bulk of his forces towards the north, leaving behind powerful rear guards which were engaging our forces in heavy fighting. After receiving this information, on the evening of 29/4 the battle group commander assessed the situation as follows: the renewed offensive activity by the 3rd Panzer Army from the southeast led to the conclusion that the enemy was again being forced to orientate himself towards the east. The heavy bombing of the area in front of the Anhalt and Kaminski groups, the very serious flanking threat from the Zamosh'ye and Tartak area appeared to have caused him to withdraw northwards into his core area in order to avoid encirclement, and more importantly to allow him to concentrate his defensive strength in a smaller area. At the same time, it was also to be assumed that the enemy had realized that he could not withstand the weight of our attack from the southwest and west and had identified the weakest part of the pocket, namely the blocking lines in the northwest and north, which were held by Latvian formations. As reconnaissance by Battle Group Jeckeln still confirmed an enemy digging in with large numbers of forces, while the known shifting of bands from the Szo lake area into the area north of Glebocki surely suggested an attempt to break out towards the northwest, during the night of 30/4 the commander of Battle Group von Gottberg grouped his attack forces in such a way as to allow the Rehdantz group, which had already been pulled out of the blocking line and assembled for an attack, to relieve the right wing of Battle Group Jeckeln in the blocking position. The forces released from the right wing were then used to bolster Battle Group Jeckeln's blocking line. After this measure was carried out, a suggestion was made to the 3rd Panzer Army that the pincer movement, for which orders had already been issued, not be carried out and that it approve the steps taken by the battle group commander. In the early morning hours, following a meeting with the commander-in-chief of the 3rd Panzer Army, authorization for the measures taken by Battle Group von Gottberg was issued retroactively.

The correctness of these measures was subsequently confirmed by the outcome of "Operation Spring Festival".

30/4/1944. On 30/4/1944 the Kaminski and Anhalt groups reached their objective of the day after overcoming weaker enemy resistance. The enemy had in fact withdrawn to the north following the difficult and, for him costly, defensive struggle. The only serious resistance was encountered in the Dubinets area. The Rehdantz overcame stubborn resistance near Fw. Hrazie and to its east. After making a stand near Skrobotuny, the enemy also withdrew to the east. The commander of the battle group was forced to make an emergency landing while flying to the forward command post. The commander was not hurt and damage to the aircraft was minimal.

The line achieved by the operations groups on 30/4 ran from Tserkovshche – Pervomsisk – Vesnitsk through Point 229.2 – Cherven – Gorka – Zamkhovo – No. 269 – Losina – southern tip of Biale Lake – western edge of Suponiec Lake – southern tip of Karavayno Lake – Horanie.

1/5/1944: Continuing its attack, on 1/5/1944 Operations Group Kaminski reached the general line Wel. Dolzy – Starina – Adveritsa against resistance that was in places stubborn. Enemy resistance stiffened in the Adveritsa area. After initially overcoming delaying resistance from rear guards, the Anhalt group advanced against stiffening opposition and reached the general line Oferovshchina – Glinishche – No. 264. The villages stormed and taken on 1/5 were heavily fortified with field and bunker positions.

While Blocking Group Grave had occupied a blocking position from the southern tip of Bialo Lake to Zaulek, during the day and night the Rehdantz group occupied a blocking position from Zaulek to Starzynka. The relieved elements of Battle Group Jeckeln solidified their own blocking position. On 30/4 and 1/5 the Luftwaffe carried out particularly effective attacks against enemy march columns of 300 to 1,000 men in the Ushachi area which had been discovered by aerial reconnaissance. Reconnaissance reported that five columns had been destroyed.

2/5/1944: During the night of 2/5 the Red air force attacked the Anhalt group's front lines and bombed the villages of Koshan and Faleczpole. A very large number of enemy supply flights into the Ushachi area were detected. At the same time, heavy raids were made against Mal. Dolzy, Zerkovshche and Starina, and the Kaminski group recorded a number of casualties. A heavy raid against the area and town of Lepel followed, and communications were disrupted for a time. Breakthrough attempts in the Krovnica area were repulsed with losses to the enemy. On 2/5 Operations Group Anhalt's advance ran into stubborn resistance in the villages of Bobovishche and Oferovshchina. After heavy fighting, the enemy was driven out of his well-fortified positions towards the north. Enemy assault and reconnaissance patrol activity in a northwesterly direction opposite the Rehdantz group's front was detected on 2/5. At dusk on 2/5 an enemy force of approximately 100 men with trains attempted to break out of the Zapole area towards the northwest. The attempted breakthrough was repulsed with the assistance of anti-tank and anti-aircraft guns, with heavy losses to the enemy. On 2/5 the Kaminski and Anhalt groups reached the general line Bogdanov – Skarschicha – Ukleinowo – southern tip of Riale Lake.

Blocking Group Grave, the Rehdantz Group and Battle Group Jeckeln continued to hold and bolster their blocking positions. Kaminski group command post in Mal. Dolzy.

3/5/1944: As anticipated by Battle Group von Gottberg, during the night of 3/5 the enemy attempted a breakthrough to the northwest in the Bojary – Bonday – Karavayno Lake area. According to prisoners, a force of about 1,500 men was supposed to spearhead the breakout so that any success could be exploited to the full. 10,000 men, including civilians, with all the supply trains stood ready to leave in the northwest part of the pocket. Already the previous day, however, the intelligence officer and aerial reconnaissance had detected the start of a massing in the northwestern part of the pocket. The necessary measures were taken and consequently the breakout attempt failed, even though it was carried out by powerful forces in a small area. Just 300 men succeeded in breaking through to the regimental command post of SS Police Regiment 26. These enemy forces were intercepted there, however. They subsequently turned south and tried to escape through the narrows between Szo Lake and Dolhe Lake. A blocking position was hurriedly put in place and foiled the attempt, so that 150 men at most escaped to the west. The enemy realized that his attempt to break out had failed, and the bulk of his forces streamed back into the pocket. 142 enemy dead were counted opposite one battalion's sector, giving some idea of the enemy's losses. As the continuing attack on the other fronts was steadily reducing the pocket, Battle Group von Gottberg was sent reinforcements to bolster the blocking line: two battalions from the Knappe Regiment, Territorial Battalion 860, Fusilier Battalion 56 and II Battalion, 32nd Regiment. These forces were used to establish a second line in the west and northwest. The failure of the enemy's breakout attempt was due to tight command and the defensive power of the SS police units deployed in this sector and the 57th Rifle Battalion. Under heavy pressure from the enemy, our forces did not withdraw to the west, instead allowing themselves to be overrun, and just 300 bandits ran into a rapidly-established second line behind the main line of resistance. After the SS police units had fought off this breakout attempt, the commander-in-chief of the panzer army sent General Staff Major Balve to Battle Group von Gottberg for the purpose of inspecting the blocking positions in the west and northwest and, if necessary, intervening. After spending several days at various command posts, General Staff Major Balve convinced himself of the correctness of the steps taken by Battle Group von Gottberg and the fighting spirit of the SS and police troops.

The Kaminski and Anhalt groups continued to attack and reached the general line Doroshevichi – Slobodka – Point 200.5 – Prudy and forced the enemy to withdraw to the north.

4/5/1944: During the night of 4/5 attempts to break through the Kaminski group's left wing were repulsed. At about 03:50 an enemy force of about 400 men attempted to break through the left wing of the Anhalt group, and this, too, was repulsed with heavy losses to the enemy. The enemy lost 46 killed there alone. According to prisoners, the enemy had massed several thousand men in the wooded area east of Suponiec Lake. Our air force attacked in strength and smashed the enemy concentration. In the Fw. Hrazie area, Blocking Group Grave repulsed a group of about 150 men. During the day the Rehdantz group conducted reconnaissance and offensive patrols and found no enemy presence opposite its front.

A further attempt by the enemy to break through at the seam between Battle Group Jeckeln and the Rehdantz Group in the Posadniki area was also repulsed with heavy losses. A group of about 2,000 partisans managed to reach the rail line, where it ran into the second blocking line. 64 enemy dead were counted in front of Armored Train 61 alone.

The Kaminski and Anhalt groups reached the line Boyarshchina – Sertshenichi – Point 83 – Osinovka. Battle Group Jeckeln's blocking position, the Anhalt Group and Blocking Group Grave were further reinforced.

5/5/1944: During the night the Anhalt Group repulsed an enemy breakthrough attempt in the wooded area east of Point 183. The Krehan Group was deployed as the second line behind the Anhalt Group. Krehan Group command post Kopylovshchina. The Kaminski Group held the line it had reached the day before and further extended the blocking position. Patrols returned with 30 prisoners. During the course of 5/5 Russian close-support aircraft and fighters repeatedly attacked the positions of the Kaminski Group. The Anhalt Group successfully carried out offensive patrols southeast of Karavayno Lake. A large number of the enemy were killed and several prisoners were brought in.

According to prisoners, concentrated offensive blows by the air force destroyed the large radio station in the town of Livny (RD 1b). The 600-Watt station, which was located on 3/5 by signals intelligence and direction finding, had maintained radio contact with Moscow.

Reconnaissance by Battle Group von Gottberg found various signs that, following the failure of his breakout towards the northwest, the enemy had massed the bulk of his forces for a breakout attempt in a southeasterly direction. The enemy's intentions, which clearly pointed to an attempt to break out to the southeast, were reported to Headquarters, 3rd Panzer Army by Battle Group von Gottberg at 20:30 on 4/5. This breakout attempt in fact succeeded, and the enemy was able to exploit his success. Not until after about 30 hours did aerial reconnaissance and intelligence become aware of this breakout and identify the location and direction of march of this partisan group. As a result of this breakthrough, which either was not noticed or not reported in time, a serious threat arose to Battle Group von Gottberg's rear-echelon units. The breakthrough had taken place in the 95th Infantry Division's sector in the Marienpolye – Shebotovo area. Battle Group von Gottberg took immediate steps to at least encircle some of the enemy forces in the Azoviny area. Nevertheless, the delay in spotting this move enabled the bulk of the enemy to escape to the south. This second pocket was created with forces of the Krehan and Anhalt groups and the Miltzow Regiment. The establishment of a blocking line Ragosino – Sadki – Zamkhovo prevented the planned breakthrough and continued march to the south. According to prisoners, the enemy forces trapped in the pocket were most demoralized by the ceaseless efforts of the air force. Furthermore orders were issued for the bandits, after burying their weapons, to try to break through the German ring in all directions.

6/5/1944: In conjunction with Battle Group Jeckeln, Operations Group Rehdantz attacked from its blocking position, overcame stubborn resistance, drove the enemy back towards the southeast and reached the general line Zapole – Girsy – southwestern tip of Bobynichi Lake. Powerful enemy forces reported by aerial reconnaissance to be massing for a breakout in the Borovye – Barbarovo – Goldinovo area were annihilated by the air force. The Kaminski Group repulsed breakout attempts in the Boyarshchina area, inflicting losses on the enemy. By the end of the day the general line Anikeyevshchina – Dvor. Sershenichi – Ostrovo had been reached against determined enemy resistance.

The Anhalt Group's attack brought it to the general line Krapivishche – Golinovo Center – east shore of Karavayno Lake. Enemy fighters over the Anhalt Group's lines in the morning hours. Our reconnaissance and assault patrols annihilated enemy concentrations in the pocket and destroyed small groups of bandits. Enemy wandering about in the pocket in complete disarray and trying to escape. Massed air attacks particularly effective against escaped bandit forces in the wooded area south and west of Asovnya, which suffered heavy casualties.

7/5/1944: Attempts by groups of 20 to 30 bandits to break out on Operations Group Anhalt's left wing were repulsed. The Kaminski Group remained in its line and offensive patrols brought in numerous prisoners and equipment. The Anhalt and Rehdantz groups also remained in their blocking position and inflicted significant losses on the enemy, who tried to break through the encircling ring split up into small groups. Numerous prisoners were brought in, including political officers, battalion commanders and Red Army officers. During the day the Rehdantz Group, in cooperation with II Army Corps, whose attack from the east had meanwhile reached Bobino Lake, advanced its left wing in the general line Ugly – Bobynichi – Dmitrovshchina. The strong enemy band forces in the Asovny area were attacked by our forces from the south. After they had broken through two security lines, they were heavily counterattacked and forced to pull back to their starting positions. After fierce fighting the enemy's efforts to break through were repulsed here too. Further breakout attempts to the west in the Szusza area were repulsed by our forces. Most of the bandit forces encircled in the Azoviny were part of the "Smolensk" Brigade.

8/5/1944: After II Army Corps reached Ryabshonki – Krapivishche, its objective of the day, the Kaminski Group was pulled out of the line and assembled in the Starina area. The Anhalt Group continued to hold its blocking position with SS Police Regiment 24 and the SD battalion, its remaining forces having already been committed to the encirclement and destruction of the enemy in the Azoviny area in cooperation with the Krehan Group and Blocking Group Grave. During the night of 8/5 and the following day, the enemy tried to *break out of the pocket northeast of Szo Lake. The forces freed up by the reduction of the pocket northeast of Szo Lake were moved to the pocket southeast of the lake, which was then also reduced. In the Samchow area, a group of about 150 enemy fighters tried to break out, but the effort was repulsed with losses to the enemy. Prisoners stated that several air attacks against the bandit forces in the Azoviny area on 6/5 had had a devastating effect. The 1st Platoon of the Multiple Rocket Launcher Battery alone inflicted losses of 25 killed and 80 wounded.*

9/5/1944: Under the command of Hauptmann Siebott, the 11th Company of SS Police Regiment 2, part of the Anhalt Group, achieved a splendid success in offensive patrol operations against a well-camouflaged bandit camp 1.5 km south of Point 187.7. Through circumspect command and a vigorously executed attack, an underground bandit camp was taken out and 307 of the enemy were killed. A great deal of booty was brought in. During the night of 9/5, our blocking position east of Karavayno Lake repulsed several breakout attempts by small groups of bandits. The offensive patrol operations carried out by the Rehdantz Group on 8 and 9/5 brought in much booty and prisoners. The enemy's losses were heavy. On 9/5 the Rehdantz Group attacked from the north and northwest to mop up what was left of the pocket. After overcoming resistance that was very determined in places, the stubbornly-defending enemy fighters were cut down in close combat. The bandit groups, 20 to 30 men strong, were made up of fanatical officers, commissars and political officers. Very well-camouflaged bandit camps and hiding places were taken out, much booty was brought in, enemy losses were heavy. The enemy encircled in the Azoviny area were attacked by our forces and squeezed into a small area, particularly onto the swamp islands northwest of Ulinets. Many of the enemy were killed, and prisoners and booty were brought in.

10/5/1944: On 9/5/44 aerial reconnaissance spotted a partisan group numbering about 2,000 in the Muskovitsa Lake area. Air strikes were immediately sent in and good results were observed. While Rear Area Commander 590 sealed off the area in the general line Lipnyaki – Beresino – Chernitsa II, and Battle Group von Gottberg occupied a blocking position in the general line Vetche – Bushenka – Saboloye – Chernitsa II, the Kaminski Group prepared to attack in the general line Vetche – Lyubovo. When the wooded area northeast of Karavayno Lake was combed again, numerous bandit groups of about 30 men, some hiding in well-camouflaged earth bunkers, were destroyed. Prisoners and booty were brought in. Approximately 60 enemy supply vehicles destroyed in the air attacks were found. The enemy forces encircled in the area southwest of Azoviny were destroyed in a concentric attack in, at times, heavy fighting. The number of enemy dead was high, prisoners were brought in.

11/5/1944: During the combing of almost impassible swampy terrain, a few small groups of partisans were destroyed or driven off to the west, and during the course of 11/5 the general line Gorochovo – Katlubishche was reached.

Operations Group Rehdantz again combed the woods in the Szo Lake area and returned with booty, however there was no contact with the enemy.

12/5/1944: The attack continued and the enemy forces in the Muskovice Lake area were wiped out. Large number of enemy killed, no prisoners could be taken as the enemy fought to the end.

Carried out under the most exacting conditions, "Operation Spring Festival", which saw the forces of Battle Group von Gottberg engaged in at times fierce offensive fighting from the first to the last day, placed especially high demands on the officers and men. The great success of "Operation Spring Festival" is apparent in the army order issued by Headquarters, 3rd Panzer Army on 8/5/1944 and the Operations Officer's daily report to Army Group Center of 10/5/1944.

"*The partisan forces in the greater Ushachi area have been annihilated. This success, achieved in at times heavy fighting and under particularly unfavorable terrain conditions, has critical importance for the overall situation on Army Group Center's northern wing and the extreme southern wing of Army Group North. The Soviet command has lost a particularly valuable region, which would have greatly benefited the enemy in an intended operation on both sides of the Dvina by restricting the amount of fighting room available to the German forces, as well as large, well-organized partisan bands.*"

"*In the rear area, "Operation Spring Festival" against the bands in the greater Ushachi area has ended. In three weeks of heavy fighting units of the army and police together with native volunteers, in extremely unfavorable weather and terrain conditions, encircled and annihilated the strong, well organized bands in the area between Lepel and Polotsk. Elements of some bandits managed to break through the encircling ring in massed night breakout attempts, however they were caught and for the most part destroyed. […]*"

Document 57

Battle Group von Gottberg's Final Report on "Operation Spring Festival"
12 May 1944

1.) Own Losses:
Killed (German police)	101
Killed (foreign volunteers)	57
Killed (Wehrmacht)	17
Wounded (German police)	361
Wounded (foreign volunteers)	224
Wounded (Wehrmacht)	40

2.) Enemy Losses:
Enemy dead counted	3,654
Enemy dead estimated	
Prisoners	1,794
Deserters	43

The enemy dead included:
Brigade commanders Alexeyev and Melnikov and the leader of the Smolensk Regiment, 1 Major, 1 Captain, 1 Lieutenant and 1 "Rodyanov" Lieutenant.

The prisoners included:
Deputy chief-of-staff of the Alexeyev Brigade, 1 battalion commander from "Zorotkin", 1 commissar from "Romanov", 1 Lieutenant from an NKVD squad, 1 Red Army Lieutenant.

Booty:

a) Weapons

3 45-mm anti-tank guns, 28 mortars, 24 anti-tank rifles, 10 heavy M.G., 70 light M.G., 86 S.M.G., 38 automatic rifles, 1,082 rifles, 47 pistols, 8 bayonets, 2 aircraft machine-guns, 17 drum magazines, 3 heavy M.G. carriages, 2 sled-mounted M.G., 2 mortar sighting mechanisms, 14 silencers, 23 machine-gun barrels, 1 heavy M.G. breechblock, 1 anti-tank gun limber.

b) Ammunition

294,710 rounds of small arms ammunition, 10,060 rounds of S.M.G. ammunition, 1,205 rounds of anti-tank rifle ammunition, 80 mortar rounds, 62 80-mm mortar rounds, 8 50-mm mortar rounds, 175 anti-tank shells, 697 mines (including 7 English), 1,343 kg of explosives, 1,155 fuses (including 25 English), 2,100 meters of fuse cord, 1 aerial bomb, 1 hand grenade cluster, 40 blasting charges.

15 cases of small arms ammunition, 4 cases of mortar ammunition, 1 case of anti-tank ammunition.

c) Other:

1 Russian transport glider, 6 saddled riding horses, 26 panye wagons, 1 set of harness, 2 shortwave receivers, 7 field telephones, 2 backpack radios, 2 radio sets, 1 km of field telephone cable, 5 binoculars, 4 flare pistols, 3 gas masks, 9 pistol holsters, 1 car battery, 1 field pack, 13 pairs of fur-lined boots, first-aid equipment and maps and other items of equipment.

Document 58

Propaganda Activity Report for the Second Half of May 1944
29 May 1944

15 May:
Report and consultation by leader of Army War Reporter Platoon North, Oblt. Busse, with St.C.Prop.

16 May:
Censorship directive with respect to the publishing of pictures of the Commander-in-Chief in the press. Pictures of the Commander-in-Chief are to be released to field newspapers in the army group area, provided there are no other generals in the photos. The civilian press may not publish anything until the Wehrmacht communiqué has confirmed Generaloberst Lindemann as the commander of an army group.

Handling of the matter "National-Socialist Russian Workers Party" (Kaminski) and the Vlasov Movement.

As per a directive from OKW/WPr., Vlasov can continue to be used for propaganda directed at the enemy. An accentuation of Vlasov as a personality among the Russians working with us is not desired. Recently the Kaminski movement, mainly in the area of Army Group Center, has been closely watched and managed by the SS. (SS-Obergruppenführer Gottberg in Minsk). At present, senior offices have no intention of bringing about a thorough resolution of this matter. Essentially they are awaiting developments in the Kaminski movement.

17 May:
The propaganda ammunition delivered by OKW/WPr. was distributed as follows:

	16th Army	*18th Army*	*Army Group Narva*
Prop.Gran. 41	*1,650*	*825*	*825*
Prop.Gew.Gran.	*5,000*	*2,500*	*2,500*
White-Red Shells	*1,200*	*1,200*	*600*

Document 59

Report by the Army High Command Regarding the
National-Socialist Russian Workers Party
3 July 1944

Since the issuing of the reference order, the NSRAP has expanded further. At present it is the strongest entity among the anti-Bolshevik organizations in the central and northern part of the eastern theater of war.

So far the principle of free play of forces has been applied to the various anti-Bolshevik movements in the east. This principle will continue to be respected, but with respect to the NSRAP it must not lead to an attitude that fails to lend the necessary support to organizations that have proved themselves in the struggle against Bolshevism. Minor considerations are of no importance when what is at stake is winning and keeping the friendship of valuable forces which can take some of the burden off the German military in its difficult struggle against Bolshevism. Requests for approval for gatherings and issuing of passes for propaganda trips and similar requests, which in the final analysis have the objective of increasing the participation of native forces in the struggle against Bolshevism, are therefore to be granted within the realm of possibility. Outwardly, however, the impression of promoting a particular party is to be avoided.

Further developments are to be monitored. Unusual events are to be reported,
[...]
at the present time do not yet lie in the German interest. It must be left to the free play of forces to determine which of the various movements wins out among the Russians.

IV. The reference order only makes reference to intervention in the movement and a direction of the propaganda spread by the NSRAP, it only characterizes such measures as not necessary. As a result, some questions have arisen, as for example the attached report by Army Group Center of 17/6/44 – Ia/Ic/SrO Prop./O.Qu./VII (Mll.Verw.) Br.B.Nr. 974/44 g.Kdos. – shows (Appendix I). The accompanying draft order to the army groups, for which approval is requested (Appendix 2), is intended to clarify the matter. The draft limits itself to the reference order, especially as it is not intended to hamper or complicate the work of the NSRAP.

In view of the military situation, a decision is requested soonest possible.

Document 60

Copy of a Telex from the OKW to the Army General Staff Concerning the NSRAP
3 July 1944

1.) Wehrmacht Operations Staff agrees with the proposed order, provided its scope is limited to the combat zones.
2.) In the rear area response to the NSRAP is a matter for the civilian administration.
3.) It is proposed that the intended order include a provision, in keeping with Army Group Center's wish (Article C of the letter of 17/6/44), that the army group high commands be given a free hand in guiding the NSRAP within the agreed guidelines.
4.) Submitted documents will be returned by courier.

Document 61

Radio Message from General Commissar White Ruthenia to the East Ministry
8 July 1944

Gauleiter Koch refuses to accept 30,000 people in the Bialystok area, request the necessary steps be taken from there.

Document 62

Letter from General der Polizei von Gottberg to the East Ministry

Below the copies of two telex messages for your information.
1. to OGRF. V Gottberg, secret
Order to evacuate Slonim, 2/7 xxx evening 12/7/44 issued by the army group. Gauleiter Koch refuses to accept Kaminski in the Bialystok area. Request the necessary steps be taken from there.
General Commissar Lida
2. to Corps Group von Gottberg, at present in Lida
Marching order for Kaminski into the Bialystok area is to be carried out, security assignments for the army group needed.

Document 63

Telex from the Plenipotentiary for the Cossack Refugees
to the East Minister Operations Staff Politics Berlin
9 July 1944

1. To the extent possible, military administration has organized the evacuation of the refugees.

2. Approximately 500 native administration officials are being sent to ZAVO in Forst.

3. White Ruthenian Order Service shall be directed to Neuhammer in Silesia and there allocated to German divisions with the agreement of the General responsible for volunteer units.

4. Evacuation of the defense village population is being carried out by HeWiFü (Army Economic Officer). Pomerania and Mecklenburg are being considered as reception areas.

5. The White Ruthenian and Russian youth organizations are being collected by Oberbannführer Schulz at the direction of the General Commissar.

6. Should the East Ministry fail to issue the necessary directive, 600 members of the active ROA shall be sent to Thorn.

7. The Kaminski shall be accommodated in the Bialystok area.

8. At present it is impossible to keep track of the refugee columns streaming back in disarray, which are being collected and controlled by Operations Staff Sauckel.

9. Figures for the refugee movement will not be available until the front stabilizes and regulated traffic is possible on the roads.

Document 64

Telex from the East Minister Rosenberg to Gauleiter Koch
Concerning Accommodation of the Kaminski Brigade
10 July 1944

The General Commissar for White Ruthenia has advised me that you, as head of the civil administration in Bialystok, have refused to accommodate the Kaminski Battle Group in that district. I appeal to you to agree to accept this brigade. Further information regarding the employment of this brigade will follow shortly.

Document 65

Telex from the East Minister to the *Generalkommissar* White Ruthenia
10 July 1944

Subject: Kaminski Brigade
Regarding your telex of 7/7/1944 I request you advise concerning the planned further employment of the Kaminski Brigade. Request further information, whether the numbers in your telex of 7/7/1944 are correct ("... Kaminski 30 thousand people")
Head of the civil administration in Bialystok has been asked by me to immediately accept the Kaminski Brigade in this district.

Document 66

Letter from East Minister Rosenberg to the Reich Minister and Head
of the Reich Chancellery Concerning the Accommodation of the Kaminski Brigade
in the Bialystok District
10 July 1944

11.
The General Commissar for White Ruthenia has advised me:
"Gauleiter Koch refuses to accept Kaminski in the Bialystok area. The Kaminski Brigade is a native fighting unit under the command of the Senior SS and Police Commander White Ruthenia and Central Russia, which to date has served well. Strength approximately 3,000 men with probably up to 5,000 family members and hangers-on.
Today I have asked cdz Bialystok to accept this group. However, as I fear that cdz will reject this request, because of the great urgency I request that you simultaneously appeal to him from there and if necessary bring about a decision. The Senior SS and Police Commander has issued the brigade marching orders for the Bialystok area.

Document 67

Letter from the Information Office of the Operations Staff Politics Concerning the Accommodation of the Refugees
21 July 1944

Concerning the accommodation of the refugees, P3 has advised the following:
1. Cossacks
17,000 men, 9,000 of them fit for military service, 8,000 older men, women and children.

The Cossacks are presently in the Siedlce area. On the Narev they are being employed to keep watch over workers constructing fortifications. It is planned to either accommodate them in Göring (Generalgouvernement) if three conditions are met:
-- Settlement area is satisfactory
-- Self-administration
-- Release of men fit for military service for service in the police to combat partisans or in the area of Triest, to which the responsible Gauleiter has already agreed in principle.

2. North Caucasians

4,000 men, 2,000 of them fit for military service.

The North Caucasians are at present south of Siedlce. It is planned to accommodate them in the Isonzo Valley. The Gauleiter has already agreed in principle.

3. Vilna Tatars

The intake of refugees has so far been small, as no concentration has taken place. Through the Reich Interior Ministry it was agreed that the entire group is to be sent to northern Styria to be used as workers. The necessary directive will be issued to the officials of the GBA in the reception camps.

4. Kaminski Group

3,000 (?) fit for military service (Kaminski Brigade), 3,000 family members, 24,000 hangers-on.

Unfortunately, precise numbers for this group, presently in the GG, cannot be determined. Consideration is being given to employing all of Kaminski's hangers-on as workers, while offering the brigade and family members to the police for anti-partisan duties. In view of the prospective use of Kaminski in the Russian matter, accommodation in the east seems advisable.

5. White Ruthenians

The exact number of White Ruthenian refugees is not known. Previously they were used mainly in the construction of fortifications on the Narev and in East Prussia. The respective Reich Defense Commissar is responsible for the refugees. The Interior Ministry has suggested the creation of refugee committees, in which the responsible departments are represented. Major Müller has been named Refugee Commissar by the RMfdbO. His functions with respect to the Reich Defense Commissars are only advisory, however he is to take care to ensure that the politically-interested special groups are held together and treated equally.

6. Special Group Flak Auxiliaries

It has been agreed with the GBA that flak auxiliaries recruited from the ranks of the refugees are to be released from labor or fortification building duties. Recruiters have been sent to the reception camps. The GBA has been advised.

The following guidelines have been issued for the work of the refugee commissars appointed by the RMfdbO:

1.) In the selection of refugees by the representatives of the GBA, families are not to be separated.

2.) *Refugees who have shown themselves to of possible use to German interests and qualified tradesmen are to be given preferential treatment whenever possible and placed in service.*

3.) Also to be given preferential treatment are the family members of the above-named circle plus German refugees who have relatives in the native units.

4.) Care is to be taken to avoid taking refugees capable of work and military service from the GBA or military administration while leaving the elderly, children, etc. behind.

Document 68

Letter from the Army General Staff to the Foreign Armies East Department
Concerning the Kaminski Party
24 July 1944

As a result of the military events of the past weeks, the matter has lost importance to the army groups. It therefore appeared sufficient to only advise the heads of the O.Qu./VII sections of the army groups (Appendix 2). In doing so, the Reich Minister's propaganda guidelines for the occupied eastern territories of 5/7/1944 were utilized.

It is requested that we be advised of any directives to subordinate offices of the command area there.

Translation of the Manifesto of the National-Socialist Workers Party of Russia!

Our homeland—Russia—created by the tremendous efforts of our ancestors, is on the verge of collapse.

Millions of Russian sons have been destroyed in the current war. Millions of orphans, widows and grieving mothers are the result of this insane struggle.

Beautiful cities, villages, monuments to culture and art, created over centuries by the work and sweat of the Russian people have been turned into ashes. Never in its entire history has our people endured such torment and suffering.

The people of Russian know that the only guilty ones are the Bolsheviks under their bloodthirsty Stalin.

They lied to our people in 1917: they used the revolution begun by the people to seize power. They promised the farmers land, the workers the plants and factories, the entire people freedom of speech and the press. The people of Russia have had to pay for their gullibility with unprecedented suffering and sacrifice. Instead of land the farmers have received the slavery of the collective farm, the workers forced labor in plants and factories. Instead of freedom the people have been given a close-meshed net of prisons and concentration camps.

The Bolsheviks have sacrificed the 170 million Russian people to their mad international plans which are directed against all of humanity.

The people of Russia have never ceased their struggle against their bitterest foe, bolshevism—but without success. A tremendously large number of NKVD executioners, mainly Jews, have stifled every attempt at resistance.

Only now, with bolshevism weakened by the war and weapons in the hands of the people, is a realization of the efforts of the Russian people possible.

History will never again offer us such a favorable opportunity and if we do not take advantage of it, Russia will go under and our children and children's children will damn us. They will say, "For thousands of years there has been no more unfit generation than that which permitted the ruin of Russia."

Every citizen of Russia must understand and feel that he, too, is personally responsible for the fate of his homeland.

The saving of Russia is only possible if all of Russia's upright sons unite, willing to wage a sacrifice-filled struggle in a powerful organization (party), which would be capable of taking on the communist party. In the knowledge that only an organized power is capable of bringing down bloody bolshevism and rescuing the homeland from ruin, we join together in the National-Socialist Russian Workers Party under the command of B.W. Kaminski, an experienced fighter for the good of Russia, leader of the new party.

The NSRAP has set as its goals:

1. The destruction of the bloody Stalinist regime in Russia

2. The founding of a sovereign state, uniting all the peoples of Russia

3. Acknowledgement of the right of self-determination of the various Russian nationalities ready to establish independent states

4. Liquidation of the class differences artificially created by bolshevism through a just, social, working order to be created in the new Russia.

Private property and private initiative will form the basis of economic policy.

1. The land must be turned over to the farmers for their own use.

2. The worker is to be turned from a proletarian in bondage into a free worker, who will also share in the profits.

3. The creative power of intelligence must be freed from political chains. Full freedom of speech and the press.

4. All property rights of former estate owners and capitalists (Russian as well as foreign) are null and void.

Against the Jewish internationalist ideas we offer the national idea, the love of country and people. We bind ourselves by a solemn oath to give all our strength and also our lives for the attainment of these goals, for the salvation of our land.

We call upon all upright sons of Russia, to whom the homeland is dear and who wish to see its people free and happy, to support the new Russian leadership and to fortify the strength of the National Russian Liberation Army—the true representative of the new regime.

Organizational committee of the NSRAP:
Mossin, Bakshansky, Vasyukov, Voshshile, Khomutov."

Document 69

Memorandum by the Reich Minister for the Occupied Eastern Territories
26 July 1944

At present Kaminski's following is believed to be approximately 27,000 persons. The brigade itself consists of about 3,000-4,000 armed men and with their families 8,000-10,000 people. The rest are party members of Kaminski, who is known to have created a National-Socialist Russian Party. We have no particular political interest in this party. It would be best if these party-liners of Kaminski's were disbanded and employed as workers. In the opinion of Professor von Mende and Dr. Knüpfer, the transfer of the brigade to Hungary planned by the police is not advisable, as Kaminski is surely only reliable if he is fighting near the eastern area and thus can always tell his people that they are fighting for their homeland. Employment of the Kaminski Brigade in the Generalgouvernement is therefore also strongly recommended. Professor von Mende and Dr. Knüpfer wish to contact Obersturmführer Pech of the Reich Security Head Office, who has asked me for an opinion on this...

Sources and Literature

Sources
Federal Archives File Collection Reichsfuhrer SS, Coblenz
Federal Archives File Collections CIC West, Army Groups Center and Vistula, Headquarters 2nd and 3rd Panzer Armies
Public Prosecutor's Office Ludwigsburg   Investigation Results Concerning the SS Assault Brigade RONA

Literature
Albrecht, Karl J.: Sie aber werden die Welt zerstören, Munchen 1954
Bim, Ruth Bettina: Die Höheren SS-und Polizeiführer, Dusseldorf 1986
Dallin, Alexander: The Kaminsky Brigade 1941-1944, Russian Research Center Harvard University, 1956
Fröhlich, S.: General Wlassow, Köln 1987
Haupt, Werner: Die Heeresgruppe Mitte, Dornheim 1968
Hesse, Erich: Der sowjetische Partisanenkrieg, Gottingen 1993[2]
Holimann, J.: Die Geschichte der Wlassow-Armee, Verlag Rombach, 1984
Klietmann, K.G, Dr.: Die Waffen-SS, Osnabrück 1965
Krannhals v., H.: Der Warschauer Aufstand, Frankfurt/M. 1964
Manstein, Erich von: Verlorene Siege, München 1979[8]
Michaelis, Rolf: Das SS-Sonderkommando Dirlewanger, Berlin 1999[2]
Michaelis, Rolf: Die russische Volksbefreitmgsarmee RONA, Erlangen 1992
Michaelis, Roll: Die Grenadier-Divisionen der Waffen-SS (Teil 2), Erlangen 1995
Michaelis, Rolf: Die Tapferkeits- und Verdieristauszeichnung für Angehörige der Ostvölker, Erlangen 1997
Littlejohn, David: Kaminski and RONA in: Foreign Legions at the Third Reich, USA 1987
Neulen, H.W.: An deutscher Seite, München 1992[2]
Preradovich, Nikolaus von: Die Generale der Waffen-SS, Berg 1985
Reitlinger, G.: Ein Haus auf Sand gebaut, Hamburg 1962
Schramm, Percy E.: Kriegstagebuch des OKW, München 1982
Stein, Georg H.: Geschichte der Waifen-SS, Düsseldorf 1967
Strik-Strikfeld, Wilfried: Gegen Stalin und Hitler, Mainz 1970
Tessin, Georg: Verbände und Truppen der deutschen Wehrmacht im 2.Weltkrieg, Osnabrück 1970-1980
Thorwald, Jurgen: Die Illusion, Zürich 1974
author unknown: Die Brigade Kaminski in: Der Freiwillige, Osnabrük
author unknown: Die 216./272. niedersächsische Infanterie-Division 1939-45, Bad Naulieim